Memoirs of the Foreign Legion

By

M. M.

[Maurice Magnus]

With an Essay by

D. H. Lawrence

Zea Books
Lincoln, Nebraska
2022

ISBN 978-1-60962-276-3 paperback
ISBN 978-1-60962-277-0 ebook
DOI: 10.32873/unl.dc.zea.1339

Published 1924 (London: Martin Secker)
and 1925 (New York: Alfred Knopf).

Text transcription courtesy
Project Gutenberg Australia.

Zea Books are published by the
University of Nebraska-Lincoln Libraries.

Electronic (pdf) edition available online at
https://digitalcommons.unl.edu/zeabook/

Print edition available from Lulu.com at
http://www.lulu.com/spotlight/unllib

PUBLISHER'S NOTE, 1924

EXCEPT that it has been deemed expedient to omit certain passages and to give some attention to the punctuation, these Memoirs are printed exactly as they were found among the Author's possessions at his death.

PUBLISHER'S NOTE, 2022

SOME passages in Magnus's *Memoirs* have been restored, and D.H. Lawrence's long "Introduction" has been placed following the *Memoirs,* beginning on page 168.

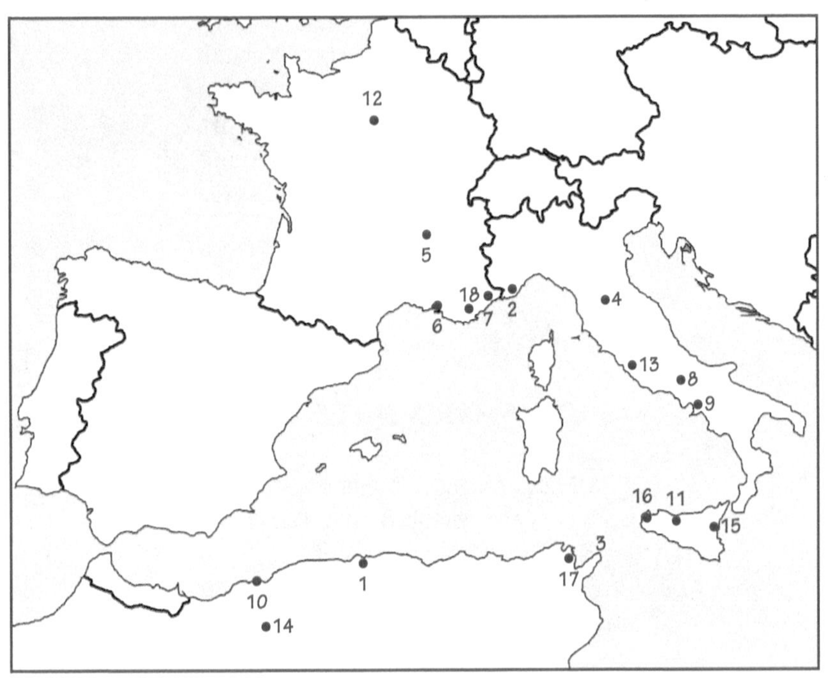

Europe & North Africa in 1914

Algiers	1	Oran	10
Bordighera	2	Palermo	11
Cape Bon	3	Paris	12
Florence	4	Rome	13
Lyons	5	Sidi-bel-Abbès	14
Marseilles	6	Taormina	15
Mentone	7	Trapani	16
Monte Cassino	8	Tunis	17
Naples	9	Valbonne	18

Memoirs of the Foreign Legion

Chapter I

SOON after Italy joined the war in 1915 I felt I wanted to do something in this great struggle and volunteered for the Red Cross Service; first in Italy, where my application was answered with "only Italians can do service." I wrote to France, and a very courteous reply came that they were not in need of any one just then, thanked me for my devotion, and would let me know if an occasion for my services presented itself. I wrote to Russia and received an extremely polite answer, in English, that their Red Cross Service was complete and that they had no need of my help. I wrote to Servia and received a curt reply that they had all the help they needed. Soon after receiving the latter, Lady X. in London, at some meeting, called upon those who were capable to volunteer for the Red Cross in Servia, as they were much in need of male and female nurses. I sent her the reply I had received through the Servian Legation in Rome. I did not offer my services to England, as I had heard that no foreigner, including Americans, could serve in the British Army or British Red Cross.

When all these attempts failed I thought of the Foreign Legion, and in the early days of March, 1916, crossed from Naples to Palermo on my way to Tunis and Algiers.

It was a very stormy night when I left Naples — the big State Railway steamers had been taken off and only the smaller ones were in service. The waves were terrific, and several times during the night I thought we had been struck by a submarine. The end seemed to have come, and from one moment to another I quite expected to see the water rushing into my cabin. Nothing happened, and next morning Palermo, with its wonderful Monte Pellegrino, hove into sight.

At this season of the year in normal times Palermo is gay. The approach of spring, the mild sunny days, the Palermotanians and foreigners driving about in carriages and cabs and promenading in the public gardens along the sea front and up and down the Corso and Maqueda, give an air of cheery carelessness to the city. Not so when I was there. Palermo was almost dismal, the streets were deserted, along the Corso and Maqueda only a few hurrying shop people and business men were to be seen. Many hotels were closed up, and the Hôtel des Palmes, where I stopped, was more like barracks – it contained exclusively English officers.

At night all lamp-posts at the sea front had blue glass; even in the streets leading to the sea the lamps had blue glass on the side which looked seaward.

About midnight of the following day I embarked on the *Cagliari* for Tunis, I had made all my preparations before turning into my berth. My jewels I had sewn into a chamois bag, and my money and necessary papers into an oilcloth bag, and hung both around my neck. I went fully dressed to bed. The only lights in the cabins and saloons were tiny blue electric bulbs, and the porthole shutters were tightly closed. Neither on deck nor on the masts were there any lights.

The next morning when I awoke we were out at sea, but still in sight of land. In fact, we remained in sight of land all day. The sea was rough, and when towards sundown we arrived at Trapani it was almost impossible to embark the passengers who had come out in small boats. Trapani looked very wonderful – the sun shone, but there was a strange white haze over the town which made it look like some white city on the eastern coast of the Crimea. The night was wild – a hurricane was blowing, and the moon, which looked strange and uncannily whitish, lighted up the haze to a radiance.

In the morning we sighted Cape Bon. I was the only first-class passenger, there were some second-class, and very many third class. My ticket was supposed to include meals, but after sighting Cape Bon it appeared no further meals were included, and the chief steward was at liberty to charge for food as he felt inclined, which he did in regular highwayman manner.

I had heard much about the flamingoes in the two lakes flanking the channel from the bay up to the town, but that day I was not fortunate enough to see any. A man standing next to me on deck, with whom I had entered into conversation, told me that he and five others had a lease for the fishing in these lakes, and that their income had been considerable, but that since the war they did not gain one-half of what they did before, owing to the fact that they could not send their fish to France any more. Soon after the war had started there was such a scarcity of meat in Tunis that a law was passed prohibiting the export of fish; in consequence, they were obliged to sell their fish in Tunis, where competition compelled them to sell it at a very much lower price than that obtainable in France.

We arrived at the quay in Tunis at about five o'clock in the afternoon. A French military physician came on board before we landed and vaccinated all the third-class passengers, men, women and children, for cholera. It was not the cholera year. Then came a French police official who took away our papers and passports, and told us to call for them the next day at the office of the Harbour Commissioner. I was not at all sure he had a right to do so high-handed an action, as it seemed to me. War-time is not the time to be without one's papers for an hour. I asked the captain, however, and found it was all right.

On landing at the customs all newspapers and printed matter was taken from our baggage, whether it was used to wrap boots or other things did not matter, and immediately destroyed. I had great difficulty in rescuing several magazine articles, which I needed for reference in my literary work, and which had nothing to do with war or politics. Finally, towards six o'clock, we were free to depart. The carriages in Tunis are good, their rubber tyres and easy springs and fast trotting horses reminding me of Russia and Oriental luxury.

The Tunisia Palace Hotel was a deserted hole – dark, gloomy, half-lit; the man at the door without collar, in shirt-sleeves, who helped down my luggage and argued with the coachman about the fare, proved to be the French-Swiss proprietor. No food was obtainable in the hotel since the beginning of the war, only coffee and bread and butter in the mornings, which I believe was brought in from outside.

The French quarter of Tunis did not interest me at all; it might have been a third-rate quarter of Nice or Cannes. Tunis itself, that is the inner town, inside the Porte de France, was very fascinating. I only felt one drawback – it was war-time and the foreigner was a very conspicuous personage in any of its streets. Most of the hotels were closed or half-closed, that is they only let rooms, and I believe the only one which gave food was the Hôtel de Paris in a gloomy noisy tram-line street, in the French quarter. The Casino was turned into barracks. Thank heaven, there were no trams inside the city walls proper. The restaurants were mostly wretched, and there was only one which was really good and that was Italian; it was on the main street of the French quarter, the Avenue

Jules Ferry. I had not the courage to go to the Arab restaurants; what with the conspicuousness of a foreigner, not knowing a word of Arabic, and being alone, I fought shy of them, although I should like to have tried them. Near the Porte de France, inside the walls, there were many little wine shops, run by Sicilians and Italians, and I used to resort to them for my wine which was invariably very good.

As soon as I had settled down and received my papers back I telegraphed to the First Regiment of the Foreign Legion at Sidi-bel-Abbès, in Algiers, reply paid, offering my services. Neither in France nor in any of her dependencies can a telegram be sent without showing one's passport. I am speaking of war-time.

Tunis was a chapter of the Arabian Nights to me – the magnificent many-coloured costumes sometimes of very rich materials, the leisurely life, the *cafés* filled to overflowing with Arabs, in whose midst there seemed to be invariably a public storyteller, the souks with their gorgeous display of carpets, silks, woollens, saffian leather goods, shoes and boots of brilliant colours, the perfume shops – it was fairyland to me. The Arab types are very beautiful, fine tall thin men with clear-cut features, eagle-like noses and noble expressions. There is much grandeur and dignity in their carriage, their gait, their movements, and their entire attitude. I felt like a mean savage cur next to these obvious products of an old and refined culture. Of the women I saw nothing; they are all veiled, except the Dervish women from the desert, who come into Tunis with their men to do their shopping occasionally. They were good looking with their olive complexions and jet black hair and piercing black eyes, but rather heavy and voluptuous in feature. Of course there were the public women in their quarter, who were unveiled, painted and bedizened, with jewels and bangles. One night I happened to go through one of these streets and witnessed a row between two neighbouring prostitutes. It was not very different from a row of their sisters in the profession in Leicester Square at midnight. The Arab called the Jewess a Jewess, and the Jewess replied: "Yes, I am a Jewess and you are an Arab, but whether Jewess or Arab or French or Italian or any other nationality or religion, in this street we are all whores."

In the souks I made friends with a most intelligent, entertaining, and charming Arab – Barbouchi by name. He sold rare and beautiful carpets and silks and other woven materials. He had been educated in Paris and London, spoke excellent French, and some English. I used to go to see him in the evening, when business was over and the bazaars had quieted down. He was a philosopher and a brilliant conversationalist. He did not like the French nor the French occupation. He told me that the Arabs did not have pleasant memories of the Turks, but they preferred them infinitely to the French. After all the Turks were their co-religionists, and had Oriental blood and imagination and understanding, a race related to them by family ties and tradition.

"In times gone by we sold Christians here in the Slave Market, and we are reproached for it, but to-day we are all slaves here to the French, and their mastery of slaves is much more subtle and complete than ours ever could have been. And these people talk of their Civilization and Christianity — they should speak of their Hypocrisy and Tyranny, to which they give a Christian mantle.

"This place is infested with spies and agents of the French police; nothing is unnoticed. You come to see me here in the evening — it is already reported at the police — you will be watched. Presently you will see many strange individuals enter this souk and look to see what we are doing. You are thinking of writing articles and a book about what you have seen and heard — you will find that the censor is already watching your mail, and your manuscripts will have those parts which are displeasing to them beautifully clipped out."

At first I thought him a bit of a crank on the subject because he did not like the French, but I soon found out that what he had said was no hallucination but very real. More than once on my way home I was asked by French detectives and policemen for my papers. As to the censor, every word he had said was Gospel truth; as much as five chapters at a time were stolen from the mails. Government or no Government, to annex deliberately the property of others is theft. All my manuscripts were registered, and my reclamations were absolutely of no avail.

"Bocha" is the indigenous Arab corn brandy, and is forbidden to be drunk by the Arabs. Of course my friend had it always in his shop, as all the other Arabs had, but it had to be kept hidden, and, before he served his friends a drink, he would go first to the front of the shop and look up and down the souks to see no one was in sight.

"The French have even forbidden us to pray for the Sultan in our mosques since the war. Whatever we may say about him as a Turk, and an old enemy of ours, he is after all the representative of Mohammed on earth, and according to our religion we are bound to pray for him."

He was a rich man and told me he had inherited his business from his father. He showed me his best and most valuable carpets. He had the spirit of the real collector, and would never sell his most beautiful pieces.

"Some time or other I shall sell them to some one I like, and who I know is as good a connoisseur as I am, and would take as much pleasure in owning them as I do."

He had very little regard for the French officials and their families in Tunis, quite aside from his political prejudices.

"They all are very common people from the provinces of France, who have either done something in France so that they cannot live there, or have come here because they couldn't make their salt at home."

The French in Tunis have the habit of "tu toi-ing" every Arab, no matter what his station in life. This not only seemed insulting to me, but when a common Frenchwoman, who was no better than a cook or a fish-wife or worse, entered Barbouchi's shop and "tu-toied" this obvious gentleman, it seemed ridiculous and incongruous.

I met many interesting Arabs there in the evenings. One old fine-looking fellow, who posed as fifty, looked like sixty, but was in truth seventy-two years old, and was the owner of the largest date palm groves in Tozeur. Occasionally he would get most amusingly drunk on "Bocha." One of his great stunts was to dance round the room, this tall dignified man in turban and gorgeous costume, looking like a Prophet with his long beard, and singing as if to himself: "I am the Bey of Tunis, I am the Bey, I am the Bey, I am the Bey of Tunis." And then he would go up to one of us and ask quite seriously: "Am I not the Bey of Tunis?"

"Of course," we said laughingly, and he enjoyed the joke, and knew that we realized he was drunk but liked him for his antics. He looked a very dear lovable man, and I was not astonished to hear that he had no less than twenty-eight children of which the youngest was five months old. He invited me to come to see him and I had a good mind to accept; it would have been an interesting experience.

Another visitor and friend of Barbouchi was a young Arab from Tripoli, who had left Tripolitania after the Italian occupation. He seemed to be a well-to-do merchant. I asked why he had left, and if he preferred the French to the Italians?

"It isn't a question that we object to the Italians and prefer the French; those of us who left, did so in protest that any European Power should come and interfere with the last bit of territory which we felt was still Arab. The Italians are certainly to be preferred to the French, they are more human and not arrogant, but we feel the injustice of any foreign occupation. Of course the day will come when we Arabs shall have gathered force enough to unite and put the foreigner out" – and after a moment's pause – "and that day may come sooner than Europe thinks. It is not a question of a Holy War – it is a question pure and simple of our rights, which we cry out for and do not get. With every new European invasion we Arabs are becoming more united, and realize the humiliating position into which we have been forced. It is Europe herself and her present methods and tactics which will be the real cause of the resurrection of Arab power."

"Is it true that most Arabs are pro-German?" I asked.

"Is it true?" broke in Barbouchi. "Of course it is true. We like the Germans, they have been always most kind to us, and we get along with them famously."

"Probably you would speak differently if you had ever lived under German rule or a German Protectorate."

"Nothing can be worse than this French tyranny. I can never believe the Germans to be tyrants."

"But I have lived in Germany and know what I am talking about."

"May be, but we, who have not had the experience, prefer the Germans to the French," he said, with a smile.

"We don't want Germans or French or Italians," said the Arab from Tripoli, "what we want is our independence, and we shall get it when Europe is least thinking about it. You will live to see the day when my prophecy comes true."

"But remember the weapons of war which are at your disposal, and those that are at the disposal of Europe. How will you be able to fight them?"

"We have some weapons which Europe doesn't know of, nor their power, and they are not made of steel, nor have they anything to do with dynamite."

Barbouchi's brother was a real Arab dandy, who was always immaculately dressed, and looked as if he had just come out of a box, very good looking, with big greyish eyes like star sapphires, and a perfect olive complexion.

"He is too good looking," said his brother contemptuously, "he ought to have been a Mullah. Not that I think that all Mullahs are good looking, but it doesn't suit him to be the father of a big family, which he is."

"Don't you like Mullahs?" I asked.

"No – I am a good Mohammedan but I don't like the priests." And we began to speak of religion and Christianity.

"I respect Christians if they really live up to the precepts of Christ. The only thing in Christianity I don't like is that you claim that Christ, who was born of a woman, is the son of God. God would not descend to have his son born in this manner. And then I don't like the idea of the Trinity. God is God – only one. I think our religion is a very rational one, and as rationalism spreads so Mohammedanism will grow. Quite aside from all spiritual matters we have one great advantage over Christianity, from a practical standpoint, and that is cleanliness. Our religion compels us to be personally clean, which is more than yours does."

It was not easy to argue with Barbouchi, for he had an astute mind, but I was quite content to listen to him, and I found later that his views were very representative of his race.

The censor was very strict in Tunis, and the news which appeared in the two paltry newspapers was most scanty and usually several weeks old. When I arrived in Tunis I read news which I had read a fortnight ago in the *Tribuna* of Rome. Barbouchi told me the Arabs knew that the real war news was kept from them; that the war was going badly, and that the French were afraid that the Arabs would take advantage of the weakness of the French situation and start a revolution. But that, he said, was quite a mistaken idea. In the first place they did know the situation, for the Arabs had some sources of information of their own; and secondly, they were not going to take advantage of it, as they had other plans which would prove more efficacious in time. "To tell you the truth, we are really indifferent about the war, for, even if France loses, we shall have to solve our problem at a future date – our time has not yet come."

Chapter 2

THE third day after sending my telegram to Bel-Abbès I received an answer: "Apply to military commander Tunis." It took me an entire day to find the military commander, for I was sent from one end of the town to the other and back again, as the various offices are distributed all over Tunis. Finally I found out that I must apply to the recruiting office, in the first instance, to undergo a medical examination.

At the recruiting office, which consisted of two or three back rooms up a dismal flight of stairs, I waited two days in succession, until I was able to see the sergeant in charge – a caricature who looked as if he had stepped out of *Le Rire*. He took my name and address and asked me if I had papers; I said I had, and showed them. Later I found out that to enter the Legion no papers are ever asked, in fact they are not supposed to be asked. He told me that if I wanted to become a French subject, I could do so, and thus enter any French regiment, whereas as long as I remained a foreigner I should have to stay in the Legion. I thought of my friend Paul S——, who was a naturalized French citizen, had fought at the front during the early days of the war until his health gave out, and who, by a retrospective law made in 1915, was denaturalized and treated as an enemy because he happened to be naturalized a few days after a certain date in 1913 mentioned by the law. He was born in Dresden, had lived in France ever since, was quite a young fellow, and as loyal a Frenchman as I ever met. The day might come when America would go to war with France. I preferred to remain an American. The day following I came for my medical examination, and waited about two hours and a half until the military doctor came. I had to strip and wait in that condition, with bare feet on an icy cold stone floor of the unheated back room, for another half-hour until the doctor could see me. He looked at my eyes, listened to the breathing of my chest, made me walk a few steps backwards and forwards, and it was over. I could dress, and got a slip with which I was to report to another office. That doctor was my first experience of being looked at askance. I did not know then why he looked at me in that strange way; I did not understand the look until I was in the Legion.

At the next office, which was open only at most unusual hours and only for a short time, I had another waiting séance. At last I was let into a room filled with many sickly looking clerks sitting at tables writing; they were dressed as soldiers, though it looked like a masquerade, and on hearing my business some of them busied themselves filling out a lot of foolscap for my registration. One thing struck me as curious – I saw the clerk fill out under the heading nationality, "Says he is an American."

"Look here," I said to him, "I am an American, and I have my papers to prove it."

He paid no attention but continued writing. I was told to return in two days. After two days I was told to return the next day, as the papers were not yet ready. I came – same story, and finally on the fifth day I was asked to sign the papers. I was called into the private office of an officer, who merely asked me: "Are you willing to have your body sent wherever you are commanded?"

"Certainly," I said, and the formalities were over. The following day I received a military railway pass for Sidi-bel-Abbès, the headquarters of the Foreign Legion.

It was a bright sunny Sunday morning when I left Tunis. For a time the train rattled along the coast, and then turned inland. Large plains with waving palm trees – now and then deserted looking villages – until we arrived at the frontier of Tunis and Algiers. Here was a customs examination. Tunis is a protectorate, whereas Algiers is a French colony. My military pass seemed sufficient – no other identifications were asked. In France and her colonies no one can take a train without a *sauf-conduit*, which is a permit to travel, obtainable at the police station where all particulars are asked as to the necessity of travelling, etc.

After passing the frontier the scenery was less monotonous; gradually hills rose, with villages nestling here and there, until the splendid heights of the Tell Atlas came into sight. The climate changed, it was much cooler, and by night it was quite cold; mists and fogs settled over the landscape, and instead of the brilliant clear atmosphere of Tunis grey clouds spread over the sky.

In Algiers I noticed that the Arabs who got into the train were of a much poorer class than any I had seen in Tunis, and also that the French passengers avoided all the compartments in which Arabs travelled. I was travelling third class, and chose specially the compartments in which Arabs were seated. They were mostly very scantily clad, some literally in rags, and nearly all were bare-legged and bare-footed. By nature the Arab is a very stately individual, dignified, and with magnificent manners, Nature's grand seigneur; he is quiet and speaks in low well-modulated voice. Here in Algiers the Arabs bore a haunted look in spite of their stateliness. Their large eyes grew larger each time the compartment door opened, apprehensively, as if expecting something disturbing to happen. Soon I saw the justice of their apprehensions. The French railway officials treated them like dogs never spoke civilly, only shouted and shrieked at them. At one station a great number of Arabs were ready to take the train on its arrival; the French official shoved them like a pack of beasts to the last railway carriage, and would not permit them to get into any other, although the train was half empty. There was not enough room for them, still he insisted upon piling them in until they stood like cattle. As they did not get in quickly enough to suit him, he kicked and punched mercilessly whoever was nearest, using horrible oaths. It made my blood boil to see it. These poor Arabs accepted this treatment without a word of protest, calmly, with a dignity that seemed superhuman to me. Now and then one would turn and give the French official a look of withering contempt, but the brute was probably too dull to understand, and would not have cared if he did. He was in power, and to him Might is Right. The poorest of these Arabs were infinitely superior in culture, manners, race and breeding to this low-down, drink-sodden French official, who was not good enough to blacken their boots, had they had any. After he had hurried them in this brutal fashion, the train did not leave for another half-hour. This incident was not an exception; the treatment the Arabs received was similar all along the line.

On one occasion a common French soldier, who was in loud vulgar conversation with his compatriots, was standing in the passage. The train had arrived at a station; an Arab rose and went along the passage, bowing in his stately manner, as if asking permission to pass the soldier who was blocking the passage with his legs. In reply the soldier glared at him: "What do you want to pass here for? You are all right where you are." The Arab did not understand him, and repeated the motion and the salute.

"You stay where you are, you are all right there," and the soldier did not budge until another passenger made it plain to him that the Arab had to pass in order to be able to get out, as he had arrived at his destination.

The courtesy shown me by the Arabs was extraordinary. In whichever compartment I entered there was a ready smile and the offer of a seat, no matter how crowded it was; it was done with a gesture of complete self-possessed courtesy and graciousness, never obsequiously, or as if in fear. It was their nature to be kind, and probably they felt I liked them. Naturally I treated them as any average decently brought-up individual treats his fellow-men. Towards the close of the day the carriages emptied somewhat, and I had an opportunity of stretching my legs; I went to lie down, and immediately one of the Arabs rolled up his *bournos* and offered it to me for a cushion, another his cloak to cover me. Their attention was touching. The French guards, who came through the train for the tickets, never attempted to make their demands civilly to the Arabs, swore and cursed, and felt so elated about their manner that they looked at me for approval. I need not say how disgusted I was, nor how much contempt I felt for these officials and the Government which tolerated such a condition. Barbouchi's words rang in my ears, and I realized that what he said must come true. No people can remain unpunished who abuse their power in this shameless manner. The day of reckoning will come when every Arab's feelings have been outraged past endurance, and then woe to the Frenchman. The ominous words I heard in the carpet shop in Tunis may mean another Sicilian Vespers, in Arab style, for the French.

The frugality of the Arabs seems to me greater than that of any other people I have come across. Some of my travelling companions were quite satisfied with some bread and dried figs and an occasional drink of water for their entire day's food. On other occasions I noticed the same frugality; oranges and bread or waffles seemed to be all the nourishment they took for the day.

After travelling all day and night I arrived in the city of Algiers early in the morning, and after a change of clothes and linen I repaired to the American Consul to inform him of my decision. I thought it would be just as well to let my country's representative know where to look for me if anything happened. He proved to be an old acquaintance, and he warned me that if I entered the Foreign Legion I would have no chance if I were taken prisoner at the front by the Germans. As a neutral I would be shot by them, and the American Government could do nothing for me. Further, that as an American, if I became an invalid for life, France would not pension me. He told me, what I had heard before, that since the war had broken out the Legion was entirely different from what it used to be, that the traditional Legionary had been cleared out, and that it was made up of enthusiasts for the Allied Cause. By the traditional Legionary he meant the professional soldier, adventurer, and deserter.

"The Legion is now a clean healthy place," he said, "with men who have ideals, and there is an American contingent, in fact several hundred Americans. At the present moment several thousand Americans are fighting in France." This sounded very encouraging, and I felt I had chosen the right course.

I had a very superficial look at Algiers, but was impressed by the utter lack of oriental life in the streets. It is a real French town by the sea, and unless one goes up to Mustapha Supérieur and sees the gorgeous semi-tropical vegetation of the lovely gardens of the private villas, there is no sign whatever that it is Africa, or the Algiers one has dreamed and read about. The houses, streets, shops, restaurants, the life, people, trams, everything is purely French. There are a few Arabs in the streets, but then one sees them in Paris too. The view of the sea is beautiful, but the sea is beautiful everywhere.

Next morning I started early on the last stage of my journey to Sidi-bel-Abbès. Although I had not been in Algiers twenty-four hours, the evening of the day of my arrival the police came to enquire who I was. I was out, so I was spared that little interview, which is never agreeable with French officials, especially police officials, unless one is in company of some important Frenchman and then they are too obsequious.

In the dining-car of the train I met a young Dane, a Mr. Stadel, who told me many interesting things about his voyage from Denmark; he was on his way to Morocco to buy a farm there. After he had sailed from Denmark on his way to England, his steamer was attacked by a German submarine and towed back to Warnemuende.

Here a general requisition was made, and all things useful to the Germans were taken ashore and paid for in German paper money. The passengers' luggage was ransacked, and all valuables of gold and silver taken and weighed. Finally, a personal investigation took place, and all the gold coin found on the passengers was confiscated, and its equivalent, at par, given them in German paper money. These proceedings took about eight days, and then the Danish steamer was allowed to proceed to England.

He envied me going to the Foreign Legion, and wished he could go too, but his health did not permit it. He told me glowing tales about the Legion and how there were companies of each nationality, having officers and noncommissioned officers of the same nationality. He was especially enthusiastic about the Danish and American contingents, all of which made me very hopeful as to the future of my life there. I did not ask him how he got his information; he spoke so animatedly and with so much conviction that I took it for granted that he had friends there, and had probably investigated it for himself. He told me:

"Let me give you some advice, do whatever you are told, never demur, and when marching, if you are dog-tired, don't drop, keep up with all the force of your will and nerves, for if you drop they will leave you there by the roadside without any ado, and you may happen to be in the Desert, miles from any human habitation. They are not very sentimental about a man in the Legion, and will let him die of hunger and thirst without a single scruple."

Then he spoke of the theatre they had in the barracks, where the soldiers often gave entertainments among themselves, what clever artists there were among them, and about some splendid female impersonators.

"The spirit," he continued, "is that of the greatest *camaraderie*, and you will not only enjoy yourself, but make many friends, and after such an exhilarating life you will go to the front with still more enthusiasm."

Naturally I was delighted. We had luncheon together and then drinks until tea-time, and chatted until it was time for me to change, about sunset, at Ste. Barbe du Tlélat. He continued on to Oran to take his boat for Morocco.

The scenery, after leaving Algiers had changed completely in character – the country had widened, the Tell Atlas were more distant, there was a greater expanse of country, an impression of vastness, the mountains seemed more like gigantic hills, habitations seemed further apart, the towns looked whiter, more silent and isolated, the earth's colour grew redder and redder, and it seemed as if we were approaching the desert.

An hour after leaving Ste. Barbe du Tlélat I arrived at Sidi-bel-Abbès. It was evening and dark. As I alighted and gathered up my various portmanteaux a sergeant on guard stepped up to me: "Your papers!" I showed him my military pass.

"Where are you going?"

"To the Foreign Legion."

"What bêtise is this? You for the Foreign Legion? You must be mad. You don't know what you have let yourself in for. What do you want to do in the Foreign Legion."

"To fight the 'Boches.'"

He laughed. "You have come to the right place – you will see enough of the 'Boches' in the Legion." I passed on. He had been drinking, and so I thought it was better not to say any more than necessary. The impression was anything but pleasant. Obviously he was a sergeant of the Legion, for I had read that the only other regiment stationed at Bel-Abbès was that of the Arab Spahis.

I took the ramshackle hotel omnibus and drove to the best hotel in town, according to Baedeker — the Hotel Continental. The town was so badly lighted that I could not see anything except that we drove through a long avenue of poplars, passed through a town-gate and then up a wide, dull, gloomy, cheerless looking street until we stopped before the dirty ill-lighted entrance of the hotel. The staircase was still dirtier than the entrance, and on the first floor in a spacious hall was the office, a sort of telephone booth with a *guichet*, in which sat, wonderfully coiffed and powdered, a Frenchwoman with a very tight mouth and sharp steely blue eyes, Madame Bourelli. Three francs fifty was the price of a room, and I was shown down a long gloomy corridor, lit by gas, which seemed on the verge of going out, to a room which was the ghastliest I have ever inhabited in my travels in four continents of the world. The wallpaper had a nightmare-like design, the furniture was old and ramshackle, the toilet dishes of the most primitive order, the bed with most unappetizing covers though the sheets were clean, and springs which had been springs probably in the time of Napoleon III; they had certainly retired from any kind of activity or resistance since. The hangings were mere rags, and withal there was an air of pretentiousness about the place which made it worse, for one could not say a word of complaint, feeling that it might be considered an insult. The stump of a candle lighted me to bed.

Chapter 3

I AWOKE the following morning with an attack of depression. The room was dismal and dreary, not a ray of sunlight shone into it. I dressed and went out. Somehow I did not have the energy or curiosity to look at the town. I wanted to know where the Legion's barracks were. I walked up the main street and finally asked some one. I had been walking in the opposite direction.

Large gates confronted me, opening into an immense courtyard with a large white building on either side and one at the back facing the gates. At each side of the gate was a small guard-house. I asked to see the Colonel, and a soldier from the guard was despatched to accompany me. He led me straight across the courtyard, flanked by two rows of trees, to the middle building. Up a flight or two of stairs and I was ushered into an office where several soldiers at desks were writing. After a moment's wait I was ushered into an inner office where I found the Colonel. A thick-set fattish man with a miscarriage of a beard, which might have had the intention of becoming an Imperial but was neglected at the wrong time, and so had degenerated into some hair on his chin. The moustache grew in patches. He had only one leg, the other was wood; he had lost it in a Moroccan campaign while captain, and in consequence had been made colonel. He had commenced as cook in the Legion. I showed him the telegram he had sent me, and he answered in a high falsetto voice that he would see if my papers had arrived from Tunis. They had not. I was then ushered to the Major's office. The Major was a fairly pleasant man with a nice twinkle in his eye and good manners. He looked me all over and seemed amused, and asked me some questions as to my profession which. I answered. He was himself interested in archaeology, and had written some things. We had a little chat, and he asked me why I had come to the Legion. When I told him he gave a good-natured smile as if he wanted to say: "I don't know whether to believe you or not, you look truthful, but it is too extraordinary – however, it is no business of mine."

He called an orderly, and I was handed with instructions to the orderly from one office to another. In one office I had to say how I got to Bel-Abbès, and if I had received my ticket and any money at Tunis, also how long it took me to come, where I had stopped, and when I said I had stopped at hotels at my own expense all further questions ceased about that subject. Evidently they had only a right to ask about it as long as I had been *en voyage* at the Government's expense. In the next office I was asked all about my personalities, father, mother, birth date, residence, what relatives living and where, etc.

A rather distinguished-looking fair young man in a very slouchy uniform, which hung on him in a debonair manner, asked me these questions in perfect English. I asked him if he were English.

"No," he answered. "I am German, and my name is Müller."

I was flabbergasted. It did not seem possible. Some time later I heard his story. He was born in Marseilles of a German father and an English mother; his father had been a well-to-do merchant there, had remained a German, and had his son registered at the German Embassy, so that there should never be any doubt as to his nationality. The father died, the war broke out, the son was heir to his father's business, he had no German sympathies, and in order to evade the concentration camp, and the sequestration of his fortune, he entered the Foreign Legion.

When he had noted all the answers to his questions he took me to my squad which was also his own. He told me I should have to remain in barracks until five o'clock as no one was allowed to leave before then. Eleven o'clock was the dinner hour. Very likely I would be put into uniform during the afternoon. His room was large, with twenty-eight beds running straight across the building, and a large window at each end, one looking into the courtyard at the front, and the other overlooking a narrow courtyard and a high wall at the back. It was nearly eleven o'clock then, and before dinner he made up his bed, the mattress of which had been doubled up to air, and the sheets and blankets folded.

Then he gave me some advice about locking away my things as they disappear very easily. "You see you are in the Legion, where there are all kinds of people, and stealing is quite an everyday occurrence."

For some inexplicable reason dinner was brought into the room that day; soup, meat and vegetable, in dirty looking tin dishes. I could not touch any of it. I ate the bread, which was good, and drank some coffee out of a tin cup. Müller warned me that I had never drunk such stuff before. I had not.

After dinner an order came that I should not remain in that room, but go into the squad which was under the lieutenantship of a Danish officer, who spoke English. So I was marched off to the third and top floor and shown into a hall room, half the size of the others, with only fourteen beds. Only the corporal was in the room when I entered, and he was lying down having a nap. The orderly who brought me gave instructions and left. The corporal arose, looked me over, smiled cynically, and took out a cigarette. He did not say anything for a long time, So I sat down on a deal bench and watched him. Then he said: "I don't know what you have come here for, but you'll find life much too hard for a man of your habits."

"If others can stand it, I don't see why I can't." He did not speak again for some time, then: "I'll put you in the bed next to Grothé, he is a 'gentile garçon,' and he speaks English."

I wondered what Grothé would be like. There was nothing for me to do. I had no reading matter with me, so all I could do was to stare into the air. The corporal was not talkative, and he made no attempt at being sociable. He kept on smoking his cigarettes one after another. The hours, sitting in that room, waiting for the order to come to be clothed, seemed interminable. Finally at four o'clock the soldiers trooped into the room returning from their exercises. Grothé was a nice soft-spoken person, who spoke English in a way. He spoke it better than he understood it, and made countless errors. I had to pay great attention to catch the exact meaning of what he wanted to say. After the soldiers had unburdened themselves of their knapsacks and guns, the whistle blew in the courtyard, and every one rushed down for *rapport*. Although I was not yet in uniform I had to go down too. A large square was formed by the soldiers, two lines deep, and in the middle stood a sergeant-major who took the roll-call from each corporal. Then he read a list of the change of guard for the next day, and the result of the medical examinations of the soldiers who had reported themselves ill, and finally wound up with reading the changes and transfers of soldiers either from one room to another or to other companies, regiments, or garrisons. Another sergeant-major stepped into the square and read out the punishments, and the *rapport* finished with an ordinary sergeant stepping into the arena and calling out the letters which had arrived for the soldiers by mail. My name was mentioned as having been transferred from one room to the other. Evidently the slightest change was reported publicly in this *rapport*.

While standing in my place during this performance I heard several voices behind me whisper: “What are you going to do with your clothes when you are in uniform?”

“Will you sell me your clothes? I shall be free soon, and shall need civilian clothes.”

“If you want to sell your clothes I know some one who will buy them at a good price.”

After the report a sergeant stepped up to me and asked me in perfect English: “What are you doing here?” I told him my reasons, and he said: “Well, my boy, you have been very foolish, but it is no use talking about that now, for it is too late. You have signed, haven’t you?” I said I had. “Kohn,” he called out, and up came a rather good-looking Jew of about thirty-five or forty, with a big black beard, dressed in a new uniform, but a common soldier. “You’d better know each other, and, Kohn, you can give this young man some advice.”

Mr. Kohn, as I heard afterwards, was a very rich Paris banker, whose father had neglected to become a French citizen, although as an Alsatian he had privileges in advance of any ordinary German. He had entered the Foreign Legion to save his fortune from being sequestered. He spoke English perfectly. Kohn told me he kept a room at the hotel where he could wash decently and have his meals, and feel like a human being for a few hours a day, and that I would have to do the same, as I did not seem to have any idea as to what I had let myself in for by coming to the Legion. He said he had entered with enthusiasm, which had waned very rapidly when he found out what a dastardly lot of people they were, and what a filthy muckheap it was. He was very bitter, and I heard later that he had had a position in the offices of the Legion, due to influence and money, but that he got very cocky there, thinking himself perfectly secure, and that some superior officer, to whom he had not lent all the money he wanted, had him put out and allotted him a place as a common soldier in a room with twenty-eight. As a clerk he had had his own room. No soldier can sleep out of barracks, only when away on permission. He was extremely acrid about everything that concerned the Legion. I listened patiently, but did not say anything. I realized that this was a man to be avoided, as it was obvious that he had got himself on everybody’s bad books. Like a great many of his race he was very patronizing and bragging. He warned me that they were all thieves in the Legion, and that I had to be very careful of my belongings; that this day I had been sized up by hundreds of eyes, that not the slightest cut of my coat had been missed, and that they judged me according to my value in money. That they would all come and want to borrow from me, and that I was not to lend them anything. That they would all want to buy my clothes, or rather steal them, as they would never pay for them, and that whatever little things I had about me would be stolen.

I had asked my corporal if I might go out at five, as I had to go to my hotel to tell the people there of my whereabouts. I was told that that was impossible, as I was not yet in uniform, and until a man is in uniform he may not leave the barracks, but I might ask the sergeant. I did, and he gave me permission, but said that he must accompany me. How true this was I don't know. However, he came with me to my room, looked over my luggage, seemed satisfied, and told me that I might store all my luggage in his room, as I should not have room in barracks; besides, it might be stolen, whereas in his room it would be perfectly safe. I thanked him, and he left telling me to be in by nine o'clock, duly impressing upon me how kind he was in leaving me alone as I was not yet in uniform, and that he really ought to follow me about until it was time to turn in.

I looked up Kohn in his room at the hotel, as he had asked me to do, and found out what arrangements he had made in order to do the same. The whiff I had had of the barracks and the soldiers had convinced me of the necessity of having a place to keep my portmanteaux, to bathe, and to write in peace and tranquillity.

Kohn shared his room with another man, an elderly dignified Jew, who was a Paris jeweller. He was in the Legion for the same reason as Kohn, that is, he was a German subject in virtue of his father's nationality, but was born in Paris. He did not speak a word of German, or any other language but French, and had entered the Legion to avoid the concentration camp, and the sequestration of his business and fortune. Evidently he had been on good behaviour, and had duly ingratiated himself in the right quarters, for some little time later he was allowed to depart in peace for Paris. He was much too old a man to do service.

I had my dinner in the hotel, and before nine o'clock returned to barracks for my first night there.

Chapter 4

AT five o'clock next morning the bugle blew the *réveil*. At 5.30 all the soldiers, equipped with their kit, assembled in the courtyard for *rassemblement*. Although I was not yet in uniform I had to go down and stand in line with the other members of the squad just as if I were going to march out with them for the exercises. I felt like a fish out of water. A tall good-looking officer, obviously a gentleman, came up to me and asked me in English what I was doing here. I was beginning to get a bit tired of the repetition of the same story. Was it really so extraordinary that a fairly decent person should enlist in the Legion? It was – only I did not know it then. He was very tactful and nice, and after he had learned the main facts he returned to the group of officers, who were holding an inspection of the troops before marching out, and communicated to them the things he had just heard. I was told later that he was a Greek from Patras whose mother was English.

A fair-haired young Jewish lieutenant, of almost miniature size, then came up to me and asked me in French if I happened to know his brother, who was a lawyer in New York, and had something to do with the Red Cross Association of the Allies in America. I did not. He was very cold and brief and haughty, and showed no interest whatever.

After the *rassemblement* I returned to my room, and sat all the morning waiting to be clothed, but there was no call. At ten o'clock the soldiers returned from their exercises and immediately went down to the *rapport*. At eleven o'clock we trooped to the dining-room, a long low one-storied building, behind the centre building, which had been the theatre in pre-war days; the stage still existed at one end, and was now used as the regiment's barber's-shop. Long deal benches and tables ran along the full length of the dining-room; the food was brought in large tin pails from the kitchen, another outhouse in the courtyard. The corporal of each squad had to write out a *bon* saying how many men were coming to dinner, and two men of each squad brought the food to the dining-room. The men of each squad took turns in serving the food out of the tin pails to each man at table. The tin dishes, forks, and spoon were provided by the Government in the soldier's outfit, but he had to provide himself with a knife. The food consisted of horribly greasy soup, great hunks of unappetizing fat, and some gritty unwashed greens. Most of the time we received bad potatoes instead of the greens. It was what the lower-class Germans call *Bürgerliche Küche*, and they all enjoyed it. The bread had been served out in the room of each squad before dinner, every man receiving a quarter of a loaf.

From eleven to twelve the canteen was open. I hurried through the pretence of eating and rushed to the canteen. This was in another outhouse, on the ground floor of a two-storied building, which contained the noncommissioned officers' mess on the upper floor. The canteen was dark and gloomy and comprised three rooms. The first room had a counter where all the indispensable necessities of a soldier were purchasable: shoelaces, shoe-blacking, polishing materials, etc. etc., and wine, cheese, bread, cigars and cigarettes; the rest of the room was taken up with deal benches and tables where the soldiers could eat and drink. The small windows were protected by iron bars like a prison, and at night two mean little petroleum lamps, suspended from the ceiling, lit up this dive-like place which was none too clean, since the soldiers who frequented it were not overscrupulous in their manners as to increasing its cleanliness. On the other side of the small entrance hall was the third room, the kitchen, where only fried eggs and chops were obtainable. The prices were not exorbitant, but certainly above what would be expected in a soldiers' canteen. At twelve o'clock every one was shooed out, and driven to a large shed where piles of potatoes lay on the ground. Each squad gathered around one of these piles and commenced to peel these black, vile, half-rotten potatoes, and not before each pile was finished were any of the soldiers allowed to go to their rooms.

There was a *repose* after that until 12.45, but in reality it was no repose, for in that half-hour the soldiers had to make their beds, if they had not had time before dinner, clean their clothes from mud-spots, polish their boots and guns, and be ready at 12.45 for *rassemblement* and exercises.

I did some more waiting in my room during the afternoon, and finally was called to the offices in the centre building (our company's building was on the left side coming in at the gate), and sent to the top floor to receive my uniform and outfit. It consisted of a cap, a pair of red trousers, two pairs of whitish linen trousers, a long blue coat, a short blue jacket, both with brass buttons, a pair of short leather leggings, a long blue sash, a whitish blouse, a pair of linen slippers with rope soles, three rough flannel shirts, three pairs of drawers of the same material, a gun, straps and leather belt to hold bayonet and cartridge cases, a *musette*, a water-bottle, shoe and other brushes for polishing, two cheese cloths, handkerchiefs, tin dishes for eating and drinking, a small blanket, a knapsack, pegs and a piece of canvas for the tent, pick and shovel, two blue neckties made of similar material as the handkerchiefs, and a pair of *brodequins*. The *brodequins* were big coarse hob-nailed boots, which had been worn by legions of soldiers, evidently, and had been repaired again and again with new tops and new soles. Their insides were disgusting and the smell appalling. They were greased to such an extent that whatever came in contact with them took the grease. Of course they did not fit – in fact not any of the things given me fitted, and the clothes had been worn by countless soldiers before me, which was shown by the many matriculation numbers in the linings. The only things that were new were the shirts and drawers, and the polishing materials and brushes. Duly dressed, and "with my knapsack on my back," I returned to my room to put my things in order.

That evening I was able to go out without an escort, as I was in uniform, but Grothé had to clip my hair first, as it was *règlement* that every soldier had to have short cropped hair. At the gate of the barracks a sergeant is on duty, whose business it is to look over each man, to see that he leaves in a clean condition – no mud-spots, polished brass buttons, two weeks the buttons buttoned on one side of the double-breasted coat and two weeks on the other side, and polished boots and leggings. If any one of these things was not in order, to the complete satisfaction of the sergeant, the soldier was ordered back without a word of explanation. It was left to him to find out the fault. It might have been the long sash, four or five metres long, which was so difficult to wind about one's waist alone, which was not just as it ought to have been; any little mistake like that was sufficient reason to be turned back.

I had put on my own shoes, as I could not wear the *brodequins*, and managed to get past the gate with the aid of Grothé, who lied that I had permission to buy my own regulation boots in town, as no *brodequins* were in stock which fitted me.

My first business was to buy a pair of good decent boots, and which to all appearances looked like the *brodequins*.

I took a look at the town. According to Baedeker Sidi-bel-Abbès is a prosperous agricultural town of thirty thousand inhabitants, was founded in 1849 on the plan of a Roman camp, with streets at right angles, and is surrounded by suburbs occupied mainly by Spanish immigrants.

The streets are wide and dirty, flanked on each side by drab-coloured houses, one or two stories in height. With the exception of four or five bazaar shops, there are only public-houses of the lowest order, and the ordinary grocery and butcher shops. A wooden shack is called a cinematograph theatre, and adjoining the public square is a regular theatre of the most primitive village type. A little iron kiosk adorns the centre of the square, where on Sunday afternoons the band of the Foreign Legion plays for the edification of the townspeople. They are a dirty-looking lot, these townspeople – sinister, lowering, slouchy, a bastard type of Spaniard, French, and Algerian.

The town has five gates, one in the middle of each of the four walls of the town, and a fifth to the north-east leading to the Arab quarter, which is outside the town across a common. Each of the four gates is called after the town to which the road leads: Porte Tlemcen, Porte Oran, Porte Frenda, Porte Mascara, but the fifth is called La Porte Cocu (the gate of the cuckold), because beyond the Arab quarter is the celebrated "Village Nègre" with Jewish, European, and Arab prostitutes.

The two main streets, which cross the town leading to the gates, are ornamented on the kerb side of the pavement with short misshapen palms, which resemble brooms; the leaves are bound together half-way up, so as to foster their growth and protect them from the street urchins. The back streets are very dismal and abound in questionable resorts of all kinds. Bel-Abbès also boasts of the "Halles," a large square building where on Sunday mornings the townspeople go to market.

The drinking-houses and eating-places are of the type to be found near the docks of any big port – dirty, sombre-looking, old, with raw wooden floors, reeking of spirits, squalid and sordid. The restaurants are no better, places such as those to which coachmen and labourers resort in northern cities, with oil-cloth table covers and leaden spoons and forks. The cuisine was accordingly bad, and in order to get any decent food it was customary to do one's own shopping, bring the restaurant keeper the eatables, and then pay for the preparation and the service.

Both public-houses and restaurants are all of the same class, only the *cafés* are a little better, although the stuff which they serve is vile and dear; they look like third-rate *cafés* in the provinces of France.

Outside the walls and all around the town are walks with fine old trees; in fact, these park-like fortifications are the best part of Sidi-bel-Abbès.

The Arab quarter is interesting, not on account of the houses, which are all European in structure except the Mosque, and look like the houses of Bel-Abbès, though they are white and pink and blue and not drab coloured, but on account of the life and movement and the picturesque and many-coloured costumes of the Arabs. The Spahis, a regiment of Algerian Arabs, whose barracks are across the street from those of the Legion, frequent the *cafés* and baths of this quarter. Their finely cut faces, wonderful dress, and marvellous turbans, are a real pleasure to the eye after all the common-place, dirty, brutal-looking, and shabbily dressed townspeople of Bel-Abbès, and the caricatures of criminal types of the Legion's soldiers.

Beyond the Arab quarter is the "Village Nègre." Every soldier of the Legion is forbidden to go there, and if he disobeys and is found out, he is liable to the severest punishment which his immediate superiors can impose on him, except sending him to "Concile de Guerre." This village consists of one solitary narrow unpaved street of one-storied houses, and each of these houses is inhabited by the typical Algerian painted and bebangled prostitutes of the lowest order. Most of the houses have one room, barely furnished with a bed, wash-bowl, and a chest of drawers; and these luridly painted women sit on their front doorsteps waiting for their customers, or rather pouncing upon their prey, when some misguided male passes the little bridge over the creek which separates the Arab quarter from the village. The Legion's soldiers are forbidden to frequent these women, as they are reputed to be diseased. A *piquet* of four soldiers and a sergeant does duty here every night, and if a soldier is caught within the precincts he is taken back to barracks at the point of the bayonet. The soldiers went just the same, I found, but waited for a night when a friendly sergeant was on duty, who would close an eye.

It was said that all these women were diseased because the Arabs frequented them, and that all Arabs were syphilitic. I have not found that to be true but just the contrary – their religion absolutely demands the utmost cleanliness of body, and especially before and after visiting a woman; besides, being Mohammedans and circumcised, they are more or less naturally protected from infection, whereas the absolute filth of the Legion's soldiers and their inability and more often lack of desire to keep their bodies clean, is most conducive to breeding infectious diseases.

Bel-Abbès possessed only one bathing establishment, whereas the small Arab quarter had no less than five splendid baths. Neither the Bel-Abbès townspeople nor the Legion's soldiers frequented any of these five; only Arabs, though Europeans were allowed to enter. The price of a Turkish bath and massage was one franc, whereas the establishment in Bel-Abbès charged three francs for an ordinary bath. The Arab baths were always full, the French baths mostly empty.

One evening when I told the landlady of my hotel that I was going to the Arab baths her eyes narrowed, and she said: "How can you possibly go to such a dirty place!"

Chapter 5

All Bel-Abbès lived on the Legion as far as I could make out. Of course there were agriculturalists, but the townspeople had no other customers than the Legion's soldiers. The Spahis went to the Arab quarter. The countless drinking shops, restaurants, and tobacconists were all for the soldiers — no one else entered them. And yet these people were indescribably rude to the soldiers. It was sufficient to wear a Legion's uniform to be insulted. No one trusted them. No matter how courteous one might be to the people, they were rude and intended to be rude. It was an antagonism which they cultivated, and which was not to be forgotten for an instant. I had my photograph taken in uniform; the photographer was more or less civil, but the woman who gave the receipts and attended to the business part was personified rudeness to every soldier. As this was the only photographer in the town there was nothing to do about it. My own experience was that the pictures were not ready when promised, and I asked, as I could not come the next day, that they should send them.

"Send them to you — a soldier in the Legion? We cannot send them — you can come here to-morrow and get them."

"I am sorry I cannot come to-morrow as I am occupied."

"Oh no you are not — I know all about it — you are free after your *soupe* at five o'clock, and you can come and get them then."

I turned to the man, and had my way, but it was just an example of the spirit of insolence which prevailed. My tobacconist, a surly man, who seemed to sell us his cigars and tobacco most grudgingly, watching us all the time like a lynx for fear we might steal something, said to me one day when I happened to enter alone: "Why are you in the Legion? You don't look like the others."

There was no small coin in circulation; chits, issued by different tradespeople, took its place. It was impossible for the new-comer to know which were good, as many of the trades people had opened a shop, circulated a few thousand francs worth of chits, and then shut up again.

Naturally their chits were valueless, and every now and then my chits were refused with contempt and a look of distrust, as if I were trying to cheat. These chits were for anything under a franc. One and two franc bills existed in Oran Chamber of Commerce notes, which were not current outside the province of Oran. Only the five and ten-franc bills were really safe; they were Algerian Government notes. Very often change could not be given in chits, and in consequence one had to accept stamps, but then in the next shop a printed notice announced that stamps were not accepted for payment!

Only wine could be served to soldiers, and not liquors, but there were places where liquors could be obtained on the quiet for double price. A law prohibited the sale of spirits of any kind to a soldier before 11 a.m., and then only until 2 p.m., and again only between 5 and 7 p.m. After 9 p.m. spirits could not be sold to any one. Nevertheless it was astonishing how most of the soldiers managed to keep perpetually drunk while they were *en ville*.

The landscape around Bel-Abbès is rather fine. The town lies in a large fertile plain, rising in the north to the Tell Atlas, and to the south to undulating hills covered with magnificent oak and pine forests. The situation is not unlike Rome in the Roman Campagna. And the plain is treeless like the Campagna.

The early morning is very beautiful when the haze lies over the landscape, midday is hot, and the scorching sun in the cloudless sky is merciless. The fields are of a rich reddish earth, clay-like when damp, and baked to breaking-point in the heat. When the weather is bad it is very bad – either blinding rainstorms, which, in their fine drizzle, penetrate to the skin, or dust storms which make it impossible to breathe or even swallow, drying the throat, and inflaming the eyes to blindness.

The nights are clear and balmy. Moonlight nights are particularly fine, and with little imagination, standing on the Common between the Porte Cocu and the Arab quarter, with the Mosque in the distance and the tall stately trees fringing the Common, one is transported for a moment to the Orient. For, although Bel-Abbès is Algiers, and ethnographically in oriental surroundings, it has in reality not the slightest trace of the Orient. The town is intensely low-class European in aspect and atmosphere, and even the better houses are of the lower middle-class order.

The Foreign Legion was originally founded by Napoleon I, and, it appears, was disbanded under the Restoration; however, under

Louis-Philippe it was resurrected, and after the occupation of Algiers by the Duke of Orleans the headquarters of the Legion were established at Sidi-bel-Abbès. All the barrack buildings belong to this period, with the exception of one which was built during the reign of Napoleon III. Structurally they are all the same style, and the inner arrangements are also of the same primitive order as in the time of Louis-Philippe.

The halls are wide, the staircases also, the stairs are worn by the tread of generations of soldiers, and to prevent their complete decay the corners are edged with iron bands. These bands are not on the level with the wood, as the wood has been worn too low, thus forming an admirable trap for tripping with the heavy *brodequins*, especially when rushing up and down the stairs in a crowd of hundreds of soldiers. The great wooden rafters of the ceiling and the walls are whitewashed; the wooden floors unpainted. In each hall hangs a large old-fashioned lantern with a tiny petroleum lamp in it. On either side of the entrance in the lower hall are about eight taps, and underneath them a tarred trough, which is the only washing convenience for the soldiers when they have time and when there is water. They have precious little time; besides, what parts of their bodies could they wash in a draughty entrance hall, with people passing up and down the stairs and past the building? The water was turned on at six in the morning, exactly a quarter of an hour after the troops had marched out. At noon the water was said to be used up by the kitchen, and in the afternoon, when there was water sometimes, one had a free fist fight to get a place, and, if not very careful, soap, towel and any garment which had been laid aside for a moment would disappear instantly beyond all hope of recovery.

There was a bath house, which was open once a week for a shower bath. The shower consisted of five fine sprays of water dripping down. But if the exercises were long that day, or the man who heated the oven was not well, then the bath was omitted. As everything had to be done according to *règlement*, so also the bath – each squad had its turn for a short space of time, and if it happened that a soldier was stopped by an officer, or had to do a *corvée* while his squad was bathing, he had to miss his bath and wait another week.

The idea in founding the Legion had been to give a man who had committed some error a chance to rehabilitate himself. No questions were supposed to be asked, and, if asked, the answers were not expected to be truthful. A man's word was accepted. Many a man had come here in the history of the Legion's existence who turned out to be murderer, embezzler, forger, or prince. It is not many years ago that a simple young man arrived, who had not much to say, and registered as John Smith, or some such name, and lived the life of a private soldier. He was a bit of a dullard, and not popular, and was generally avoided by every one, which he took very indifferently. Altogether he was very apathetic. After he had been in the Legion some time he fell ill, was taken to the hospital, and died. Two months after his death a German battleship arrived at Oran, and several high naval officers travelled to Bel-Abbès, and, with all due formality, asked the Colonel and authorities for the body of John Smith. John Smith was no other than a nephew of Emperor William II, and the body of the German Prince was transported with full military honours to Oran, and taken to Germany on His Majesty's cruiser.

The times are countless, when a detective from some part of Europe has entered the Legions barracks, and, when the company was at dinner, has looked for his man, tapped him on the shoulder, motioned him to follow, and disappeared with him – no one ever knowing who he was, what he had done, or what became of him.

I was never able to find out who the German Prince was, but I imagine it must have been one of the three sons of Prince Albrecht of Prussia, Regent of Brunswick, who had such unfortunate endings. They were the *bêtes noires* of the Kaiser. He literally hounded them to death, and wrecked each one's life – and incidentally confiscated their fortunes, which were reputed to be the largest of any of the Royal Princes. The last of the three, Prince Friedrich Heinrich, fell from an aeroplane in 1917 in the British lines and a week or two later died from his injuries. Prior to the war he had been an exile from his country, and had spent most of his time in Italy.

Chapter 6

I WAS but a few days in the Legion before I realized that I had come to the wrong place. First of all there were no contingents of different nationalities with their respective officers, as Mr. Stadel and others had told me. French was spoken – bad French by Germans, Greeks and Spaniards. There was one Englishman, one Dane, one American nigger, a few Armenians, a number of Spaniards and Greeks, two Corsicans, a few Turks, Russians, Egyptians, Portuguese, Servians, Italians, Arabs, Negroes, many Algerians, some Jews, very few Frenchmen, and the rest Germans.

The marches, the desert, the shooting, the Arab encounters on the Moroccan railway, the watch-fires, was it all a dream of Mr. Stadel? The officers of different nationalities? One Danish lieutenant, two Greek lieutenants, a Corsican captain – the rest Germans.

Secondly, there were no idealists or enthusiasts for the war in the Legion, as the American Consul at Algiers had told me. The typical Legionnaire existed as he had existed ever since the foundation of the Legion: the murderer, thief, cut-throat, deserter, adventurer, embezzler, forger, gaol-bird, and fugitive from justice. The only exceptions of a different category were the few German-Frenchmen who entered in order to save themselves from the concentration camp, or to save their fortunes from being sequestered, or both.

The Legion was the stamping ground of the typical ex-German as he has been described for generations. Seventy per cent of the Legion were Germans, and it was German food, German manners, German discipline, German militarism, German arrogance, German insolence and German arbitrariness. One of the majors was a German-Alsatian, the Jewish lieutenant had a German name, every sergeant-major but one was a German, every sergeant but two was a German, the cooks were Germans, and the infirmary nurses were Germans. The severity of the punishments was decidedly German, It was a German regiment of the lowest type transplanted to Africa. The soldiers spoke German among themselves, and aired only German sentiments. They retained all their German habits of excessive drinking, eating, smoking, swearing, and blaspheming.

There was not a man in the Legion who could be trusted either as to his word or honesty. There were no morals – not even the morals of the *Apache*, who at least protects his associate in crime. It was a crowd of men nowhere else to be seen.

The humane among us always believe that, no matter how low or bad a man, he can always be redeemed with love or kindness or decent treatment, and that somehow his heart can be touched. Nothing of that kind here. Such a man did not exist. They were hardened old criminals, who were past all touching of heart. Any such attempt would have been construed as a trap, and any apparent kindness or friendship was treated with suspicion. Genuine feeling was unknown in the Legion. There was nothing to redeem; a man was a living shell, with his soul dead, with no conscience or scruple, without heart or feeling, with only a belly to feed and fill with drink, and sexual organs to serve him for his depravities. To rob openly, to steal secretly, to murder when lust prompted, were all one to him. There was no friendship, no self-respect, no respect for others, nothing was sacred. Everything was calculated, every feeling only existed theoretically, was called into service to obtain money, drink, food, tobacco, and animal satisfaction. And having once succeeded, the victim was publicly laughed and jeered at, treated with contempt for his stupidity and softness, and then bullied by others, who exploited their knowledge of him and finally harassed him into submission, until any attempt to retain self-respect was impossible and the last ray of decency was extinguished. He was made a beast of so often that he himself became a beast like the others.

The human brain is not made of steel; it is malleable and impressionable; and the strength of numbers and its force is overpowering. A man cannot swim against the stream, and once in the vortex of human depravity, where there is no religion, and where ethical values have never existed, a man, if he has any stamina in him and doesn't fall at once, is slowly attacked by the innumerable, subtle, invisible tentacles of wickedness and vice, daily, hourly, in speech, suggestion and action, and life is made a mental and physical torture for him in hundreds of ways every hour of the day and night, consciously and unconsciously, until he yields to the surrounding influences; and once brought down to their level there is no hope of his resurrection. To get there means the killing of everything good that was ever in him, beyond all hope, and with it appears a carelessness of self, and a gradual awakening of a sense of enjoyment of the cruelties and depravities of their life, until he, like the others, can no longer live without their brutal pleasures and vices, and becomes like them in thought, in apathy, in degeneration, with the same fixed idea that nothing matters except the coarsest, most brutal and physical satisfactions. Everything must be sacrificed for that. The ethics of the decent world serve to play with, not to be acted on, or believed in.

I had thought that in my many travels, in my knowledge of all sorts and conditions of men, I had met the worst class which existed, the lowest types. I found I was mistaken; it was only here that I met them. I had never met them before. What I had met were ideal types of ruffians, thieves, prostitutes, and thugs, of which one reads in books, types that had personality, a sense of humour and a heart underneath their badness, and always a sense of honour, even if only among themselves.

But my remotest imagination had never pictured the type I met here, a type absolutely foreign to me, of which I had had no previous conception. There had always been a basis in common from which I could grapple with low types, whereas here I stood before an enigma – these people were outside anything I could tackle. Even if I had understood them, there was no common ground, no point of contact; I had to become one of them first. And once there, I would have had much common ground, but it would not have been of any use to me, for then I could not have been of any help to them. I should have been where they were. It was the dregs of the lowest of human society which gathered here. No such collection is to be found anywhere else in the world, not even in prisons.

In prisons there are bound to be persons who are good but have failed; probably through a temptation, a wave of temper, a weakness, a first offence. But whoever came here was a hardened old sinner, who had been in prison many times and never dreamt of reform or betterment, but who came here because he could be his hard-hearted self, in all his viciousness, together with the others like him, and be protected by the law.

Here the code was: do as you would not want to be done by, but don't be found out. The victim is the guilty one.

A man is not punished for stealing, but the man who has his things stolen is punished. The murdered man is buried, the murderer must not be found out. I had come to the refuse-heap of Europe, and I had to stick to my guns in order not to land on top of it too.

Two thoughts occupied me after my first glances at the Legion and the life and the men – to keep myself straight at all costs, and to get out.

Chapter 7

WITH my advent in the Legion I received quite a number of offers of friendship. "You look like a decent chap – why on earth did you come to the Legion – they are all thieves and cut-throats here? You must take great care of them. If you want me to I'll be your friend – you can leave your things with me. I'll take care of them, otherwise you will have everything stolen. You must not trust any one. They will try to get everything you have away from you. I'll give you the tip as to who you can trust. Sorry I am for the day I came here."

Another one: "I am an Arab – you know," and he winked. "I'll be your friend – you understand – but you must lend me forty sous now – I need them. I'll be your friend always. You know my friend the Spahi – he is a great friend of mine."

"What was that Arab saying to you? You must not trust him, he is a rascal. I have been ten years in the Legion and I know something about it. You go your own way, don't associate with any one – they are all bad. If you want anything or are in trouble come to me – I'll help you."

These and similar propositions were made to me by the dozen. Most of the faces of the speakers were so much against them that there could not be a moment's doubt as to their hypocrisy and ill-intentions.

It was the usual thing for a new arrival, who looked as if he had either money or clothes, to be spotted as a natural victim, each one making free and unscrupulous use of calumny and malignity at the expense of his brother soldiers to gain his point, and become the one confidential friend of the innocent and then rob him completely.

As all these propositions were so baldly obvious, I did not pay any more attention than if they had never been made. But their suppositions that I might be taken in were evidently well founded, for I saw very soon to my intense amazement how others who came after me were taken in by these declarations of friendship by the very first suitors. A Dane was one of them. He was taken in by a thick-set blonde German from the "Wasserkante" in Hamburg, with large blue eyes that were calculating and hard as steel. The Dane trusted him absolutely, thought he was his only friend in the Legion, and the German showered attentions upon him. He sold him his clothes and shoes for about 10 francs, and his steamer rug for about 2.50 francs; then bought him a knife out of that money, which had probably cost 1.50 francs, and charged him 4.50 for it, telling him how clever he was to have got so much, for if the Dane had tried to sell them himself he would not have received more than 9 francs, and would have had to pay at least 6 francs for the knife! The Dane swallowed it all, almost fell round the German's neck in sheer gratitude, and went to every one of the squad praising the cleverness of the Hamburger. But when steely Blue Eyes saw that the Dane had nothing more, and received no money from home or anywhere else, but depended upon his 2.50 francs pay every ten days to buy his necessities, he dropped him and was seen no more in the vicinity of the Dane. He had profited probably to the amount of 60 francs by him – a good deal for a soldier in the Legion.

The Spahi, to whom the Arab referred, I had met in the train, after leaving Ste. Barbe du Tlélat on my way to Sidi-bel-Abbès. He was a fine looking chap, who spoke tolerable French, and when I told him I was going to the Legion, said: "You will get on there and be a sergeant in no time, for I am sure you know how to read and write, and any one who knows how to read and write gets promoted at once. I do not know how to read and write and so I shall never get on."

He told me many things about Bel-Abbès and the life there, and about his wife in Oran, and how much he loved her. He had just been staying with her for five days. "The French Government will always give you leave for a few days if you can prove you are going for purposes of procreation." (I don't remember if he used these words but that was their meaning.) He said that he had made good use of his five days.

I had not yet had supper and I told him so, and asked him if he knew of a simple good restaurant in Bel-Abbès. He volunteered to show me about – he himself had not yet supped, so after I had left my luggage at the hotel we went to a small restaurant together. Since he had been so kind I insisted upon paying the modest little bill.

Soon after I had settled down in my squad I was given to understand that, being a new arrival, it was expected of me to stand drinks to all the company of my room in the canteen. I gladly complied with this, and after *la soupe*, as supper was called, we all met in the canteen. I cannot remember the number of bottles of red wine that were drunk, but it was a goodly number, and I had the satisfaction that they were all pretty tight when the canteen closed at 8.30. They were all heavy drinkers, and it did not take them long to get enough; a glass was one swallow. Of course cigars and cigarettes were included in the treat. I had taken a pick-me-up before I went to this initiation party in order to appear as cheerful as possible. It was hopeless. I have never been in a company which, with all the wine and smokes and good cheer I was ready to bring, was so absolutely heavy and dull. Some spoke a little, some answered at intervals in monosyllables, others only listened, but one and all only leered at the wine and seemed to wonder how much more they could put away, and to wait for the feeling of drunkenness to come over them. There was no *esprit*, no jokes, not even vulgar ones, no one became talkative or sociable – it was like a herd of beasts, whose business it was to get drunk. All my attempts at hilarity fell flat. But they were satisfied – absolutely satisfied, as I heard later. It was what they wanted: all the wine they could drink and all the cigarettes and cigars they could smoke; the rest did not interest them.

One little incident was characteristic. I had placed a lot of packages of cigarettes on the table and invited each one to help himself. Towards the end there were some packages over, and, when it was time to go, in a trice they had disappeared, each one asking the other: "What became of the cigars and cigarettes which were here a moment ago?" No one knew.

Chapter 8

ALTHOUGH my squad consisted of the men in my room I did not go with them to the exercises, but was allotted to the squad of the *jeunes soldats* at the *rassemblement*. This was a squad quite apart, into which all new-comers were sent, no matter how young or how old. After the exercises each young soldier returned to the squad of his room. Once the primary instructions of a young soldier were completed he entered his room squad as a regular soldier, joining them in their exercises. Some of the "young soldiers" were over fifty years old, had been in the Legion before, had left when their time was up, and returned to sign again; nevertheless they had to go through the school of the *jeunes soldats*. One had the decoration of the *croix de guerre*, others were mere boys. There was no specified time for a man to be a young soldier. It depended on himself and the goodwill of the sergeant. Several had been there as much as six and eight months and were no farther advanced in the simplest methods of instruction than the man who had been there a week. The usual time was supposed to be about three months, but I heard there was no fixed rule.

Acharock was the sergeant of the young soldiers during the first days of my arrival. He was a Frenchman, handsome, dark, quick, nervous, irascible, severe but just – one of the very few who was just. He had at the end of his tongue the longest list of animal names applicable to his soldiers which I have ever heard, and they were curiously appropriate. His rebukes and scoldings were made impetuously, and apparently without sufficient reason, but a few days convinced me to the contrary. He scented ill-will and reprimanded it; but where he found good intention and honest effort he was lenient, indulgent, kind and helpful.

The programme of the day was as follows: *réveil*, the bugle call, at 5 a.m.; assembly of the troops 5.30; march out to the *champ de tir*, where the exercises took place, 5.45, and return to barracks at ten o'clock. Immediately after the return, report in the courtyard; dinner at 11, followed by the arduous and tiresome job of peeling half-rotten potatoes until 12.15; repose until 12.45, which, as I have said, really meant cleaning up and getting ready for the afternoon exercises at the shooting field; march out at 1 o'clock, and return to barracks at 4.30, followed immediately by another report, which lasted until supper at 5, when the soldier was free until 9 o'clock, the hour of *appelle*. There was no bugle or whistle for the *appelle*. At 9 o'clock sharp an officer made the rounds to see that all those who had no midnight permission were in their rooms, and to make note of those who were missing. The door used to burst open as if a cyclone had struck it, and the officer would look about to see that every man stood to attention at the foot of his bed, if he had not gone to bed before. If a man came in after the *appelle* he was punished, and further permission to go out not granted. Some of them used to come in for the *appelle* and go out again, scaling the outer walls, but this was a dangerous proceeding, and was only done by those who were very much in love, and who were deprived of all midnight permissions for very long ahead. At 10 o'clock the bugle played for the last time and all lights had to be extinguished.

Between 5 and 5.30 a.m. the soldier had to dress, attend to his chores, have his gun and *accoutrement* in perfect condition, take his coffee, or *jus*, as the soldiers called it, make his bed, sweep from under his bed, and, if he was room-guard for the day, he had to attend to those duties too.

On our return to barracks we had barely time to go to our rooms to take our things off when the whistle blew for *rapport*. This report took an hour or an hour and a half, and very often prevented the soldier from going to the canteen after dinner before it closed.

The potatoes had to be peeled by every one of the soldiers after dinner, even by those who dined in the canteen.

The afternoon report was the most tedious, as every one was anxious to dress and be ready to go out at five o'clock, but the sergeants used to take special pleasure in prolonging this function, so that the soldier who dined in barracks was late for his *soupe*, and the soldier, who did not was deprived of part of his free time.

The doctor of the regiment was one of those supercilious arrogant Frenchmen, who enjoyed the honours given his position, without in the least feeling that these honours implied duties on his part. His arrival in barracks in the morning at about eight was announced by a special bugle call, and those, who had reported themselves ill in the morning at the *réveil* to their corporal had to troop in front of his door and stand there waiting until it suited His Excellency to receive them. These miserable creatures, ill as they reported themselves, had had to appear at *rassemblement* at 5:30, and were not allowed to return to their rooms until after the doctor's consultation. Tall, cadaverous looking, with a pointed beard, hard cold blue eyes, and a gait as if he were really too good to walk the earth, he looked at the soldiers as if they were cattle. They may have been worse, but that was no reason why a man, who professed to be a gentleman, should show such a feeling.

After the soldier had stated his ailments, the doctor would look at him, and, as the case might be, open his mouth, look at his tongue, sound his chest, feel his pulse, or look at his eyes, prescribe something or nothing without a word, without giving a diagnosis, and with an *allez* dismiss him. No name was given, just the matriculation number. The Dane, who had syphilis, which he got the night before leaving Copenhagen from "a very respectable girl of one of the best families," and, who having been *en voyage* for a couple of months, had never been properly treated, was in a very bad way, and tried to explain, in his gibberish of French-Danish-English-German, what was the matter. The doctor glared at him, paid no attention to what he said, told him to shut up, and that he shouldn't eat so much soup, and gave him ... a purge.

At the report the patient would find out what the doctor had written down. *Consultation motivée* meant that the patient was justified in consulting the doctor and therefore would not be punished for reporting ill, but what was the matter with him the patient did not find out. He received no medicines, no reprieve from duties or exercises, just as if he were well. His ailment was considered so slight that no attention need be given it, and that he was fit for duty.

However, when the doctor's verdict was *consultation pas motivée* the soldier was punished with prison or *salle de police* for several days. The doctor considered him perfectly well, and that reporting himself ill was a ruse to evade doing duty.

A man who had been wounded in the Gallipoli Campaign, but was healed, reported himself ill. At the report *consultation motivée* was the verdict; the next day the man was in agonies and reported himself ill again, but as before, *consultation motivée*; the third day the same thing, not a word could that poor suffering wretch of humanity get out of the doctor. Finally, on the fourth day, it was no longer *consultation motivée* but "infirmary," the fifth day it was "hospital," and the sixth day he was dead. No one ever knew the cause of his death. Even among that lot of hardened old criminals a wave of indignation at the inhumanity swept through the Legion. This was not the only case, there were many others like it, only it was very typical of the *régime*. A man with an open sore on his foot, which was obviously from syphilitic causes, was told to sit a couple of hours exposing it to the sunlight! There was a young fellow who had consumption, and sometimes he was in a very bad condition; he was treated with aspirin as if he had a cold or a headache. A diagnosis was never given. Anyone with an eye of intelligence could see that the young fellow was in the last stages of this virulent disease. At the report it was always *consultation motivée*, and he had to go on doing his service.

A man was never sent to the infirmary until he could not stand up any more, and then he was usually ripe for the hospital, and the hospital meant the beginning of the end. When at the report "hospital" was pre scribed, we were sure that that man was doomed, and had but a few days to live. They did not want anyone to die within the precincts of the barracks, and so they shipped the dying off to the hospital, which was in the town; the infirmary was within the grounds of the barracks.

I shall never forget the sight of the man who, when he undressed himself, was a mass of running sores and was ordered to be bandaged up with a liniment – *consultation motivée*.

The infirmary was a gloomy looking place, and the chief nurse, a fat German-Pole, who had got the position through some influence, had very little else to do than drink enormous quantities of brandy, which he was generous enough to offer to his friends when they visited him. As most of the soldiers who were ordered to the infirmary were ready for the hospital, the place was more like a railway station, people coming and going, and waiting for the next train. Their next train meant hospital and death.

I suffered with my heart at the *pas gymnastique* exercises, and a bronchial trouble of my youth, which I thought I had outgrown, started again with fresh vigour, so much so that even my sergeant made me stop running on several occasions. I consulted the doctor at a time when I was free, so as not to have to report ill; he gave me a cough medicine – *consultation motivée*.

Chapter 9

ON rainy days we had *Revues*. Reviews of the gun, of the room, of the bedstead, of the *accoutrements*, etc. This meant that we had to take the entire gun apart, clean every part of it, and place the different parts on our beds for inspection, or the room had to be thoroughly cleaned, or the bed taken apart, and all bedbugs removed. The sergeant would come first, and then an officer for the inspection. Then we would have theory lessons. We were called into one of the bedrooms, and a Prussian sergeant would give us a lesson. His French was invariably much too abominable to be understood, but no intelligent answer was expected, only a parrot-like reply to the stereotyped question the sergeant found in a book for that purpose; all one had to do was to remember exactly what he had said, and repeat word for word. In fact unless this method was pursued, the sergeant would get very angry and make the soldier repeat word for word as he had said it, if necessary prompting him. He himself did not understand the lessons, so he thought it would be on the safe side to have the answer repeated in this manner. The lessons consisted in learning the names of the parts of the gun, or how to obey orders, or how to salute an officer, or what to do when on guard at night at the approach of a stranger on forbidden ground, or the duties of a soldier when he rises in the morning.

"And what is the next thing you do?" the German sergeant asked, referring to the toilet of a soldier.

"I wash my face," answered an especially black nigger.

"With what?"

"With shoe-blacking."

"No, with soap," corrected the sergeant seriously.

The nigger grinned.

"With what do you wash your face?" he asked again without moving an eyelid.

"With soap."

"Quite right."

"When somebody approaches you say 'halt' and 'who is there,' and if you receive no answer you call again 'who is there,' and if the individual does not answer the third time you fire. Now then, what do you do when an individual approaches?"

"I tell him to stop three times, and if he does not answer I fire."

"No, you idiot, you say 'halt!'"

The soldier stands in silence listening.

"What do you say?"

"Halt."

"Repeat word for word: 'I say halt.'"

"I say halt."

"All right and what else do you do?"

"I fire if he doesn't reply after the third time."

"No, you elephant, you ask 'who is there,' and if he doesn't reply you ask again 'who is there,' and if he does not reply after the third time 'who is there,' you fire. Now what do you do?"

"I fire if he does not reply after the third time to 'who is there.'"

"Ass! repeat word for word: 'I cry "halt" and ask "who is there," if he does not reply I ask again "who is there," and if he doesn't reply the third time I fire.'"

"I cry 'halt' and ask 'who is there' and if he does not reply I ask again 'who is there,' and if he doesn't reply I ask again 'who is there,' and if he doesn't reply the third time I fire."

"Good."

But nothing was said as to what was to be done if the stranger did reply.

If a soldier presumed to ask a question of his own accord, to gain information, he was told: "Shut up; listen to what I am saying, you will find out in time," and the sergeant went on with the next question. He could not have answered anything that was not in the book, and in this manner covered up his ignorance.

When the weather was threatening we used to have our exercises on the field across the way from our barracks, which was the *champ de tir* of the Spahis, or when that field was engaged by the Spahis themselves we marched to the Common between the Porte Cocu and the Arab quarter.

On Saturday mornings we did not go to the *champ de tir* but marched with music through the dismal town to beyond the railway station, where there was another field, the name of which I have forgotten. Then a general review was held, our costume on these occasions consisting of white trousers and the short white blouse without any knapsack, just the necessary belts and straps for gun and bayonet.

On Saturday afternoons there were no exercises and we were engaged in reviews of rooms, guns, *santé* (showing the doctor our masculinity to prove that no venereal disease was being kept secret) and any other review which was on the list of the *règlement*. These afternoons the Captain would utilize to command individual soldiers to his presence to air his grievances, or give special instructions. I too was ordered to the almighty presence.

"What is your profession?"

"I am a writer."

"I suppose that is a man who makes literature?" I made no answer.

"You are to grow a moustache."

"Bien." I had not yet got accustomed to say "Oui, mon Capitaine."

"Avez vous compris?" he thundered at me taking my docile answer as an evasion to obey orders, whereas in reality it was the natural expression of the feeling that an order was a command about which there could not possibly be any discussion. "You are to grow a moustache."

"Oui, Monsieur," I said, but he glowered at me as if I were not to be trusted.

"Grothé, I forbid you to cut any man's hair à *la phantasie*. Every soldier is to have his hair clipped close. Avez vous compris, Grothé?"

"Oui, mon Capitaine," and Grothé saluted.

"Have you got your hair cut à *la phantasie*?" Grothé took off his cap. He had been to his Arab barber friend the night before and had just had his head shaved in true Arab fashion!

Sunday was washing-day. It was the only day in the week when the soldiers had any time to do the washing of their trousers, shirts and underwear, which was done in big troughs under sheds in the courtyard. Any man who wanted to go to church had to report the day before and ask for permission, as no soldier was allowed to leave barracks before 11 a.m. on Sunday. Mass was at 10. The sergeant-major Ferez, one lieutenant, and two or three common soldiers, were the only representatives of the Legion I ever saw in church.

Every Tuesday night there was a night march. The bugle for *réveil* was blown at 3 a.m., at 3.15 there was the assembly of the troops, and at 3.30 march out. A certain point was chosen as a destination where a short rest of an hour was made, and the troops re-entered barracks at about 9.30.

Every Thursday was a manoeuvre, for which we started at the usual time for marching out, laden with full kit, weighing about forty kilogrammes, flasks filled with water, and food in our *musettes*. The march on these occasions lasted about five hours, and we covered about twenty kilometres before we reached the forest outside the Porte Frenda, where the manoeuvre took place. The march was very exhausting on account of the intense heat and the heavy weight of the kit. The knapsacks of the Legionnaires are made of wood, covered with canvas, which helped to increase the weight, and the coarse shirts and extra woollen trousers and other antiquated wardrobe, which was not used in the present war at all, made the luggage very cumbersome and heavy. We sweated blood, and the poor devils who had reported themselves ill but had not been granted any respite from their duties could not keep up with our pace and naturally lagged behind.

A sergeant was commandeered to watch them and walk with them. Some of them, who had sore feet, aggravated by the impossible *brodequins*, suffered excruciating pains. The Germans and Northerners did not seem to mind the *brodequins*, while all the soldiers of the Latin and Mediterranean peoples, who had small, slender, and delicate feet, suffered intensely.

Every hour a rest was granted of ten minutes in which a soldier could eat and drink, if he had anything with him.

Sometimes dust storms would come up suddenly, which scorched our skins and throats, or with unexpectedness a blinding drizzling rain would start, which drenched us to the skin. No return to barracks was made for a little thing like that. Once arrived at the forest, the sergeants were assembled under the officers and given the lie of the land and plan of the manoeuvre which was to be enacted. On the sergeant's return to his company he gave his orders and the soldiers followed blindly. Of course no common soldier knew anything about what was taking place. Once our sergeant and company were taken prisoners, and he was sadly reprimanded for it. Another time we took a company prisoners, and that is all I could ever make out of the manoeuvres. Every thing else was a Chinese puzzle to me.

About noon the bugle was blown for *rassemblement*, and we assembled near the provision waggons which had come out after us. One or two soldiers of each squad acted as cooks, camp fires were built, and the greasy food, now spiced with pine-needles, dead leaves from trees, dust and dirt, and a few sticks and cinders, was prepared in large marmites. The soldiers gathered about and came to get their rations. On horrid days, when it was pouring cats and dogs, the food was more watery than greasy – I don't know which was preferable. In the afternoon, the manoeuvres being virtually over in the morning, we had some exercises in the forest, and then marched back so that we arrived in barracks at about 4.30, hot, exhausted and drenched to the skin from rain or perspiration. The moment we reached the Porte Frenda the band struck up and kept on playing until we reached barracks, just as if we were returning from a picnic. Many a man, who had collapsed from exhaustion, or whose feet were so sore he could not go on, had to be carried on a stretcher, but then the provision waggon had to pick him up outside the town gate, so that the people did not see the gruesome sight of so many disabled soldiers.

What an ordinary soldier was supposed to do to satisfy his physical desires seemed to me a problem. To the "Village Nègre" he wasn't allowed to go; there he could have found satisfaction for 50 centimes. The women in the French public-houses cost anywhere from 10 to 20 francs. The poor devil of a soldier only had 5 sous a day!

If the soldier was more or less good-looking, and had tolerable manners, could not afford the public women, and did not go to the "Village Nègre" on the sly, he could try to find a widow, or an adulterous wife of some petty French official. This was not very easy in a small place like Bel-Abbès, where everything was known, and where a *cocu* husband could not remain *cocu* very long, especially when his wife's lover was in uniform and in the Legion at that.

Some of them managed it. The little Corsican corporal made love to a widow who had a beautiful daughter. After he had ingratiated himself with the widow, he proposed to the daughter, and thus made them both his mistresses. The marriage was put off until after the war – and then the corporal confided to me that he expected to return to Corsica alone.

Or there was Grothé, who, through his hair-dressing proclivities, got to know all the *bourgeoise* women of the town, including the wives of the officers of our regiment, and only had to take his pick. He was a good-looking chap, and in a dull place like Bel-Abbès there are some very respectable women and honest wives to all appearances, who like a change. But then Grothé was fortunate and was rather an exceptional case. To be a ladies' hairdresser stood him in good stead.

The soldiers who played in the regimental band were better off than the private soldiers; they had some pay, bedrooms to themselves, and the privilege of staying out every night until midnight. Whether they got into the band by influence, or money, or only on the strength of their talents, or all three, I was never able to find out. They must have had money from somewhere, for they spent comparatively much for soldiers. Among them were several who managed to make some financial arrangement with an Arab, who procured for them young Arab girls for mistresses. But I heard that this was rather an expensive proceeding – certainly nothing for the average poor Legionnaire. No wonder that other forms of vice were rampant.

* * *

It was on these marches that I first realized the position of the "jeunes filles" or "girants" of the regiment. They were evidently public property.

"Well dearie where is your protector today? Why doesn't he carry your pack?"

"Can't you walk? Did he hurt you last night?"

"I'll carry your pack if you are tired, but you must let me come to see you tonight."

"I hear you have a new lover—how are you getting on?"

These and other similar remarks were shouted across from one column to another.

After one of the night marches one of the "girants" returned in exhausted condition. During the march it had been evident that he was in great pain and continued to walk with much difficulty. The Lieutenant saw the situation and made inquiries. When he heard that the "girant" had had a particularly wild night with his lover he was merciless, and made a point to keep him up to the march at any cost. The consequence was that the "girant" simply collapsed on a bench the moment the soldiers returned to barracks, the perspiration streaming from his forehead. He could not drag himself upstairs to rid himself of his "accoutrements", ready for the Report, and some one, probably his lover, took off his things and carried them up to the room.

At the next Report but one he was condemned to imprisonment for 15 days for sleeping with another soldier. And after that he had to sleep in the Guard-House, at the gates of the barracks, in order to prevent further violation.

Most of the "girants" were quite young fellows, who had been picked up by some man going to the Legion, either in Marseilles or in Paris, taken him along for company, and during the first days of passionate friendship induced him to enter the Legion too, then later deserted him and exposed him to the onslaught of every one else. The "girants" were well established personalities in the Legion. Every one knew who was a "girant" and if he was protected by anyone or if he had become public property.

At night after the "appelle" and the bugle call for silence the men of the piquet in the courtyard saw dark figures gliding from one building to another, soldiers going to their lovers. It was prohibited that a soldier should visit any other room after "appelle", but the piquet paid no attention officially — it was an understood thing.

One night when I had a permit to stay out until midnight, which could be obtained every Saturday if a soldier had been on good behaviour during the entire week and had not been punished for anything, I was accosted by an older soldier in the town:

"Where are you going at this hour?" he asked, "to some nice 'girant'?"

"No," I said.

"Well then to a woman."

"No," I said, "I am going to a bath."

"I bet you are going to a 'girant'. Tell me where he lives," and chucked me under the chin. He had been drinking and the friend who was with him realizing the situation said: "Leave him alone — he isn't that kind."

On another occasion I was just going out of barracks when the French Sergeant Fenet, who was on guard at the gate, stopped me. He was a real French "Apache" type. He had been drinking. "Guarde à vous," he yelled and I stood attention. He looked me over, then came up to me and pinched my cheek and said, "You are not bad — I would not mind sleeping with you. But why don't you grow a mustache? It is a dead giveaway to have no mustache."

I made no reply — I trembled with rage and would have liked to have thrown him down. Something in my expression made him realize what feelings he had wakened and he let me go at once.

Another time when I came to the gate, an officer stopped me: 'Why don't you wear a mustache? Only 'tapettes' (the French term for men-prostitutes) are clean-shaven."

"Most men in England and America are clean-shaven, and they are not 'tapettes'," was my impetuous reply, which I had to pay for later by the definite order from the Captain already alluded to to raise a mustache.

Even the Arabs were aware of the "girants". One evening I went to a bath to which I had not been before, where I was treated with great courtesy, which is very unusual for a soldier of the Legion. The attendant helped me undress, gave me one of those massages in the hot room which only an Oriental can give, a massage that awakens every sense in one's body. He was extremely attentive, and although his massage ended in something akin to caresses, he did not go any further. After he had deposited me on the rest-lounge, he sat down beside me.

"There are many young 'girants' in the Legion?"

I did not answer.

"I know there are – will you try to bring some of them here?"

No answer on my part.

"I will give you something for each one you bring."

My curiosity was aroused: "What will you give me?"

"Oh will four or even six francs for each one be enough?"

"I suppose so – but what will you do with them here?"

"Not for here – I have a house where Arabs come."

Since I had never been approached on this subject before in any of the other baths, and since the attendant seemed to treat his proposition as a matter of course, I could only draw the conclusion that the "girants" had their customers in some of the Arab houses, his man being one of the few who, as yet, had no "girants" to offer his customers.

One evening on my way to the barracks, after a bath, an Arab approached me. "I live here in the neighbourhood. I have a shop and make and sell burnooses. Will you come and see my shop?"

I could not imagine that he expected to sell a burnoose to a poor legionnaire, but I had had many surprises and wasn't going to fight shy of this one.

"Certainly, with pleasure."

In a God-forsaken street, close by, he opened the shutters of a shop and bade me enter. He lit a little olive oil lamp and asked me to sit down.

The shop was hardly a shop, but a workroom where remnants of cloth were lying on the floor. The glimmer of the lamp threw long dark shadows. A few cupboards, with glass doors filled with cloth standing rectangularly as partitions, formed a vestibule. He motioned to me to step behind the cupboards where I found a large improvised sleeping apartment, with a flue for a charcoal stove at the further end of the room where he seemed to do his cooking.

"I sleep here," he said, coming up very close to me. 'Will you stay with me the night?"

"No thank you, I must return to barracks."

"But one of your German sergeants often comes here and sleeps with me all night. Why can't you?"

"Because I have no permission."

"If you had a permission would you stay?" he asked leeringly.

"I have never permission to stay out all night, and, if I had, I would want to stay with a woman."

"Yes, I too like women very much – but your sergeant is just like a woman for me."

I told him it was late and that I had to go. I'll give him credit that no "grand seigneur" could have been more courteous in understanding and letting me out, as if he had had no other intention but to show me his shop.

The bath house of the barracks was a long low narrow building in the middle of which were the bathing booths, with a corridor running around them. The soldier entered a small dressing booth from the outside corridor, this led into a second booth in which there was the douche, which again led into another dressing booth where another soldier, who had entered from the other corridor, was getting ready for his bath, both taking their douche in the same douche room.

One day an Armenian from Egypt, a big strong fellow who had been watching me go into a booth, entered the corresponding one on the other side. I thought he looked strangely at me. We happened to enter the douche room at the same time, which was barely big enough for two but there is never any time to wait one for the other. I saw he entered in a state of physical excitement, but naturally paid no attention and commenced my bath. I tried to keep as far away from him as the narrow space would permit, turning my back to him. Suddenly I felt his body close to mine, but in such a manner as to leave no doubt as to his intentions. I moved away pretending not to have noticed, and turned facing him, so I could watch him. He seemed to have stopped his persecutions, when as I leaned down to wash my lower extremities, he deliberately tried to assault me in the face. My disgust and indignation gave vent to a volley of contemptuous language which completely cowed him, and he withdrew, murmuring an apology that he only tried to please me, as all the Englishmen in Alexandria had liked that sort of thing and that they had given him from 3 to 7 shillings into the bargain!

Chapter 10

CAPTAIN B—— was the name of our captain, commonly called "the Telephone Captain" or "Captain Hallo-Hallo." During the Gallipoli campaign he was usually in the line of the second and third trenches, and whenever he thought his life in danger he fled to a telephone booth and found it necessary to telephone. He was a Corsican, medium in height, with long Kaiser-like moustaches, trying to look important, but on closer examination the air of importance was an actor's mask; he had a weak sensual mouth and a receding chin. He was a typical bully, who is always a coward. He shouted and shrieked at every one, thinking that necessary in his position of captain; he could not be civil if he tried, only when he was with the Colonel, and then he wasn't civil but seductively sweet, like a woman of the streets trying to gain her point. He had been a common soldier, worked himself up to sergeant, and then, for some inexplicable reason, he was made captain just before the Gallipoli campaign, where he proved such bravery!

One of the stories was that he shot his own men on the battlefield, when he suspected them to have seen some of his particularly cowardly actions. The Corsican corporal spoke of him quite openly as "that assassin." Fenet, the French sergeant, tried everything to get himself before the Council of War, in order to be able to get a hearing and denounce the Captain. But the Captain condemned him to all the penalties in his jurisdiction, but never sent him to the "Concile de Guerre."

Every three months a report came out praising the non-commissioned officers for their good or excellent work and behaviour. On one of these occasions the report came out praising nearly all the German sergeants and never mentioning any of the few French non-commissioned officers. Fenet was furious, for, whatever might be said about him, he was a good soldier. In consequence he did not turn up at the next *rassemblement*, nor for any of his duties.

In the evening the Captain called him to his office. Fenet was a short stocky fellow, with a slouch of a walk and a devil-may-care manner.

"Why didn't you go to the exercises to-day?" asked the Captain.

"Why? You low-down beast! Do you think I am going to take any more orders from such a cowardly brute as you, you dirty swine, you assassin. You think you can treat a French soldier the way you have treated me any longer, and give all those Boches praise and distinguish them with merits and pass me by, and not suffer for it?"

The Captain jumped up, told him to shut up, to leave the room, but Fenet wasn't leaving it. More language passed, the Captain tried to ring the bell, Fenet prevented him and forced him into a corner, where the Captain drew a revolver. Fenet, realizing the situation, shouted: "You can go and shoot us on the battlefield, but you won't do it here," and hurled the lighted petroleum lamp at the Captain, which just missed him and crashed through the window. The next moment Fenet had the Captain by the throat, wrenched the revolver away from him, and threw him on the floor.

The crashing window, the scuffle, the thud of the Captain's fall brought the soldier-clerks from the next room to the scene of action, and the Captain rising quickly, pulling himself together, just managed to gasp, "March this man off to prison," and Fenet was marched off.

The commotion had also brought the Lieutenant to the room. The Captain made no remark, but walked out with the Lieutenant to the nearest *café*, where he told him what had happened. They sat in front of the *café* on the terrace, or sidewalk, talking, when suddenly Fenet stood before them, and in a loud voice for all the habitués of the *café* to hear, denounced the Captain, calling him all the names he had called him in his room, and challenging him to send him to the "Concile de Guerre," so that he could show him up at last, and let every one know what *canaille* he was. The Captain turned pale; both he and the Lieutenant had risen. They drew their revolvers, and at pistols' end saw him back to barracks and into prison.

How Fenet had escaped no one ever knew. He was quite content; all he wanted was to make a public scandal and get the Council of War. We heard later he was condemned to only fifteen days' prison, but we never saw him again.

The Captain could not stand me. I was an eyesore to him. I did not know why for a long time, until some one told me: "Don't you know that the Captain is furiously jealous of you? You, an ordinary soldier, dining at the hotel every night, and obviously spending more money in a week than he has in a month. All his life his great ambition was to dine in that hotel, and now that he is at last able to do so, he sees you, an ordinary private soldier, dining in the same room."

I began to understand the cold haughty looks he gave me when he saw me at table. I always rose and saluted when he entered and left the dining-room, as was my duty, but he never condescended to reply. The Major and another officer, who used to dine with him, had not taken that attitude, but replied to the salute as they would to any soldier. In order not to arouse his ire more than necessary I decided to dine in a private room, where he would not see me.

The Germans in the Legion were a disloyal lot. I never let any one know that I spoke German or understood it, so they conversed very freely among themselves before me. Sometimes it was very difficult to seem indifferent, and appear not to have understood what they said. Even Grothé, who was supposed to be my friend, said things about me which were anything but friendly. They had nicknames for all of them – the Dane was "the long phenomenon"; in my presence they spoke of me as "he," but what they called me behind my back I was never able to find out.

"He says he writes history, well, if he does, he must be a good liar."

Everything I did and said was criticized, credit was never given for a decent action, but it was discussed what my motives might be, which, of course, could never be good. They read the papers ardently, and were delighted at the French set-back at Verdun and the German victories. Their idea was that no one but a German could be a good soldier. And often I heard:

"Look at them – they call themselves soldiers, and think they can beat our well-trained German army."

When the news came of a German defeat: "Never mind – they will win yet; you know that when a man has to do something out there (meaning Germany) he has *got* to do it." And when they read of the appeals for money for Red Cross purposes in the English and French papers, on account of the tremendous losses: "It stinks somewhere; things are not going for the Allies so well as they say. It is sure to end badly for them."

When the French tricolour was hoisted in front of the barracks every man who happened to be in the court-log yard, had to drop whatever he was doing and salute *garde à vous*. Nothing seemed more farcical. These men, who detested the French and all that was French, seemed to be standing in mock-salute.

The Germans were not sent to the front, neither in France nor at Salonica, after the first experiences, when invariably at the advance of the enemy the German Legionnaires deserted by the dozen to the German ranks.

The Legion is a German regiment in France, and why France tolerates its existence is a puzzle. It is like nursing a viper at one's breast.

The Arab officers of the Spahis across the way were officers in name only, whereas French officers were really in command. The Arab soldiers, whom the French are afraid to trust, are more trustworthy than the German Legionnaires, for an Arab would not become a French soldier unless he had French sympathies, whereas the Germans entered the Legion simply as a make-shift, or to evade prison, and have absolutely no sense of loyalty to the country they serve. No doubt they have been good fighters in pre-war days in Morocco and Indo-China, but when their own country is at stake "blood is thicker than water." They have one trait in common with the French, which is probably the reason why the French trust them – they dislike and despise the Arab. They are a danger to France and the French Government would do well to dissolve the Legion.

Everything in the Legion was based upon German discipline and German militaristic ideas. The sergeant-major, who read out the punishments daily at the Report, was a type of mediaeval executioner. His cold steel blue eyes narrowed with cruel delight when he announced the penalties, and looked about him to see the effects of his words. Often he would add a few words of his own: "and this is not all – here is another list of offenders of the *règlement*" or "this is a very lenient punishment – the next time it will be more severe."

The men condemned to prison were by no means free from the daily exercises; they formed a squad for themselves and were marched out of prison, which was alive with vermin, especially lice, with dirty white trousers stamped all over with the letters H.S. (*Hors Service*), to the shooting field with the rest of the soldiers. Every one meeting them in the street knew by the H.S. that they were "out of service" – prisoners. The dirtiest chores about the barracks were allotted to them, such as cleaning the lavatories, which on account of the shocking habits of this low-bred scum were usually in a terrible condition. Most of the soldiers did not mind the prison; on the contrary they were rather proud of it, and it was proverbial that a man who had not been in prison often was not a good soldier. But there were a great many drawbacks to having been in prison, quite aside from the discomforts and the humiliation. A man who had been imprisoned could not ask permission to go out until midnight for a fortnight, or a month, nor was he entitled to a vacation of two or three days, when such was granted at Easter, and other festivals of the year.

The slightest offences were often punishable with imprisonment, and serious ones were passed over with "Salle de Police" or "Guarde de Chambre"; it depended on the humour of the Captain, the Executioner, who I believe had his say too, and the victim.

As I have said, 70 per cent of the Legion were Germans; of the remaining 30 per cent of other nationalities, the Greeks, Armenians and Turks were the lowest type. Slip-shod, useless, idle, lying, gluttonous and undisciplined, they resembled lazy swine more than human beings. The Spaniards were the best type. They were gloomy but proud fellows, who did their work grumblingly, but did it, and did it fairly well. They resented being called down and insulted by petty German officers.

The Italians, Egyptians and Portuguese, who had enlisted before the war, desired to be returned to their own country when their countries declared war – but in vain. There was so much red tape, and the queries and replies were endless; not one had been repatriated since the beginning of the war, and I am speaking of April, 1916.

One of the negroes was an American, but he was so insolent in attitude and speech that I avoided him. The French-speaking negro was an enormously tall fellow, whom the sergeant called the "cigone." He looked good natured, but later I found out that he was very vicious.

The dozen or so of Frenchmen were mostly men who had done something or other in France which would have meant prison or worse for them, and so they had come here. Of course there were a few exceptions, such as Acharock and Ferez, who were born fighters, and had entered the Legion for adventure, had fought bravely in Tonkin and Morocco long before the war, but they were obviously fish out of water, and did not fit into the frame of the Legion at all.

The Englishman played in the regimental band and kept very much to himself. He told me he had applied to be returned to England but had not succeeded. He had a young Arab girl for a mistress.

The Dane had come to see something of the war, so he said, and the Jews to save their possessions because their nationality was uncertain.

The Austrians and Germans were nearly all old professional Legionnaires, and had signed for seven, ten and fifteen years. Some had signed a second time. Their antecedents were more obscure than those of the other nationalities – they kept closer together, and did not let out their secrets.

What brought the Spaniards and Portuguese to the Legion I never found out, unless it was for the same reasons as the others. But they were certainly the best element in behaviour and appearance.

Chapter 11

THE only English-speaking officer was the Dane, young, tall and blonde, who limped slightly in consequence of an illness he had lately received from one of the fair sex, and for whose knowledge of English I was exchanged from one squad to another the day of my arrival. After I had been in the Legion a couple of weeks he deigned to come up and speak to me. He had not much to say – a few questions and in reply to my answers a few grunts. It was not until his countryman arrived, "the long phenomenon," that he came oftener to the *jeunes soldats* to exchange a few words with him, and incidentally to say something to me just because he thought he ought, and not to make his interest in his compatriot too obvious. He supplied him with Danish newspapers and books on the quiet, and showed him all sorts of little attentions.

At me he grunted.

"You have been to Italy – the Italians are no good; they have no army, they will never do anything in this war [this was in March and April, 1916]. Anyway they have only two regiments that count, the Bersaglieri and the Alpini, and those two regiments won't win the war."

I ventured to remark that the Italians were the only ones of all the Allies who were fighting on enemy's territory all along the line.

"That doesn't mean anything – they have an easy job of it – neither rain nor mud as at the French Front."

"But they have to combat snow and cold, which the majority are not used to, coming from Southern Italy and Sicily, where ice and snow are unknown."

"Well, they won't do anything, they have an easy job of it. I tell you that this war is going to be won in France by the French Army – the only one which counts for anything. All the rest are no good."

At any rate he was honest in his convictions and loyal to the country he served, which was more than could be said of the Germans.

He was of no help to me, and I might have been in any other squad for all the advantages I had from him or his English. He never troubled himself about me, either with advice, or a kind word, or influence.

The nice Greek officer left for Verdun soon after I arrived. He had an extraordinarily young and handsome orderly who accompanied him. I regretted to see him leave, as he was the only officer in the Legion who was a gentleman, and to whom I could have fled in urgent necessity, and who would have understood and helped me. Some people don't need to talk, they know each other by instinct.

Acharock, the French sergeant of the *jeunes soldats*, who was such a terror to every one else but me, also left about the same time, so I lost the only two possible friends, who had any influence, at one blow. Acharock had had enough of the Legion and entered a French regiment in France.

The day for the official presentation to the Colonel arrived. This had been spoken of as a particularly important event for some time previous. For hours we stood in the blazing African sun in front of the outer door of the Colonel's office until it finally opened, and he came out with the Captain, who introduced each one of us, giving the particulars which we had officially registered. The Captain's voice was sweet as honey when he spoke to the Colonel. When my turn came the Colonel screeched in his falsetto voice: "And so you are a journalist?"

"No," I replied, "I am a *littérateur*." "Ah, that is something more, I suppose."

Age, name and nationality were perfunctorily asked, and passed over, and with an "allez" from the Captain in a strident voice, we were dismissed.

Another day we, the young soldiers, were told that we had no exercises in the afternoon, but were to present ourselves at the Doctor's office in the Infirmary for "incorporation."

We had to strip, then the Doctor examined heart, lungs, tested breathing, etc., while we were made to cough, and weighed and measured us, had everything written down in a big book, and also mention made of any marks on the body and deformities, evidently for identification. One soldier, an Austrian, had tattooed on his chest the words "Leide ohne zu klagen," which were also the last words of Emperor Frederick III to his son, the ex-Kaiser. This performance of registration made us physically a part of the regiment. We had not yet given the oath of allegiance to the French Army, which is only given after a man has been a soldier for three months.

A few days later we received the first injection. Again we were released from the exercises. The same performance took place – we were herded together in front of the Infirmary, where we had to wait for hours until His Majesty the Doctor would see us. Then we had another long séance of waiting in the waiting-room, and finally with bared shoulders we came into the presence of the great man. A bit of iodine was rubbed into the skin, and the needle inserted. The day after each *picure* we did not have to shoulder the gun, nor go out for exercises, but were ordered to do *corvées* about the barracks, sweeping the stairs, or the yard, or going to the bakehouse, which was some distance from the barracks, with large hand-carts, which looked like tumbrils, to fetch the apportioned rations of bread. There was a storehouse next to the bakehouse, where the loaves were stored on racks, each apart from the other, to get stale. We never got fresh bread, it had to be two or three days old. A line of soldiers was made from the man who took the loaves down from the racks to the man outside the window who threw them into heavy coarse sacks and into the tumbrils, passing them from one to the other with their dirty greasy hands. At the window a sergeant counted the loaves as they were passed out. Back at the barracks, the sacks had to be carried up to the fourth floor of our building, where the bread was dispensed for the whole company shortly before dinner. It was the *garde de chambre's* duty in each room to represent his squad, and get the rations for his men with a *bon* from his corporal, saying for how many men bread was needed. The bags filled with bread were extremely heavy, and the weaker of the men could not carry them up alone, although the attending sergeant tried his utmost to force them, using vile language, kicks, and threats of punishment. It ended mostly by the stronger men carrying up the sacks themselves, and giving the weaker men something else to do, watching the carts, emptying the bags, or taking the carts back to the shed.

Other *corvées* consisted of taking the food at midday to the men on guard at the hospital and the town-prison, and taking their places as sentinels while they ate. Sometimes our chores consisted of cleaning the *marmites*, the cooking pots which had been used the day of a manoeuvre. They had to be scrubbed, but nothing was given a man to do it with, he had to find the means himself. Soap was dear, and the soldier needed that for washing his clothes, so he ended by scouring the *marmites* with a handful of gravel and earth, without rag or brush.

Our injections were many – for typhoid, smallpox, cholera, and tuberculosis. They were administered to us at intervals of about a week or ten days. The effect of each was more or less virulent, developing fever by night and lasting nearly always the next day, accompanied with headache. Some suffered more than others, but the symptoms were always the same. The place of the *picure* remained sore for about four days, sometimes more. Each one of our injections was registered in our military books. These military books registered everything about a soldier, his origin, description, displacements, punishments, merits, imprisonments, etc., from the very beginning of his military career.

We had four kinds of uniforms, that is, we made four uniforms of our outfit. The uniform *en ville* consisted of the red woollen trousers and the long blue coat and blue sash, the uniform *campagne d'Afrique* of white trousers and the long coat and sash, and the full-dress uniform of the red trousers and the short blue coat without sash. The fourth, used for the Saturday review days, consisted of white trousers and white jacket or blouse, with the ordinary leather belt for cartridge boxes and bayonet. Sometimes, when our clothes were completely soaked from the rain, we were allowed to put on the full-dress coat, but usually this was reserved for special occasions, reviews, visits of the General, etc.

In addition to the prison as a means of punishment men were often condemned to "Salle de Police"; this meant that a man had to stay in the "Salle de Police" his free time during the day, and sleep there on the hard planks during the night, only going to his squad to change his clothes and do his duties there. The most with which a sergeant could punish a soldier officially was *garde de chambre* for a certain number of days, which meant that the man had to do the *corvées* of the room and not leave it at any time except for exercises, not even for meals. Other punishments had to come from higher quarters, which the sergeant could very easily incite.

To be appointed for guard duty was not a punishment, but an ordinary duty, although it was like a punishment. Guard duty at the guard house at the entrance of the barracks meant being on duty in full uniform with gun and bayonet for twenty-four hours with no proper sleep or rest, or any kind of recreation in any part of that time. The young soldiers were never trusted with this onerous office. But the *piquet* at night often included a young soldier. Four men and a sergeant were chosen every day to do picket duty. The soldier, instead of being free at 5 p.m., had to present himself immediately after *la soupe*, in uniform *en ville* with gun and bayonet, and he and his companions marched through the town to see that the Legionnaires off duty were behaving themselves. The march ended up with a visit through the "Village Nègre," the forbidden territory, to bring back at the point of the bayonet any soldier who had forgotten the *règlement*, and to whom the punishments in store for him bore no terrors.

The moment we appeared in this disreputable street all the doors of the fair inhabitants closed at once, almost automatically, so that if any of them harboured a soldier he was advised and well hidden. Of course if he happened to be friendly with the sergeant on duty he could stand in the doorway of one of the houses and the sergeant would not see him.

What puzzled me was, that, although we looked very fierce with gun and bayonet, our guns were never loaded, and every one must have known that. For picket duty the number of our men was sufficient to overpower one or two culprits, but when we had to take a band of prisoners, who were to go to the Council of War, from the barracks prison to the town prison, I did not see what we could have done if mutiny had broken out on the way, as they outnumbered us greatly. Before we escorted the prisoners we were lined up before the sergeant in charge, told of the crimes that the prisoners had committed, and that if one of them escaped on the way from the barracks to the town prison we should be held responsible, and would have to face "Concile de Guerre" ourselves. These prisoners must have known that our guns were not loaded, as on some previous occasion they must have done this duty themselves.

They had everything in their favour to escape: they were lightly clad, whereas we were heavily clad with heavy shoes, gun, bayonet and what not; in a few moments they could have reached the gates of the town, which were never guarded, not even by a policeman, and once out they could have spread and disappeared in the country. Many had deserted in this manner and had made good their escape.

An Italian, who was in my room, one day disappeared. He had been in the Legion quite a number of years, had asked to be repatriated, but no attention was paid to his request. When he found it useless to agitate further he seemed to acquiesce. He had very little to say to any one, was civil enough and did his work well. He got permission for a few days' leave, as there were evidently no punishments against him, and he never returned. No one ever knew what became of him.

Although everything that happened, decent and indecent, was read out at the report, the desertions were never read out. We only heard of them by chance. When a man deserted it was only known to the men of his own room, and if one of these had a friend in another room the news spread.

Every man who deserted was spoken of with envy – of course it meant first and foremost that he had money, for without money a man would not get far. Desertions were spoken of as a common thing, it was only a question as to how to get the money. Even my corporal, who prided himself on being a faithful soldier, boasted of the many chances of escape he had had with different men who had money and liked him, and who had offered to help him to desert with them.

Chapter 12

THE distance from the barracks to the *champ de tir* was about 4 km., and we walked this four times a day. After the *rassemblement* the sergeant or lieutenant reviewed the soldiers to see that each man's kit was in good order, that no straps were missing or undone, that the shoes were clean, that the whitish grey trousers of the uniform *campagne d'Afrique* were immaculate, that the gun was not rusty, and that the knapsack contained the regulation weight for that day. If any one of these things was not in order, the soldier had to return to his room and remedy the neglect, and if it should happen that he was not back in time when the troops marched out, he was meted out severe punishment. But even if he were back in time he was not spared some sort of punishment.

Everything was punished – everything that was not strictly *règlement*. It was as bad as the word *verboten* in Germany. The word *règlement* got on one's nerves.

We marched out with music only on days of the big march and manœuvre; at other times there was only the monotonous tramp, tramp, tramp, with a voice thundering out occasionally "un – deux, un – deux," to keep the troops in step, or the enraged yelling of "gauche, GAUCHE, GAUCHE," for a soldier who was out of step.

It was extremely difficult to keep in step, owing to the fact that so many of the soldiers could not march at all, that is, they had a slipshod walk, a slouchy shuffling way about them. They had never been taught to walk properly, and if they had had any shoes at all, they had been in all probability down at the heel and out at the toes.

It was a great relief to walk behind or next to a good soldier; it was easy to keep step then, but there weren't many good soldiers among the *jeunes soldats*. The keeping in step was kept up while marching through the streets of Bel-Abbès. The moment we passed through the Porte Tlemcen, and got into the country, the command was given *pas campagne*, which meant that we could carry the gun at leisure on the strap, and walk in single file, one column on each side of the road. Although it was no longer necessary to keep step we had to keep close to each other in order to make no spaces. Even that was difficult for the slouchy devil-may-care boys and men.

In the early morning the air was usually very fresh, in fact sometimes bitingly cold. We marched out before sunrise. The roads were muddy, the thick red clay sticking to the boots most persistently. Now and then on the outward march to the field we had to line up four abreast and do *pas gymnastique*. This was more than some could do with about 20 kilogrammes of baggage on their back, which was the ordinary weight. This mode of running was not really so very quick, but it was the continuance, the compulsion to keep in step with the others, until the signal for halt was given, that made it so fatiguing, and many were obliged to fall back when their breath gave out, which was punished.

On both sides of the road were ditches and hedges, and beyond well cultivated fields. Little Arab boys used to follow the Legion columns and sell oranges and big puffed-up waffles to the soldiers. We were allowed to eat going *pas campagne* – and even smoke. They all smoked incessantly.

Sometimes when marching we met large families of Arabs, the man going ahead in patriarchal fashion, and the women, veiled, following behind, the children mostly led by the father. I used to wonder if this would not be a good way to escape, to make a friend of an Arab and dress myself up as his woman. Being veiled, and the absolute rigid law that an Arab's wife is not to be touched, which has to be respected by all Europeans, would protect me, and I could play the deaf-mute in order to hide my ignorance of Arabic.

The *champ de tir* was a big open field, the road running alongside of it for the most part covered by weedy sward and stones. In some places the soil was hard and good for exercises, but the greater part was rough and muddy, and covered with high grass. I imagine this is all as it should be, in order to accustom the soldiers to be ready under any conditions. The field was edged with maple trees. All through the field ran trenches, very primitive trenches, which had no resemblance to the real trenches in Europe. They looked more like plain dug-outs. I don't believe the officers knew how a trench ought to be made, or they considered these trenches merely as good practice for the soldiers to use their pick and shovel. The ground chosen for the trenches was hard and mixed with small and large stones; it seemed to me as if this part had been a dumping ground for excavated earth and had been stamped down.

The exercises were extremely monotonous. There was absolutely no variety for a *jeune soldat*. "Demi-tour-à-droit" – "demi-tour-à-gauche" – "armes sur l'épaule" – "garde à vous" – "repos" – "présentez armes" – "plus sec" – how tired I got listening to these eternal repetitions! Occasionally my head became quite dizzy and the movement was never right. That is, probably it was right, for when a superior officer came along to find out how a man was getting on the sergeant would say that he worked well. The drill was evidently intended to train a man to do the exercises mechanically, but that depended largely on the individual mentality. In my case it was the everlasting repetition which so fuddled my brain that I could not do the movement at all. If there had been some change, and then a return to the movement, it might have had a different effect. Inwardly I wept when I had been tried with one movement so long that I could not do it any more. A man must have a special mentality to profit by such a drill. Your attention is required, your thought is required, but when once used it has to go to sleep and become mechanical. Difficult proposition that. How the others felt about it I don't know. I don't think they thought about it at all, and if they did, they could not have expressed themselves. It was certainly hard for some of them, and obviously quite beyond their power to obey the commands correctly. That mental reflex action, which was to be brought about by continual repetition to make the movements mechanical, did not work with everybody.

There were other exercises for the older soldiers, bayonet practice, and bayonet fencing with muzzle masks, skirmishes, attacks and shooting. I heard a good deal of shooting on some days, but I myself was only allowed to shoot once in six weeks – the only time I ever shot in my life! The targets were at the further end of the field. It was all theoretical practice, how to handle a gun, how to aim, how to shoot when kneeling, or when lying down, or when running. How this would have worked with a loaded gun, and when the time for shooting came, is another matter.

One of the malicious tricks of the sergeants when in a bad humour was to order the exercise *à genoux* on a muddy day. This ruined the white trousers completely, and entailed washing them that day, for each man had only two pairs, and had to look immaculate twice a day before going out to the field.

On cold mornings we had games for a quarter of an hour – jumping and running games, and leap-frog, when the men with their big heavy hobnailed boot's jumped over their fellows in such an awkward fashion that good swift kicks on the head were the result. Very often this was quite intentional and terrific rows would ensue, each one yelling in his own language. The patience of the sergeants was of the smallest. Orders were shouted louder and louder, and when no response was made to his orders the petty officer would fly into a towering rage. The fact was that many of the poor devils did not understand a word of French, and others couldn't understand the sergeant's French. There was a Spanish sergeant, a mean creature, who took violent dislikes to some of the soldiers for no apparent reason. If he disliked any one he tormented him at his exercises until the man could not do anything correctly any more, no matter how hard he tried. He was the type of man who would have won honours as a professional torturer in the Middle Ages. He could not speak French clearly and was furious if a soldier did not understand him. "Don't you understand French?" he would bellow, and the soldier had not the courage after that to say, "Yes, but not *your* French." Instead of saying *un deux* to keep his men in step it was always "hunk dooz" – the rest of his French being similar in pronunciation.

On one occasion the corporal, a mean looking German, with a bullet-head and cold watery blue eyes, who, I am sure, had waited upon me as a steward on a North German Lloyd steamer some years before, flew into such a rage because an Arab soldier could not understand him, that he took his gun and gave him such a whack over the head that the poor fellow collapsed, unconscious, with blood streaming from his mouth. Just at this moment the Colonel came riding into the field, as was his wont every day, to see how the exercises were going on; he noticed the commotion and asked the corporal to step up and explain. This low-down creature flatly denied he had done it, and claimed it was his *élève caporal*. The schooling corporal stepped up and took the blame upon himself, for, as he explained to me later, it was easier to take the punishment than have the corporal degraded, and earn his everlasting hatred and persecution. Persecution was a fine point in the Legion and reached into the most intimate parts of one's private and soldier life. In this way, however, he would earn the gratitude of the corporal, and get more easily promoted after he had served his punishment. This was too much for me. During the "pause" which followed (there was a pause or rest for ten minutes every three-quarters of an hour), I went up to the sergeant who had been friendly to me the first day and had introduced me to Kohn, and who spoke English so perfectly (he was a Count de R——, whose history I shall relate later), and told him the true circumstances. He reported it also in an unofficial way to the Danish lieutenant, who in turn spoke to the Captain. The corporal had watched this performance, and when the exercises recommenced, and we stood in line *garde à vous*, he demanded what my conversation had been with the sergeant and lieutenant. I answered that I had told what I had seen with my own eyes. The Arab had been standing next to me but one. His face was a study, a mixture of hatred, meanness, slyness, and fear, but he could say nothing.

The affair came to a strange close. The Captain, who hated me, would pay no attention to the matter, and ended up by saying that if the corporal did do it he did right, very likely the Arab deserved it – anyway the corporal was not to be punished, or even reprimanded, and he would talk to the Colonel. The Colonel was under his thumb. Nothing happened. What is the life of a poor Arab in the Legion? The Arab after his collapse was kicked in his unconscious condition to arouse him to continue the exercises, but he would not move, in spite of the fresh water another soldier had given him, bathing his temples and washing his blood away. The Arab was taken to the Infirmary, where he remained for a week or so, and then was put into prison for want of discipline and disobedience. I never saw him again.

Chapter 13

THE mail department of the Legion was a most irritating institution. All letters received and posted were subject to the censor of the Regiment. I never found out who the censor was, or who wrote "opened by military censor." I heard that Count de R——, on account of his perfect knowledge of English, was called in to interpret my letters for them. The contents of the letters was not treated confidentially, as was evident from all sorts of curious point-blank questions asked me by different officers, which showed me that parts of my letters were not clear to them and they wanted elucidation. The outgoing letters underwent the same inspection. There was a military envelope, which could be had for the asking, in which letters could be posted without a stamp, but then the letter or card had to be put in the letter-box in the precincts of the barracks. I never used the envelope, nor posted my letters in that box, but preferred to pay the regular postage. Even then I heard my letters were not safe, since the small post office was entirely subject to the Legion, so that when my handwriting became known they picked out my letters, and sent them over to the Legion, to have them read before sending them off.

The letters were given out twice a day in the courtyard at the *rapport*, in the morning and in the afternoon. One of the sergeants distributed the mail by calling out the names, and woe to the man who did not rush out immediately at *pas gymnastique*, salute properly, when his name was called, salute again on receipt of his missive, and disappear quickly at *pas gymnastique*. For registered letters and money orders it was different. The name of the recipient was called and ordered to appear at 5 p.m. at the Waguemestre (obviously a corruption of the German word *Wachmeister*). That worthy took his time. Five o'clock was the hour for going out, and so he seemed to delight in being late in his office. If a soldier was willing to wait until the next day, because he had an engagement at that hour, the Waguemestre would get very furious and have the man reprimanded next day at the *rapport*, make him stand in line, and take him by force to his office. But that was not all – in order to receive a registered letter or money order the soldier had to ask his sergeant to come with him and sign for him first, then only could the soldier sign himself. The whole performance took place in a small room, where the other soldiers and sergeants were waiting for their money. The sums paid were called out loud enough to be heard at the other end of the barracks. The annoying part was that not only every one knew what you received, but every one speculated as to how much they could borrow. And woe to the man who did not lend to the sergeant when that individual needed it. He had the best knowledge as to how much you received – and the sums he would borrow were in accordance. Life would have been made unbearable both in barracks and on the *champ de tir* if you refused him. The power of a sergeant over a soldier is tremendous, and he can create thousands of petty difficulties and annoyances which can break up a man completely. The torture that a man of that stamp can invent is incredible in its baseness and fiendish cruelty.

But it did not end here – the soldiers passed the word to those who were not present as to how much you had received, and the precarious ones came continually: "lend me 20 sous," "lend me 40 sous," "lend me 100 sous"; all duly armed with marvellous tales of explanations and vows as to its quick return. If you did not lend, they got nasty.

I decided to receive my money at the post office without the sergeant. At the post office I found that this was impossible; anything addressed to the Legion must go to the Legion, and be delivered to the Wague-mestre, and by way of the sergeant on to me. I thought of having my money addressed to my hotel, but that was against the *règlement*, and if known at the Legion could be stopped; besides, if I did it I could not receive the money because I was an ordinary soldier, and it is against the rules of the French post office to deliver money to an ordinary soldier. Could I receive an insured letter? No, that was the same as money.

The problem was finally solved by my having my money sent by cheque in a registered letter, not insured. But then a new difficulty – no one would cash my cheque! Finally I had to send it to the American Consul at Algiers and he returned me the money in an ordinary registered letter, which was always risky. This final method was the result of long and hard experience, and after endless, delays and returned letters with the excuse of "insufficiently addressed" and "not deliverable to an ordinary militaire."

It was impossible to get any bank in Bel-Abbès to trust one either to cash a cheque or change foreign money. Not even the hotel proprietress could do so. For me it was out of the question to pay a visit to the bank, as no soldier was allowed out of the precincts of the barracks, or "the regiment wherever it found itself," until 5 p.m. Banks close at 3 and 4 o'clock.

Count de R—— was one of the very few gentlemen in the Legion, and I was rather glad that it was he who had to translate my letters. I did not mind him knowing my affairs, and I knew he would be tactful if some particular passage might prove embarrassing for me. He realized that what was in my letters was only a question of private family affairs, and could be of no military interest. The officers were curious – and suspicious – -why had I come to the Legion – evidently I had money – what had I done – what was my real name – was I a spy – was I an envoy from the French Government to investigate the Legion – did I belong to some detective bureau trying to find out some one – would I pick out a man one day and walk off with him, telling him he was wanted? All these questions had been asked behind my back, sometimes within hearing distance. And answers would come, "You mark my word, he will disappear as quickly as he appeared, and no one will ask another question. I bet the Colonel knows what he is here for." Then there were others, who said I was under the special protection of Count de R——, and that life was made easy for me by him. This was because once after five o'clock I had gone to his room and had had a chat with him. I wanted to borrow a book – a book on the Legion, which has the reputation of being an excellent account of it, but after reading it I realized that the authors had never even put their heads inside the barracks. Count de R—— was a sergeant, and two sergeants always occupied one room. An orderly came in to do the other sergeant's *truc*, and heard the tail end of our conversation about the dance, modern plays, music, books, etc. That was Greek to him, and he suspected we talked in cipher.

A sergeant can get eight days' prison for talking to a common soldier outside the barracks not on official business. Count de R——, an excellent pianist and musician, an author of plays, knew every one worth knowing in the world of art and letters in Paris, London, and Vienna, and we had some friends in common. His great grandfather had fought at Waterloo under Napoleon I. His father died when he was a mere baby, and his mother, an Austrian, had married a second time her cousin, a Herr von A—— of Vienna, who adopted the baby. Count de R—— became Herr von A—— of Vienna and Paris. When the war broke out in 1914 Paris was alive with detectives stopping everybody in the streets, asking for identification papers and making arrests. Count de R—— had been out to Isadora Duncan's Temple of Art, the Pavillon de Bellevue, and cycled back to his house at La Muette. It was getting dusk and the air was hot, heavy and sticky – there was that peculiar feeling in the air that omened evil happenings; he was tired and without courage. All sorts of thoughts occupied him. What was he to do? He was a Frenchman, true; still, politically he was an Austrian. It was getting darker, no lamps were lit, he arrived at the Avenue Henri Martin, was almost at his door, when he was suddenly surrounded by dark figures and commanded to show his papers. He thought his perfect Parisian French would carry him through. His papers were his condemnation. He was marched off.

It took months to prove his strange family affairs, and to show his ardour and enthusiasm for the patriotic cause he volunteered to enlist and go to the front at once. But he was allowed only to enter the Foreign Legion, and when I met him, after a year and a half of war, the French courts were just commencing to reinstate him into his rights as a French-born Frenchman, and his own name – a great grandson of one of Napoleon's officers.* He told me that even at the front he was turned back from entering second and third lines because he was a foreigner. Finally he fell ill and was sent to Bel-Abbès.

No one who has once served can be quite *reformé*, and even if he is going to be *reformé* he will be held in uniform on the list for months and months, and then some easier post will be found for him, which he can fill in spite of his ailments. This is done to save pensions.

Count de R——, who was a fine fellow, rather delicate in feature and figure, with jet black hair, a little black moustache, olive-coloured complexion, large brown eyes and very beautiful teeth, was very *simpático* to me. He was clever and had a great deal of charm, although he was without much moral courage. It may be that that was taken out of him

---

* Footnote: June 17th, 1920. I have just heard that Count de R—— is still waiting for his naturalization, which, according to his war engagements, was supposed to have been automatic upon his discharge. After six years, and after fighting at Salonica, in Macedonia, in Morocco and in France for five years, a French born son of a Frenchman is treated as an enemy in his own country, unable to earn his living on account of his political nationality – afraid to move in order not to lose his inheritance.

by his experiences in the French army. He was continually afraid of doing something that might give food for gossip, or was not quite according to *règlement*. The principal motive for this was probably that he did not wish to be humiliated by his superior officers, who were all of them his inferiors, and who were fully aware of that, and duly hated him for it.

Sometimes, when I had permission to be out until midnight, we met clandestinely in the back room of a *café*, where we were let in by a back staircase, and chatted. His views, in spite of his French origin and sentiments, were a bit German *au fond*. He did not see the wrong side of what the Germans had been doing up to that time. "The French ought to do the same," he said. "It is, or ought to be, tit for tat." He called it piffle and stupid sentimentality to fight shy of anything. The Germans were quite right in what they did – they were out to win – and if the French had any pluck at all they would do the same. As to their destroying works of art, that could not be helped – and yet he was an artist himself. This opinion was very different from the one Henri Cain held, who said to me, when I went to see his Fragonards in Paris in 1915, and found only bright green squares on the faded green walls, "Yes, my Fragonards are in my caves and cellars here and in the country. It does not matter if the Germans blow me up – but a Fragonard...."

When I held forth about my ideas of art, and what its preservation meant to all future generations, he said, "Then you think less of a hundred old women being blown up than of a work of art being destroyed?"

I had to say "Yes."

Chapter 14

QUITE unexpectedly one afternoon the General arrived. The troops had marched to the *champ de tir*, the guard at the gate was asleep, the guards inside the guard-house were telling smutty stories, when the toot-toot of the entering automobile brought them to their senses. Great consternation and confusion; but it was too late – the General had come in without receiving as much as a salute. Where was the music, the bugle, the "Marseillaise" that should have been played? He poured out his ire on the poor one-legged Colonel, and he in turn gave every one his due or rather what was not due. Who knew the General was coming? No one. If he had announced his visit, no such message arrived, and the Legion isn't lying in wait every day for a General.

When we returned from the shooting field we heard the news, and also that the next day we were to be reviewed by the General on the field at the further end of the town beyond the railway station. We had to look very spick and span, and we did.

The General took quarters at the hospital, a two-storied building with a portico, standing in a pretty garden behind the barracks of the Spahis; it looked as if it might have been a country villa at some time in the past.

Next morning we marched out to the field and the General came galloping up an hour late. He was a man of medium height, thin, bony, with white hair and moustache, a typical irate looking Frenchman. He galloped about for a few minutes, talking to the Colonel, making himself very important, giving orders here and there, and then galloped away. This time the music kept playing, and both at his entry and exit the "Marseillaise" was duly trumpeted out.

On our return to barracks we found the old fossil had graciously consented to talk to any soldier who had a grievance to make, or who had some question of importance to ask. All he had to do was to mention the fact to his sergeant, and he would place the name on the list to be presented to the General.

This was welcome news indeed. There were so many who had not been released although their time of five, seven, ten, or fifteen years (or whatever time they had signed for) was up, and all their requests to Captain and Colonel to be discharged fell on deaf ears. There were others who had been degraded from the ranks of corporal, sergeant, and even sergeant-major, and their good conduct as soldiers did not help to reinstate them. Then there were some who had signed for a second time in the Legion – had been there seventeen years – had fought bravely in Tonkin, Morocco, and Gallipoli, and had never received a decoration. This was their opportunity; they would speak. Some had made an appeal to be transferred to regiments in France, and no answer had come to that. There was a little fellow who had entered before he was of age, and he was sick and tired of the Legion; besides, he was consumptive and his mother wanted him back in France; she made the proper claims in the proper places, but had no answer. In the meantime the boy was wasting away. There were those who wished to be repatriated and those who had private grievances.

The sergeant Steinmann, a typical Prussian bully, mean, brutal, domineering, ignorant, sly, and cowardly, and usually in a nasty temper, was most indulgent, and listened to the troubles of each and agreed that they had a right to speak to the General. It was evident he too had something to ask, and probably that something demanded the good-will of everybody. Those who were going to speak to the General dressed up in their best uniforms, the red trousers, the long blue coat with the lower lapels buttoned up, and the long blue sash.

The toot-toot of the motor-car announced the approach of the important person (the hospital was within a stone's throw of the barracks), the "Marseillaise" played, and out stepped the living skeleton. He did not look *simpático* to me, so I did not think I would have my say to him. I watched from the window how all the petitioners were lined up, standing at attention. There were about thirty or forty of them. And then behold – a spectacle.

The General looked at them, did not speak to one of them, but commenced a loud harangue:

"What have you come here for? To speak to me? Don't you know it is against the *règlement* for a common soldier to speak to a General? You have come here to air your grievances, I suppose? You have come to the wrong place. It is not my business to listen to all your stupidities. I dare say all of you get what you deserve, and probably you are treated much too well and much too indulgently. Why have you waited all this time to come to me? Why have you not made your petitions in the proper places with your own immediate superiors? Go back to your rooms and behave yourselves, and don't ever forget that when you want anything you must ask for it according to *règlement*. I am surprised you should be so forgetful of the *règlement*, but I am glad to see that there are not more of you. Be glad that I am not having you punished for presuming to speak to me. *Garde à vous*," and, on a wave of his fossilized hand, the soldiers disbanded crestfallen to their rooms. Then we went to see the Colonel.

Later we heard that he looked over the book for punishments and complained bitterly about it: "There are too many, and that is a bad sign – a sign of lack of proper discipline, otherwise there would be no necessity for so many punishments." He was right, but he did not know the Legion.

The bugle sounded, the "Marseillaise" played, and the General tooted out of the courtyard. I did not see him again until later in Oran, where a very similar performance took place.

We, who had had no petition to make, were severely reprimanded for having dared to look out of the window while the General was there!

A few days later we heard that a Polish sergeant, Astrovsky by name, had died at the hospital after many months of suffering. He had been wounded in Gallipoli and never recovered.

The morning of the funeral we were told to dress in our uniform *en ville*, and silently we marched to the gates of the hospital. For hours we waited – we arrived there about 6.30, and it was fully 9.30 before there was any sign of a *cortège*. Finally the coffin was borne out by soldiers, and placed on a hearse. The band played a funeral march and we proceeded down the main street to the church. A short ceremony was held, nearly all the soldiers refusing to enter the church. They made it obvious, standing there in front of the church, that it was repugnant to them that any church ceremony should take place. Many turned their back to it and scowled. What was it in their inmost nature that they should resent the church in this challenging manner? Was it tradition, or memories which they preferred to forget? Was their hatred the outcome of fear, and their contempt to make themselves and others believe that they defied religion? Yes, they defied it, but their attitude showed that deep down they believed, and were afraid, otherwise there would not have been this voluntary show of disdain, but simply indifference. After the blessing of the body the *cortège* moved on. The hearse was covered with flags of the Allies, and the coffin with the Russian and French flags. The officers and soldiers walked behind the hearse four abreast. We passed down the main street to the Porte Frenda, and then outside the walls past the Common where we exercised when the weather was bad, alongside the Arab quarter, and finally down a long narrow country lane to the cemetery.

The Captain was too busy to come – there were no exercises that day on the shooting field – and so he was represented by the little fair-haired Jewish Lieutenant.

The cemetery was quite a distance from the town. Tall cypresses lined the principal avenues; the tombs were mostly tasteless, heavy, voluptuous-looking monuments, which reeked of vulgarity and wealth. These and the simple graves were so thickly covered with the traditional French bead wreaths, and artificial and bisque flower arrangements under glass, that it was not possible to read the inscriptions. I have never seen anything quite like it, and I have seen many French cemeteries, but this one outdid them all. There was not a fresh flower to be seen anywhere – only the abominable glass beads. It seemed that one of these abominations was brought once a year, and with the years piles, and veritable towers, had accumulated on the graves.

It is a hilly cemetery, and occasionally from the top of a little hill one had a fine view of the panorama of the large plain of Bel-Abbès, edged with the distant mountains, and quite close to the low houses of the town and the Arab quarter, and a little beyond the Arena, where in days gone by, when the Spanish population had more to say than to-day, bull fights were performed. But now it is falling into decay, with grass growing over its ruins. At the furthest end of the cemetery a grave was opened for the dead sergeant. It was a remote spot of the cemetery, but in the midst of many graves. We soldiers could only stand about in scattered groups, wherever we found room in the narrow spaces between the graves.

The Lieutenant spoke:

"We all knew Sergeant Astrovsky" (we did not – no one knew him in my squad, and we had quite a number of old soldiers) and then he held forth about the virtues of the man as a soldier. He tried to be touching, and he spoke well, only the absolute lack of any mention of his family, or country, or any reference to him as a man, a brother, a comrade, or a being who had human impulses and affections, made it seem cold and unnecessary. Was this man only a piece of artillery – only a machine that now out of use is put away?

No one wept, no one shed a tear; the indifference was horrifying, no one cared. The Lieutenant was sorry to lose a good soldier – that was all. The others thought probably he was better out of his misery, and that at the hospital there was one burden the less. What may that man's life have been, what his antecedents, what brought him to the Legion, what did he feel when he knew he was going to finish there? No one knew him whom I knew – no one seemed to take any interest.

The flags were removed, the coffin lowered with a salute instead of a prayer, and we trotted slowly home ward as silently as we had come.

Chapter 15

MY room was a hall room; as I have said, it was just half the size of the other rooms, and opened out on to the large stairs. The other rooms on my floor contained twenty-eight beds each – in mine there were only fourteen beds. There was just space enough between the beds to squeeze through. The beds were hard and uncomfortable, and consisted of an iron frame with thin bands of wavy steel across it, as an apology for a spring; the woollen mattress was so thin that these steel bands were distinctly noticeable on one's anatomy; the sheets were of the coarsest linen, and the heavy blanket was made of a dirty looking felt. Opposite the door was a large window with old-fashioned small square panes. Seven beds stood in a row on each side of the wall. In the middle of the room stood a long deal table and two benches. Above the table a coffin-shaped box was suspended from the ceiling by two large iron rods. Attached to the bottom of this coffin, which had a shutter on each side and contained the tin dishes of the men, was a dirty little petroleum lamp, by the light of which no one could possibly read. On the walls behind the beds, 2 ft. above them, a shelf of about 1 1/2 ft. in width ran along the entire length of the room, and the space above each man's bed was the part allotted to him for depositing his clothes. The clothes had to be folded and laid in such a manner as to form a perfect square tower, with not an edge of anything sticking out. This was an art not easily learned. Next to this tower, each man had a little wooden box in which he kept his personal treasures. Under the shelf were hooks on which to hang his *accoutrements* and *musette*, and, in order to keep these hidden, a regulation towel was nailed to the edge of the shelf hanging down full-spread, like a curtain.

The fourteen men in my room formed a squad – the occupants of each room formed a squad no matter what the size of it might be. A curious medley of men they were. The corporal, a small stocky Frenchman with a bullet-head, wide forehead, and hair cut like an *apache*, looked in his uniform like one of those bloodthirsty soldiers of the French Revolution who would have cut the heart out of an aristocrat and strung him up at the next lamp-post. He never wore socks nor foot-rags, but only the filthy heavy greasy regulation *brodequins* – and he never washed his feet. He had registered as a Belgian, and had signed for five years under a false name. No one knew his real name, but we all knew that he was the youngest and most notorious *maquereau* in Paris. His last "affair" had been rather risky, and to evade punishment he thought it might be well to disappear for a few years, until the Paris police had forgotten him. He was a perfect type of bully and it was simply impossible for him to talk to any one in a decent manner. He always shouted at his men and ordered them about as if he were a slave driver, which in truth he was. He was sulky and had not much to say, and even in return for the cigars I brought him occasionally to ameliorate his temper, I only heard a grunt instead of a thank you. He spoke some Italian, though I don't know where he learnt it – he said he had never been to Italy. A great friend of his was another *maquereau* from Marseilles, who was in the same room with us. They called each other by their first names, which was very unusual in the Legion, and exchanged many recollections about the prostitutes and women who had kept them. The Marseilles pimp's name was François. François was just as filthy personally as the corporal, and he shirked his exercises and duties under every imaginable pretext. For shirking the exercises he was punished, about which he did not care; and, as for shirking his duties in the room, no one was quite his equal in foul and vile language, so they allowed themselves to be bullied.

Next to my bed was Grothé, the barber. He was a ladies' coiffeur from Paris, a German, who, at the outbreak of the war, preferred to enter the Legion than go to a concentration camp. This also entitled his wife and children to an alimony from the Government, but at the time I knew him, after a year and a half of war, his wife and children were still waiting for that alimony to come. He was a decent chap, in fact the only decent chap of all the ordinary soldiers, and he assisted me wherever he could. He had come with a few thousand francs to the Legion, but was compelled to spend it all very soon. Then he commenced to give English lessons à la Berlitz Method in Bel-Abbès in his spare time, and to *coiffe* the wives of the *bourgeoisie*, and thus earn a little money for himself. He was of good middle-class family, Germans who lived in Neuchatel; he was to have been an architect, had studied a few terms, then run away to Berlin, where he had had a very stormy existence for some weeks, until he met a man he liked, who was a ladies' coiffeur and who took him to a coiffeur's exhibition. When Grothé saw this display of historical and modern coiffures, he knew that all his life he had wanted to do nothing else but make such coiffures for ladies. He studied and made so much headway in a comparatively short time, that he took medals and prizes at all the great coiffeurs' competitions in Berlin, Paris, London, Rome, and Vienna. Then he settled in Paris, and was one of the leading coiffeurs there, counting the best women of the Faubourg St. Germain among his clients. History to him meant the headdress of the time and nothing more, either his disgust or his admiration for it was accordingly. There was something very attractive about him – he was a tall, well-built chap, with a good complexion, regular features, fair hair and blue eyes, and his voice was soft and winning. He could tell his fellow-soldiers the most naked truths and they could not reply, he said it so nicely. He always won his point and he never made enemies; he was always diplomatic and understanding; he listened to all the cackle that was told him, and repeated it only where he thought it might do good. I was surprised that he never got himself into trouble considering that he had many opportunities. But soon I found the answer to this phenomenon; what with his barber talents, and his always having some money, he put every one who might be dangerous to him under obligation. He was one of the three barbers of the regiment, and was the best, so that all the officers and sous-officiers wanted him.

When he came to the Legion his superiors asked him to be barber, but he refused and said: "I have come here to be a soldier and not a barber. I am not a barber. I am a ladies' coiffeur and I don't want to be a men's barber."

They worried him, they maltreated him, they made his life a hell. On one occasion they had thrown a gun at his shins, so that he broke down and had to be taken to barracks on a stretcher, and in consequence was in the infirmary for a long time. They criticized whatever he did, and found fault when no rational being could have found fault. They made his life unbearable every moment of the day, and when he complained, he always received the same answer: "Well, why aren't you willing to be the regiment's barber, and life will be much easier for you?" He gave in finally.

In his habits he was clean, probably the cleanest of any common soldier in the Legion, and I was glad to have him as my neighbour in the room. On the other side of my bed was the Dane, the only Dane except the Danish officer in the regiment. He didn't speak a word of pure French, but only an extraordinary mixture of English and German, neither of which he could speak separately, and Danish. He was a tall fellow with thin blonde hair tending to baldness, although he was only twenty-two years old. He arrived soon after I did, dressed in very second-rate clothes, with a steamer rug under his arm. No one knew where he came from. He told us he had run away from home in order to see something of the war, that he had gone to England and worked in a munition factory, then wanted to join the British army, but, being a Dane, was not accepted, and finally went to the French Consulate and signed for the Foreign Legion. He thought he was going to be sent to Lyons to be trained there for a few weeks, as he had done his military service in Denmark, and be sent to the front. Instead of which he was sent to Africa, which he only discovered when he got to Paris – too late to do anything. That was his story; how true it was, especially the latter part of it, is a matter of conjecture. He was the sort of a person who meant well but always did the wrong thing. His blunders were so continuous that one could only ascribe it to soft-headedness. His face was horribly pockmarked from the syphilis he had contracted. He was in a bad state; when he undressed he was a repulsive sight – his body was covered with bluish and copper-coloured spots and sores. He talked loudly in his sleep, and kept it up so long that every one in the room awoke, and then they woke him to keep him quiet. The disease may have touched his brain. He was always complaining, especially about the food, that he did not get his right portion, or that some one else deprived him of something that he should have had; also that he had no money, and that I had, and that for that reason every one in the room was down on him. This was not quite true. According to the standards of the room he was their "better," and so he ought to have had money for them to profit by, but they were principally down on him because he did everything upside down, had no consideration for any one, made noises when silence was unwritten law, and altogether upset the calculations of the entire room continually. He was an inveterate smoker and a great eater, eating all his own bread and that of all the others, when he got the chance.

I think the Danish officer, who was a poor boy himself, was angry with me that I had money to pay for things when his *protégé* had to do without, and that he, an officer, could not help him. The truth is that I had only enough to keep body and soul together, and to spare myself too many degrading humiliations from those who had the power to make my life a continuous torture if they chose. But if a man in the Legion had any money beyond his five sous a day paid him by the Government every ten days, he was considered rich. And if he could pay for a man to do his *truc*, then he was considered very rich. The *truc* cost only 5 sous a day, and every man who could afford it had his *truc* done by another soldier who hadn't any money and wanted to earn something. The man who did the *truc* had to keep the other man's gun clean, polish his boots, knapsack, *accoutrements*, brass buttons, brush his clothes, make his bed, sweep from under his bed, carry the food from the kitchen to the dining-room when it was his turn, wash his clothes, and do all the work when it was his turn to be *garde de chambre*, inclusive of staying in for him.

If a man could afford to have his *truc* done and did not have it done by some one in the room who needed the money, fault was found with him for not doing his work properly, until he would give it up in despair and have it done.

The man who did my *truc* at first was Wolters, a big burly German, with fair hair and blue eyes, and a heavy sulky expression. He had little to say, and, when he had, he spoke in a deep bass voice in abrupt sentences. He never looked a man in the eyes, and he had a hunted look about him. I always felt that he was watching everybody out of the corner of his eye. His exact history was a mystery, but it was well-understood that he had committed some blood crime in his own country. He had been in the Legion for seventeen years or more, had fought in Tonkin and Morocco and never been promoted. The only thing that interested him was money. He would do anything to get money, which he spent in drink. The moment he got it he would go to the canteen and not stop until his last penny was drunk away. He always said that the only thing worth while in life was *saufen*. He did my *truc* and also the corporal's. He really did not have the time to do both and his own work, but he kept it up until a curious thing happened.

The sergeant Steinmann took great pride in being friendly with the little Jewish Lieutenant. When on the march they often walked together, and, as the sergeant loved to gossip and brag on every occasion, he told the Lieutenant that I had money, and how nice it was that I had my *truc* done. The Lieutenant was a quiet crafty creature and listened to whatever Steinmann told him in perfect good humour. Next day an order came that the sergeant wanted to see me and Wolters.

"A complaint has been made by the officers that you have your *truc* done for you."

I was speechless – it was the usual thing which every one who had the price did, even the corporal, who I don't think had a private income.

"It is against the *règlement* for you to employ any one to do it. And you, Wolters," he said turning to him, "are not to do it any more. You," to me, "are to be a good soldier and learn to do everything yourself – these are the instructions from the Lieutenant." When I looked round Wolters had already left the room. I found nothing to say. Fenet (this was before his disappearance into prison), who lived in the same room with Steinmann, spoke up.

"That dirty Jew and that other swine Levi have their *trucs* done, and every one knows it, and many of the others besides. Why shouldn't this man have it done? It is ridiculous and absurd – either it is a dig at Wolters or at this man here. You go and employ some one else if Wolters won't do it for you, and don't you pay any attention to this rot."

When I returned to my room I found Wolters sulking and swearing, and when I asked him if he would continue to do my *truc*, he said, "No, get Chivinsky to do it."

Chapter 16

THE Pole took up the *truc* work reluctantly at first; he was frightened that he was going to be reprimanded too, but it was understood he was to do it on the quiet. He was another one of those who did not have much to say. No one knew his history or why he was there. He had enlisted for fifteen years, and at the end of that period had signed again for another fifteen years. He was still a young man — was born in Hamburg of Polish parents, but was quite German in manner and sentiment. He looked the Slav type, high cheek bones, fair hair, a *retroussé* nose, which was rather red at the tip from over-indulgence in alcohol, and not big in frame, but rather medium-sized. He was very suspicious, and I had the feeling that he mistrusted everybody and everything. I tried to be friendly with him, but he would not let me, nor would he be friendly with any of the others, not even superficially. But he mistrusted me more than the others.

I wasn't his class, I always read that in his expression and attitude, though he never cringed or was servile. The others were *merde*, as he expressed himself, though he did not treat them with bald contempt. They were his equals, and he looked at them as such, but he harboured a secret disdain for whatever they did. He did his work well and conscientiously, as most of the Germans who were there. He had had syphilis, and he warned us all not to drink from his cup or use his eating utensils. Whether he did this for humane reasons or because he did not want the others to use his things, I could never find out; anyway the warning was effectual.

Our room was conspicuous in the regiment for having no thieves in it, probably because it was so small; but still things were stolen by outsiders. All my room-mates except Grothé were drunkards. Schmidt, the bugle player, drank every pay-day until his last penny was gone and he had to be carried into his room. He had been in the Legion many years, had been sergeant and sergeant-major, but had been degraded so many times that there was no possible chance of his ever rising again. He was a middle-aged little bit of a fellow, with very short legs; he was bald, had a weak face, a long flowing moustache, which he put into a *Bartbinde* every morning, and was an incessant talker when he was not drunk. He was a German who had become a naturalized French citizen, and was the only man in the room who said he was a soldier because he enjoyed it. He had a devil-may-care nature, and was the sort of a man who could never be made to do anything unless he lived under a severe discipline. He played the bugle magnificently – in fact was the best of all the bugle players. When he was drunk he did not hesitate to ask any one for money, and if he succeeded in borrowing any he promptly forgot all about it, and absolutely denied having done so if reminded. It may have been that in his addled brain he did not remember, but if he failed to borrow any money he became extremely abusive; his seemingly good-natured face changed to that of diabolic satyr, and with a drunken smile he would make the most sarcastic and cutting remarks – remarks with a grain of truth in them, the sort of thing you felt had been said behind your back in perfectly sane and sober moments. One of the tricks of the Legionnaires, when drunk, was to sell their long sash for which they could always get six or seven francs. This was considered a terrible crime though it was done very frequently. It entailed that the man who had sold his sash had to steal another, and the robbed one had to do the same, and so on, as no soldier could appear without one, until finally some quite innocent soldier would get the punishment for being without his sash. One morning, going to the exercises on the Common, we found a man drunk in a ditch with his sash gone. He, having been caught red-handed, was punished himself, but usually some one else had to suffer. The old soldiers always wore their sash; even when it was not a part of the uniform they wore it under their coat.

The bugle player's neighbour was an Italian, a silent fellow who looked pensive and lowering. After he had done his work and had a moment to himself, he would sit on his bed perfectly immobile and brood, never saying a word. Sometimes I talked to him in Italian; his face would light up for a moment, he would seem quite pleased, but very soon he would relapse into a *si* and *no* and *chi lo sa*, and the conversation would come to a finish. This was the man who deserted when given permission for a few days' leave.

After five days' absence a man is a deserter, but even then it can be forgiven, of course allowing for the suitable punishment, if he returns within eight days – after that, if he returns, or is caught, it means *Concile de Guerre* for him.

After five or six days the Italian's packet of clothes and belongings were removed from the room. He had not returned and he was not caught. He had made good his escape.

The man who had the next bed was a real German, Michel, dogged and ignorant, the ignorance which is afraid of everything and everybody. He did what he was told, shirked work wherever he could, and did not hesitate to tell the most flagrant lies. But the lies were usually so obvious that they could not do any one any harm. It was said that he had a very terrible history. He had gone to the 2nd Regiment of the Foreign Legion at Saida before he came to us – why, no one knew. He was that heavy peasant type who would put up with anything, partly out of fear and partly because he thought it was his lot, but bearing a grudge against the powers that be for it, a quiet rankling grudge which waited for the day when abuse and bad treatment became unbearable, and then – a club or an axe or a crowbar, anything that was handy, and the momentary tormentor's head would be smashed to a pulp. Whether that was his history in his native land, who knows, but he came near doing this sort of thing with a sergeant at Saida, who hovered between life and death for many months. He was court-martialled and condemned to *Travaux Publiques*. When I saw him he had just returned after five years of this most terrible of French punishments. He was a young chap, and had the biggest appetite of any one I had ever met. After a few weeks with us he was sent to Morocco to do military service. He was glad to go – he hated the barrack-life and the exercises and the persecution of his tormentors. He was the type a sergeant or petty officer could not resist tormenting, on account of his stolid stupidity and his irritating manner of not showing the slightest sign of interest in what was told him. In Morocco he had to look out for himself, he was a soldier, had his post with two or three others, and his only duties were to protect himself and his companions from attacking Arabs, and prepare his food. He was just a piece of soldiery on the outskirts of the desert, living continually in bivouac. There was no one there to shout at him, or kick him, as long as he behaved himself with his companions, and he wasn't the man to look for trouble with his equals. There was a broad satisfied grin on his face when he left.

One of my room companions was particularly repugnant to me – Hüebner. He was a low-down criminal type. The shape of his head and ears, and the curious formation of the extremities, all bore signs of degeneration. He had small steely blue eyes, and a nasty hard mean mouth. He never talked to any one in the room unless it was to make some biting venomous remark. There was always murder in his eyes, a sneaking back-biting murder. He never did any one a favour, and watched with the eyes of a lynx everybody's work, which, if not done according to *règlement*, was promptly reported by him to the sergeant, or some other superior in power. He was hated and avoided by every one in the room. He set up a hue and cry if a window was opened at night, and complained bitterly about the cold he had caught, and, in order to prove it, would wear a white handkerchief as a bandage over his ears or his cheek for days. He was the type who would never do anything unpremeditated, and who hated the human race just on principle. He was a person to beware of – a man who would approach you from behind and murder you in cold blood, knowing exactly how much money you had with you, and what his gain would be; also, he would be perfectly sure he was unwatched and would not be discovered. There was something inhuman about him – no heart, no feeling susceptible to the weakness or foibles or sentiments of human nature. A hard calculating character, who took the world and the people as so much prey, like a wild animal that knows no mercy and understands no language but that of its most elemental desires.

The room was small for fourteen men, and the air was stifling. All these unwashed creatures, who were busy all day cleaning clothes, boots, beds, guns, *accoutrements*, and what not, had no time nor convenience, and often no taste, to clean their dirty sweaty bodies and feet. After a march, when they came in dripping with perspiration and black with dust, they changed their shirt but did not wash. The exhalations were frightful and insupportable. Often I would get up in the middle of the night and open the window for an hour to let in the balmy air of the African night. No one could possibly feel the worse for it, and they didn't, unless I was caught, and then I would hear complaints from all sides about fever and ear-aches, colds and pains in the chest, from the effects of that little fresh air.

How ghastly those nights were, with the moonlight shining on those recumbent figures, snoring, moaning and talking in their sleep! The strange noises, the heavy breathing, the restlessness of the sleepers, the stifling insufferable air, and the stench made it impossible for me to sleep; and, if I did drop off into a doze for a little while, in my dream I saw the same room with the moonlight pouring in, while the sleeping figures rose and committed dreadful deeds in my sight, and I powerless to scream or move or stop the crime. When I came out of my nightmare, bathed in perspiration, it would take me minutes to realize that it was not true, and that I had been dreaming.

There was an Armenian from Egypt, who slept next to the corporal, a short stout fellow who spoke some English. He cursed everything in the Legion and continually enlarged upon the wonders of the English Army in Egypt, the British soldiers' food, their pay, their treatment, and their motor-cars. He moved heaven and earth to get back to Egypt and enter the British Army, but one day he had evidently been too loud in his complaints and his cursing of France and everything French, and he disappeared from our midst. At the *rapport* we did not hear his name called among the punished or transferred, and we knew he had not deserted.

What became of him — who knows? Things like that happen in the Legion.

Chapter 17

THE discipline of the room was very severe. Each day one of the inmates was *garde de chambre*. This meant that in addition to all his regular work he had to do this extra service. He was obliged to rise before the others, a quarter of an hour before the *réveil*, and go downstairs with a slip of paper from the corporal, mentioning the number of occupants of the room, to an outhouse, where the stuff served as coffee and called *jus* by the soldiers was given out in big tin pails. On his return he had to serve each man with the "juice." His next duty was to sweep the room. Each man had to sweep under his own bed first, and fold up his sheets and turn the mattress half over to air; then the room-guard had to sprinkle the middle part of the room and sweep the dirt out of the door on to the landing, which he took turns in sweeping with the room-guard of the adjoining room. The finishing touch of cleaning was to place the two benches upside down on the table, and to supply the room with a pail of drinking water. The room-guard had to be ready for the exercises like all the rest of the squad, and on their return he was not allowed to leave the room again. He did not have to go to the Report, but he had to sprinkle the room again and sweep. There was an awful amount of sprinkling and sweeping, but that did not help the filthy, never-scrubbed, unpainted boards of the floor at all. His food was brought to him. If any one made any dust or dirt in the room he had to clean it up. In the afternoon he had to go to the exercises, naturally, and after his return he was forced to remain in the room for the rest of the evening. His supper was also brought to him. He had to sweep about four times a day, and supply drinking water quite as many times. On days when we returned soaking wet from our exercises in a blinding rain, it was also his duty to bring up hot *jus* to warm our insides. The men took turns for room-guard duty, so that each man's turn came about once a fortnight, unless some one was punished and received several days' room-guard duty.

Our brooms were stolen very often. Brooms were not supplied by the Government; we had to buy them ourselves, therefore they were particularly desirable. They were made of palm leaves and were used until they became short thick stumps and no longer deserved the name of brooms.

A favourite story was told of a sergeant who came into a room and found the floor dirty and shouted: "*garde de chambre*, sweep the room."

"But I have no broom."

"It doesn't matter, sweep the room anyway."

We had to supply ourselves with soap for washing our clothes; it was not supplied by the Government. Soap was dear, and was difficult to keep in the most lockable box. It was a necessity, and the man without money or soap had to steal it somewhere, as we were compelled to look immaculate. The few things we had, had to be washed continually, and on damp days it was impossible to dry our clothes, so that we had to start out with damp things on our bodies.

Shoe-blacking and socks were not supplied by the Government either. Most of the men did not wear socks but foot-rags, which they claimed were cleaner [?] and protected the feet better against the inner roughness of the *brodequins*. Some, as I have said, did not wear anything on their feet but their boots.

The stairs were very unsafe during the middle of the night. I was warned not to go downstairs at night to the lavatories, which were some little distance from the main buildings. Many murders and robberies had taken place on these stairs. A man who went down to the lavatory wasn't going to leave his money — if he had any — at the mercy of his room-companions, so it was quite certain that he had it on him. The stairs were ill-lighted by the solitary petroleum lamp on the ground floor, and sometimes that wasn't in function. Murders were committed for reasons of grudge, for robbery, and sometimes for the pure pleasure of murder. When anything like that occurred there was a stir in the barracks for about a day, and then a hush. No one knew who had done it — many were suspected — violent threats would be uttered by the executioner at the next report, referring to the matter in a veiled way, and there was an end to it. If the victim had not been silenced completely, he had nothing to say. He had been robbed, he never knew by whom, and he had, after all, been warned not to go downstairs at night!

After some weeks Count de R—— took me aside and told me quite seriously that this was no place for me, and that they would always be suspicious of me, no matter how good a soldier I might become, or how I might ingratiate myself, that it had nothing to do with my personal attributes, but that I was and always would be a sheep among the wolves.

"There is really no earthly reason why you are here," he said. "You have not done anything wrong, and you were not forced to come here on account of your status in France. Well, no one is going to believe that you have come here for idealistic purposes of doing your share to aid the Allies. They could not understand that; and any one can see that you are not a soldier born, and that you have no love for the life. Besides, the greatest objection they will have always is that you are not one of themselves. I would advise you to get out if you can – something sinister might happen to you if you don't. That is all I can say."

I thought it was quite enough, and I realized that what he told me was the truth. I was the butt of the officers, who were suspicious of me and partly jealous, and did everything to humiliate me, and make me feel as cheap as possible. I was the butt of the petty officers, who wished to ingratiate themselves with their superiors. I was the butt of the soldiers who thought I was not one of them, and I was the butt of others who were jealous or bore me a grudge for not lending them unlimited money. Quite aside from what Count de R— had told me, everything had begun to pall on me, and I wondered how I could continue to stand it. The horror of the sleepless nights, the stench of the room, the vile language of my companions, their thieving – which was so much the order of the day that it was a surprise if anything stealable wasn't stolen – their continual attempts to embroil me in their lies and discredit me, their evil-mindedness, which attributed every action to the lowest motives, their physical filth, and finally their drunkenness and habits, revolted and disgusted me to such an extent that life became an unbearable burden.

The disinfected clothes that I wore, and the bed-bugs in the bed, brought loathing to every one of my senses. The food which I should have to eat if my money gave out was nauseating. The lack of any kind of equable companionship was distressing and depressing. The continual necessity of having to scent danger, among those I should have been able to trust under normal conditions of life, became maddening. The physical strain of carrying the heavy kit, the long marches, the lack of sleep and proper nourishment, both at the canteen and hotel, reduced my weight from 140 lbs. to 115 lbs. within a few weeks. My feet, in spite of wearing my own shoes, became a mass of sores, and the toe-nails discoloured. My back and shoulders were in continual pain. My moustache worried me, and my short-cropped head made me unsightly.

The field with the exercises, and the eternal repetition of the movements which left no room for improvement and gave no chance to learn anything interesting, useful or practical, seemed a desolate waste of time to me.

The officers, sergeants, and corporals, with their fiendish cleverness in breaking the spirit of the strongest, and their unscrupulous methods of accusing a man of crimes he had never committed and punishing him for them, the absolute impossibility of being able to save oneself from their jealousy, spite, wrath, grudge or vindictiveness, their brutal treatment, their inexorable cruelty and endless exacting of property and money to satisfy their insatiable desires, and finally their disloyalty, their utter lack of any patriotism or ideals for the great cause for which the Allies were fighting, made me feel the hopelessness of the attempt to be a soldier, and I felt convinced I could not do my share in the great struggle by this means.

The most fiendish mediaeval torture chamber could not have been devised more cleverly than the methods employed for systematically breaking the spirit; first, until there was no resistance left to struggle against any one, not even against one's own self; and then commenced the breaking up of the body until it became degenerated and befouled, and when there was nothing left worth the name of human man, he was thrown down, trampled on, like dirt under foot or vermin, and life crushed out or thrown to the cannons for fodder.

I had not entered the Army, such as it is understood, a body of men, clean in mind and body, with ideals of sacrifice and splendid manhood, ready to lay down their lives for a great cause, kept in good condition against the frailties of human nature by a sharp discipline, directed by men of high moral values, who knew and administered justice – but a prison, full of gaol-birds, whose keepers were more rascally than themselves, and whose existence, under the name of a military institution, was a farce.

What would happen if my money gave out, and I should be able no longer to appease the pockets of the vultures who had me in their claws?

Every man, who is not living only an animal existence, is aware that there is a certain value attached to him and his capabilities, which he wishes to make the most of for himself and his fellow-men. What value had a man here theoretically or practically? His physical surroundings were degrading, mentally he was tormented and tortured until all attempt to consider himself a unit for good was thoroughly exterminated – and as to his soul – well, that was denied him as a foregone conclusion.

I was wasting myself, my substance, my energies and what capabilities I had – it was suicide mentally and physically.

How to get away? was the question that revolved itself continually in my mind. Count de R—— 's speech had been curiously appropriate, and if I had not formed any definite decision before, this was the last straw which spurred me to immediate action.

I wrote to the American Ambassador in Paris, and told him my case, explaining the impossibility of the position, and how totally different the conditions were from what I had thought, and asking him what I could do to get away. No answer came.

Then quite unexpectedly came an occasion which seemed to blow a good wind. At the *rapport* one day I heard that the applications for the Easter holiday permissions had to be made that day. I was dumbfounded, I had had no idea that such permissions were granted. At once I made my application, although I was warned that I should not get it, being a *jeune soldat* and not yet three months in the service. It is only after three months, when a man has sworn allegiance to the French Army, that he becomes a regular soldier. If he deserts after that the punishment is Public Labour or Death. If he deserts under three months he can only get about thirty days' prison, at most two months.

Fortunately I had told Grothé that I would like to go to Algiers for a day or two, and that it would be nice if we could go together. He had never been to Algiers, and was delighted with the idea, and accepted my words as an invitation, and also made application for a permission. It was due to him and all the intrigues of his diplomatic nature that we achieved our purpose. When objections were raised as to my being a *jeune soldat*, Neuhold, a sergeant-major who was fond of Grothé, was appealed to; and, when he saw the opportunity of getting his friend an outing for nothing, he stood up for me, and weighted down the scales in my favour by saying, "But he is going with Grothé, and Grothé is a *vieux soldat* and to be trusted."

I had been careful not to make myself culpable during the time I was there, for had I been punished with imprisonment I should have lost the privilege of asking for a short leave of absence for a year.

To every one's surprise three days' permission was granted to me and Grothé. I had to register where I was going, where I was going to stop in Algiers, and then received a military permission to travel to Algiers and back, which had to be stamped by the military authorities on arrival in Algiers, and again before leaving. On showing this permission at the station at Bel-Abbès we were accorded a reduction on our railway tickets.

It is a fourteen hours' journey from Sidi-bel-Abbès to Algiers, and, as there is no night train, we had to waste a day of our precious liberty in travelling. We went third class. The train was packed with Legionnaires, and before the day was half over not a single soldier was sober. Most of them were going to places en route, only one or two as far as Algiers. The train was a pandemonium, and I did not know at what moment we would get into a row ourselves, for it is not easy to evade a drunken man in a packed railway compartment. Some of the sights we saw are quite indescribable. The brutality, vulgarity, and absolute abandon of these low-down creatures the wildest imagination could not have conjured up if one had not been brought face to face with the reality.

The carriage was used as a lavatory. The jokes which were bandied about reeked with filth and depravity. Fights took place every few minutes. Food was denied, and then given to an unconscious victim to eat. Bottles were used as urine vessels, and handed to the unsuspecting as wine. They blasphemed and cursed and rolled about in physical abandonment. Dirty, filthy, bleeding, dishevelled, they were pushed out of the carriage at their respective destinations, often to fall flat on the ground, and remain there to the accompaniment of the uproarious laughter of their companions.

Involuntarily I asked myself what must have been their early surroundings and antecedents. I had never come in contact in my life with any phase of human society where such individuals as I faced now could have sprung from, and I had thought that I had had some experience in life.

What terrified me most was the fact that I was brought in such close contact with men whom it was impossible to measure. They were so entirely out of my depth. I had nothing to go by; it was this uncertain unintelligible quantity, which upset all my calculations as to reading human nature and dealing with it accordingly. I was at sea. A great fear came over me — fear, not such as comes to one in face of a great catastrophe at sea or on land, when one looks death straight in the face and "good night," but a fear of some terrible impending tragedy, where one is a negligible quantity, incapable of averting it, knowing one will be drawn into it, feeling the incapability of dealing with the problems, and going to a destruction worse than death, something which is completely outside of one, and for which one is not in the least responsible.

It was late when Grothé and I arrived at Algiers. We went to a second rate hotel, the best that was open in war-time, and to bed — he to sleep the sleep of the just, I to gloat all night over the clean fresh fine linen and soft bedding, and the luxury of a room to myself.

Chapter 18

NEXT morning I put on my civilian clothes. What a relief to get rid of those dirty heavy soldiers' clothes, and not to have to wind the putties round one's legs! I had been warned not to wear civilian clothes, as it was against the *règlement* and likely to be punished with imprisonment. However, I had plans of my own, and Grothé was not the one to object or find fault or squeal. A feeling of potency came over me when I was well-shod and wore clothes that fitted. Before leaving Bel-Abbès I had been asked by several petty officers, "Are you going in uniform to Algiers?" I had answered, "Certainly," knowing full well that it was a trap. Probably they felt that I wasn't at all proud of my shabby uniform, and was anxious to get into civilian clothes. Grothé, who had remained in uniform, took my military permission to the "Commandant" to be signed, so that I was relieved of that duty.

I started out, and whenever I met an officer quite involuntarily my hand went up just ready to salute when I remembered that I was a free man if only for a few hours. What a privilege to go into a bar and order any kind of a drink and not be refused or be told "militaire is not served here!" I was walking on air. I sped to the American Consul and told him what sort of a place was Bel-Abbès, and that I could not and would not stay under any circumstances, and asked if he could help me, or at least advise me what I was to do. He was a charming man – I had met him years ago when he was Vice-Consul in Berlin. He listened attentively and then said:

"I do not think the American Embassy will help you; they do not care to interfere with the interior workings of the French Army. More or less you are out of their jurisdiction when you enter the French Army, although by rights you have not given up your American citizenship. There is some talk that the U.S. Government wants to make some changes, and that an American who enters a foreign army is going to lose his citizenship."

This was another blow. It increased my determination to get out.

"But I will tell you what I can do for you. General Bavouzet is in command of the Army Corps here, and a great friend of mine. I will speak to him, and see if he can't transfer you to Lyons."

I was grateful, and he took his hat and coat and we went round to the headquarters of the Army Corps. The Consul told me to wait downstairs. I waited, and in about half an hour he came down and told me to come up. We were ushered into the General's private study. The General was perfectly charming, delightful in manner, a soldier and a courtier with a kind face and an understanding eye. He received me most kindly. The Consul told me afterwards that when he had told him about me he had asked if I were in uniform and when he answered "no," he said: "Well then, I can see him, for if he were in the uniform of a common soldier it would be against the *règlement* to receive him."

I told him that I had entered the Legion to fight the "Boches," and instead of that, I was trained, shouted at, and compelled to live with a regiment of "Boches" Quite aside from my personal distaste in the matter, it was hardly a fair position that I should be in a company of men, all Germans, who knew me to be an American who had come of his own free will to be trained to fight their own countrymen; also that my feelings were rather strong, and that I had a sincere desire to get away from the "Boches," not to live with them. I mentioned the fact that there were seventy per cent of Germans in the Legion, that nearly all petty officers were Germans, and that the regular officers were pro-German, as was clearly shown in the last *trimestre* report, in which the Captain praised all the German petty officers, and not one Frenchman. All this was evidently new to the General, as he seemed greatly interested and surprised.

He was most cordial, and we talked for about a half an hour. It was a great satisfaction to my vanity to be accepted again as an equal by an officer, and not to be treated as the scum of the earth. He took my name and matriculation number, the company and the regiment, and told me he would see what he could do. I knew he was all-powerful in military matters in the Colony of Algiers, and his pleasant twinkle assured me that he was going to do something, only I did not know how soon. From what I had seen in the Legion I found that military matters moved at snail's pace, and that everything had to go through a hundred hands and pigeon-holes. I allowed myself small hope as to the "how soon."

On my return to the hotel I told Grothé what I had done. His eyes fairly dropped out of his head with surprise, and he could not get over my *toupet*, as he called my action. That I was not sent to prison for having dared to go to a General in civilian clothes was beyond him to understand. And as to having seen and spoken with him, it all seemed to him quite fantastic.

"In a fortnight you will have your papers and be transferred to Lyons," he said.

That evening I was invited to the Consul's house to dinner. They had a beautiful house at Mustapha Supérieur, standing in a large garden, overlooking the bay and Algiers. The Consul's wife, who was one of the most delightful women I ever met, was a most vivacious *raconteuse*. She told me many things about Algiers, and about French Society and its corruptness. It appears that all the influential people who were at the head of politics, and indeed the authorities in general, had had something in their past which made living in France impossible, and through influence they had received sinecures in Algiers. Once there, they played the high and mighty the moment they got the chance.

The pasts of most of the wives of these high officials seemed to have been anything but brilliant. Women who had been other men's mistresses, women who had been cooks while a first wife had been alive, and chambermaids who had been the mistresses of their master before they entered into matrimony, these were the society women of Algiers. Having had such doubtful antecedents themselves, they did not give credit to any one else being any better. The acridity of their intrigues and their venomous remarks, if my informant can be believed, savoured of the back-stairs. And, having risen in position, they did not deem it necessary to guard their reputations from further onslaught.

Their ideals about the war can be judged by what a woman said to the Consul's wife at a bridge party. Speaking of a young American who had joined the Foreign Legion, she said, "Did he join in cold blood and with premeditation? Impossible! Surely it must have been in a moment of mental aberration, or under the influence of drink." Nothing would induce her to believe it was enthusiasm for the Allied Cause.

The ladies of Algiers did not speak any more of Eau de Cologne, but called it Eau de Pologne.

It was at the time that Portugal declared war on the Central Empires, and their remarks were suitable to their character. "Oh, that little country – it doesn't matter whether she joins or not."

It seemed, from everything I heard, that Algiers was packed with *embusqués*, who took any kind of small official position in order to have an excuse not to fight.

Next day, Easter Sunday, the Consul and his wife and I were invited to Mrs. Arthur's, whose house is supposed to be the most beautiful Arab house in Algiers. It stands in a large magnificent garden filled with the most luxuriant flowers. I shall not make the mistake of mentioning what flowers, as Robert Hichens did. He filled Mrs. Arthur's garden, in a chapter of one of his books, with rhododendrons, and when she wrote asking if he did not know that rhododendrons didn't grow in Africa, he changed the chapter in the second edition.

Mrs. Arthur was a very beautiful old lady, and very interesting, with a great deal of charm. Her house was wonderful. There was nothing in it that was not purely Arab, and yet it had all the comfort and luxury of an English home.

The open courtyard with its fountain, the banks of flowers, the exquisite Arab furniture and gorgeous hangings, the wonderful collection of Arab weapons and ornaments, made one feel as if Aladdin's Lamp had been rubbed.

She told me that one day two Arab women visited her and begged her to allow them to see again the house of their childhood. She was most interested, naturally, and showed them about, and inquired how the house had looked when they had occupied it; and then she changed it accordingly, so that the house was not only Arab in general aspect, but also in detail and atmosphere. She told me that she intended to leave the house to the State as a museum.

Some English officers visited Mrs. Arthur during the afternoon, well-fed good-natured men who were in Algiers on a provisioning commission. They were interested to hear about the Legion, but I held back. It wasn't time to talk – not yet.

Later we visited the Norwegian Consul and some other friends, and finally we returned to the Consul's house to have dinner under the trees of his garden overlooking Algiers and the sea, which seemed a mass of liquid fire in the light of the setting sun.

What a beautiful day it had been, warm and still, a cloudless sky, the scent of flowers everywhere, and Mustapha Supérieur the garden spot of Algiers! How pleasantly the hours had passed among these charming people; what a relief to feel once more like a human being, to be amongst one's own, and not to feel an outsider! This little whiff of civilization just bucked me up sufficiently, so that I felt I could stand Bel-Abbès a little longer, especially with Bavouzet's promise ahead, and Grothé's certainty that it would not be longer than a fortnight coming.

Grothé in the meantime had enjoyed himself on his own, and, Baedeker in hand, had gone to see the sights of Algiers. He seemed very happy and contented with his visit.

Another night in a good bed, and next morning, clad in our soldier's uniforms, we both left Algiers to return to Sidi-bel-Abbès.

Chapter 19

ON my return to barracks I found the corporal of our squad leaving. He had enlisted for five years, his time had been up some weeks before, and he had not been discharged. In spite of his appeals and reclamations he had received no hearing, and no attention whatever had been paid to him. His method of further procedure was simple and effective. He did not go to the exercises, and did not plead illness or any other excuse. He had asked repeatedly to see the Captain, which request was refused him, or rather the answer given amounted to the same thing: the Captain could not see him then, but at the same time made no future appointment. He was punished with prison for not appearing at the exercises, but in prison he continued to refuse to do the exercises or anything else he was ordered to do. The matter was reported to the Captain, who commanded him to his presence.

"Why do you refuse to do exercises? Are you ill or what is the matter?"

"Mon capitaine, I am not going to do any exercises, nor anything else I am ordered to do, as I am no longer a soldier by law."

"Why not?"

"Because I enlisted for five years and my time was up three weeks ago. I have asked for my discharge and it has not come. I shall do nothing more while waiting for my discharge."

"What are you kicking about? Have you not everything you want – a bed to sleep on, your food, and your clothes?"

"Yes, mon capitaine, but before I came to the Legion I had had a bed to sleep on, and food to eat, and wore clothes."

"What do you want now?"

"I want my immediate release."

"But this is war-time, and in war-time you are compelled to continue to serve, whether your five years are up or not."

"In the first place, as I registered as a Belgian subject, which was accepted as true, I am outside French jurisdiction, and therefore free to offer myself to my own country, and even if I were a French subject, since my term of five years is up in the Legion, I am free to return to France and enter a French regiment, which is my intention, but I do not intend to serve in the Legion another day. You may report this to the Colonel."

"Allez."

Within twenty-four hours the corporal had his discharge. He was refused his request of travelling to France in his uniform, but received the habitual civilian's clothes given those who are discharged, a pair of trousers and a jacket of the cheapest shoddy, "qui coute dix-neuf sous," as the soldiers used to say, and a cap. When he left he looked absolutely the part of the Paris *apache* and *maquereau* for which he was known.

The day after my return an order came that there would be an all-day march and manoeuvre the next day, and an encampment in the forest at the end of it for the night, and return to barracks the day following. Many of the soldiers reported ill. At the *rapport* an order was given that no one was exempt from the march except those who were considered incapable by the doctor, and those who reported themselves ill without cause would be punished with a fortnight's imprisonment and lose their permissions to stay out once a week until midnight for two months. Still many insisted on reporting ill-The chief cause was sore feet. It seemed miraculous to me that there were not more frequent blood-poisonings, for the open sores on the feet of the soldiers were most conducive to it, especially with their inability to keep clean. The doctor used to pass over these things as of no consequence, and considered that they could do service any way, unless the sore was so big and inflamed that the man had to be carried into the infirmary. In many cases these sores were caused by predisposition, poorness or illness of the blood, but in most cases they were caused by the ill-fitting and heavy *brodequins*.

We marched out as usual at 5.45 a.m., but with music and with kit complete. We had our knapsacks tightly packed with all our clothes, pick and shovel, parts of the tent, blanket, water-bottle filled to the brim, cartridges in our cartridge cases, gun and bayonet, and private provisions in our *musettes*, the entire load weighing about forty kilogrammes.

The moment we got outside the town gates the music stopped, and then we trudged along the sunny dusty treeless road hour after hour, our load getting heavier and heavier, and the sun hotter and hotter. Just as on the regular manœuvres, a halt of ten minutes was made every hour, to quench the thirst of our parched throats. Many men dropped behind, unable to continue at the rate we were marching, and always a corporal or a sergeant was commissioned to stay with them, just like a penitentiary, fearing the convict might escape. After all, that is exactly what the Legion was — a penitentiary — under another name.

One man, an Armenian, dropped by the roadside overcome by the heat. He had fainted. Two corporals were ordered to stay behind to take care of him. They bathed his forehead, and when he came to, gave him some water and helped him up. After a few paces he fainted again, and then I lost sight of him. We trudged on in the scorching sun. Before the morning was half spent a great number had become invalided, and finally formed a company for themselves under the charge of several sergeants and corporals, and followed as best they could.

About an hour before we reached the forest I collapsed, overcome by the heat and fatigue. Steinmann, the sergeant, who had been borrowing from me through Grothé, felt he had been deprived of all the money which ought to have come to him, for the luxury of a trip to Algiers for two represented a fortune to him, and this money he would have extorted from me, had he known I had so much. He felt himself cheated, and was going to make me suffer for it. I was lying flat on my back on the sun-baked earth, unable to move; he flew in a rage about me and insisted upon my rising and continuing, but I was too far gone and did not care. In his rage he kicked me with his heavy *brodequins*, which brought me to, but I could not have budged if I had wanted to. I was completely exhausted. In my dazed state I heard him say, "That is simply because he is wearing his own boots. When he gets back to barracks, he shall have the regulation *brodequins*. I'll show him."

There was never any singing on these marches, and although one hears and reads so much of the good humour and cheeriness of the soldier, I never saw any of it.

The superiors in the Legion *tu-toied* the soldiers, and the soldiers *tu-toied* each other. Every one was a *camarade*, but that did not mean anything, for whenever I asked if So-and-so was a friend, the answer would be "Oh no, he is just a 'camarade.'"

One of the principles of etiquette was, when you were asked if you were tired, never to say yes. If you did say yes, you were reprimanded immediately and told, "Even if you are tired you should never say so."

I got very thirsty, naturally, in that broiling sun, and drank up all my water. This is supposed to be the worst thing a soldier can do; it reduces his resistance to nil, and the sergeant warns the new soldier continually not to drink. But I heard later from Ferez, the French sergeant-major, that while water is the death of an old soldier, and he knows it, it is the death of a young soldier not to drink. Young and old, in this sense, means whether he is young or old in the service, irrespective of age.

We marched about twenty-five kilometres before we reached the forest by round-about ways; a manœuvre took place in which blank cartridges were fired, and after about two hours of this sort of thing the bugle was blown for *rassemblement*, and we gathered at the edge of the forest for the encampment.

Tents were pitched. Each man carried a sixth part of a tent, as six men slept in a tent liked packed sardines. The place chosen was so far from any well that it took several hours to fetch the necessary water for cooking in canvas buckets. The provision waggons had followed the troops. Wood was gathered by the soldiers, fires were made, and the cooks of each squad prepared the greasy rice and hunks of fat in the dirty marmites. *Jus* was also one of the delicacies which they made.

I had provided myself with some hard-boiled eggs, cold meat, cheese, and cognac from the hotel, and found a shady place under an old oak tree, where I could eat my food in peace.

Ferez came up to me: "Why on earth are you in the Legion? You have no business to be here. You have some grey hairs, and are much too old to carry the pack and survive. I can see you have never been a soldier before." And then he told me of all the vagabonds, thieves, murderers, and others he had met in the twenty years he had been in the Legion. He was only a sergeant-major, but he had more dignity than any of the regular officers.

On this occasion I got to know Serbo better. Serbo was a sergeant belonging to another company, and the only gentleman in the regiment, Count de R—— excepted. He was a very charming and cultured person, with an extremely amiable disposition, and, from everything I had seen, invariably kind, understanding, and tolerant. No one knew what had brought him to the Legion. He had arrived, not many months before me, with many trunks and portmanteaux, from Monte Carlo, enlisted, and had his voluminous wardrobe sold at public auction. From his conversation I gathered that he must have been in the diplomatic service. He had travelled extensively in Russia, England, France, Germany, Italy, and the Balkan countries, from which latter he hailed. It was said in the Legion that he was a Servian Prince, but, from some of the things he said, I believe he was a Greek. No one knew his real name.

He and Count de R—— and I sat under that tree and chatted, exchanging reminiscences and anecdotes about places and people we had known. For a short hour Paris, Petersburg, Berlin, Vienna, London were brought back to our mental vision, and Isadora Duncan, Marie Tempest, Cosmo

Gordon Lennox, Siegfried Wagner, the Moscow Art Theatre, Nijinsky, and the Russian Ballet were discussed. For a moment we forgot that we were in uniform, and in Africa, until the foul language of the dirty soldiers and a whiff of the beastly smelling food brought us back to reality.

Count de R——'s position was particularly incongruous. His son was a full-fledged Frenchman, whose career was the army. He had been educated at St. Cyr. At that moment he was captain at Corfu, and if Fate willed it that the father was sent to Salonica, it might happen that he, a simple sergeant in the Legion, would have to stand *garde à vous* to his own son.

The Spahis, who had been manoeuvring the same day, were encamped on the same ground but apart from us; that is, they occupied the right side and we the left side of the encampment, and between the two camps the Spahis' horses were tied.

Towards sun-down the encampment was entrenched, and low fake fortifications were raised, the wooden *mitrailleuse* was put on a high earth platform for defence, fires were lit, supper was cooked, the watch and guard were distributed, and we were free until we retired to rest. But we were warned that there would be an attack during the night, so that we were compelled to retire fully equipped with bayonet and full cartridge cases, and gun in hand.

The aspect of the camp was truly magnificent – the low tents of the soldiers, the tall tents of the-officers, the watch fires, the sentinels, the gorgeous costumes of the Spahis, the splendid Arab horses hitched together, here and there some soldiers gathered about a fire, on one side the dark forest, and on the other the wide vast plain which seemed to stretch interminably into the gathering mist. The damp rich odours of the earth and pines, the neighing and stamping of the horses, and the gradual silence which crept over the scene, held one's breath.

Sleep was not possible for me, especially in the small tents with five unwashed fellows, who had been marching and manoeuvring all day under a pitiless African sun. I sat outside in front of the tent, contemplating the scene and musing upon the entire life of the Legion. How incongruous it seemed in comparison with this really wonderful scene, which only showed the beauty, the colour, the mystery, and the fascination of adventure and the life of warriors! Impatient words struck my ear from the interior of the tent – it was the Dane's voice; a hoarse guttural voice replied imperiously, "Taisez vous" – it was the big nigger speaking.

Chapter 20

AT dawn the camp was broken up – there had been no night attack. We packed our tents, levelled the earth where the fake fortifications had been, and made the place look as if we had never been there.

The road that was chosen for the way back was still longer than the one we had come. Clouds gathered during the morning, and by the time we were well under way the heavens opened, and it poured in torrents. We were drenched to the skin, and the red mud was so deep that we stuck at every step.

Our columns moved at snail's pace over the roads, which did not deserve the name, and we reached Bel-Abbès after seven hours, with a ten minutes' halt every hour, when we could have reached our destination in about three hours had we taken the most direct route. It was one o'clock when we entered the town with the flare of trumpets and the band playing the "Marseillaise" – a dirty, bedraggled-looking set of vagabonds.

I had just changed, gone to the canteen to eat a chop and a fried egg, when some one came up to me and said: "You are going to Lyons." I was aghast – had Grothé broken his promise and gossiped? No one but he knew anything about my plan, and the result of my visit to Algiers. I was doubly suspicious because I had discovered at the hotel in Algiers that he had told the porter of my visit to the General. I pretended to know nothing, waiting to see how much was known. At that moment Grothé himself came up: "They say you are going to Lyons. An order has come for your transfer." This was quick work indeed – still I did not think it was possible; but the next moment an orderly came to tell me I was to present myself immediately to the sergeant-major, Neuhold. I went; it was true. The order had come the day before while we were on the march.

"This order arrived yesterday," said Neuhold, "and you must leave by the next train, otherwise we shall get into trouble. The next train is at four o'clock, and you must get your new outfit for France first. There is no time to lose – come at once with me to the dressing-rooms for your outfit."

"But I can't leave at four o'clock; I have no money. I am expecting a registered letter with money at any moment. Besides I must pack my things at the hotel, and pay my bill there. I understood the steamers for France left only on Saturday – to-day is Thursday."

"You must go at once, these are marching orders. Any way I must get you ready so that you can leave by the four o'clock train for Oran. Then you can talk to the Major and explain, and probably he will allow you to stay over and arrange your affairs."

Oran is only about two hours from Bel-Abbès, and I did not quite see why I should be sitting at Oran, waiting for a steamer, when I could wait here for my money and attend to my affairs.

The military railway and steamer pass was ready waiting for me. We went to the dressing-rooms; I had to give up all I had received when I arrived, except my underclothing and the *musette*, and received the equivalent of each piece according to the present uniform worn in France, that is, sky blue breeches and coat and overcoat, putties and boots. This time each piece was new. It was a great relief not to have to get into another set of disinfected worn-out rags. Each piece I returned was registered to see that nothing was missing, and each new piece which was given me was registered, all of which took considerable time. Then I went to my room and packed things according to *règlement*, otherwise it would have been impossible to get everything into my knapsack. It was about 3.30 before I was ready to present myself to the Major. He tried to be kind, but he could not give me any more time to stay – I had to leave that day – these were the orders from the General. I asked whether I might stay until the last train for Oran at 8 p.m. and he granted me that request. I went to the hotel and packed. At five o'clock Grothé came to help me, and I gave him instructions what to do with my luggage after I had telegraphed the money for my bill. I explained the position to that dreadful landlady, whose eyes narrowed still more than on former occasions, as if she were about to say in her sharp metallic voice: "What game is this Legionnaire up to now?"

The food at the hotel had been abominable: wonderful French menus with most elaborate names, and nothing to eat. The usual thing was a watery soup, or a sardine and an olive, a vegetable done up beyond recognition, a very meagre meat course (a second helping was charged extra), another vegetable, and an orange. The habitual orange was called "fruits," and the meat received an extraordinary name, with which it had no relation, but usually consisted of boiled beef, disguised with different coloured sauces. The dining-room was as ill-lighted by the weak gas as the halls, and was no more conducive to appetite or cheerfulness than the food. On the whole, what with eating something at the canteen at midday, my dinner at night at the hotel, my hotel room, and all the extras, it cost me as much to live at Bel-Abbès as at a first-class hotel in Florence or Naples. But then I would not have lost twenty-five pounds in weight in six weeks.

Grothé and I were just having dinner, when a Greek sergeant was announced. He was sent by the regiment to take me to the station to see that I really left. He had scarcely sat down to have a glass of wine with us, when the waiter came in and said that the Danish lieutenant was in the next room and wanted to speak to me. He had always avoided me, except to tell me something unpleasant, and whenever he had entered the dining-room he had rarely found it necessary to return my salute. Altogether he was a boorish fellow, and I wasn't keen to comply with his request. The Greek sergeant told me that he was furious that I was being sent to Lyons instead of his compatriot, to whom he had promised his transference soon. He wanted to know what I had done to have my transfer effected. While I had been packing the Dane had tried to pump me, but I was too busy to answer, so he had evidently reported to his officer friend. I did not see any reason why I should give any explanations, in fact I did not feel I had any right to do so, for the General's sake; besides, neither of the Danes had shown me anything but hostility. His order to see me was no longer an official order — I was out of barracks, and to all intents and purposes had left the Company and Bel-Abbès at 4 p.m. I sent an answer, to be given him after I had left, that I was sorry, but had had no time to see him at the last moment.

Grothé and the Greek sergeant saw me off. It was a happy moment when I saw the lights of Bel-Abbès fade in the distance.

At Oran I evaded the military guard at the railway station, and jumped into the omnibus of the best hotel and drove there. The rule is that a soldier of the Legion must go to the fort to sleep, when he is in transport, and be kept there like a prisoner until it is time for him to embark.

My first work next morning was to shave my moustache. I had never worn a moustache, and in all those weeks I could never get over the irritation it caused, or the feeling that I had something dirty on my face.

Oran is a very desolate looking place. The town lies high up on cliffs and the highest point is crowned by the fort. The streets leading down to the dockyards and quays are dirty and abound in shops of ship materials, drinking places, and ship-broking offices, such as one sees in any small port. The harbour is tolerable. The upper part of the town consists of two – and three-storied buildings of European structure, with innumerable third-rate shops of every description, and is as dirty as the lower part. The modern cathedral is about as ugly a building as I have ever beheld. The Arab quarter is insignificantly small, and what there is of it is spoilt by European invasion. Oran is more Spanish than French, and lacks the merest pretence of being anything else but commercial and third rate.

At the steamship office I was informed that a private soldier cannot travel first class, but that I could travel second class if the *sous-officiers* on board did not object. Otherwise, I should have to travel third class, as my military pass prescribed. I made a note of the supplementary fare I should have to pay for second, and went in search of money.

I had no money, not even enough to pay the hotel, only my cheque book, and I had had ample experience at Bel-Abbès to know how difficult it was to cash a cheque. Oran did not possess an American Consul, so I repaired to the British Agent, who received me very kindly. He telephoned to Algiers to the American Consul, and forthwith cashed me a cheque. At first he could not understand why I had entered the Foreign Legion, but when I explained the original motives he was quite touched, and we parted very good friends.

The embarkment of the troops and officers was to take place at 4 p.m. on Saturday. The S. S. *Sidi Brahim* was a medium-sized Mediterranean steamer, and at the moment carried troops only. I arrived in ample time, and from the second-class promenade deck was able to survey the spectacle of the embarkment. The troops were all natives, and were lined up parade-like on the quay. The colours of the uniforms were magnificent. The Spahis took first place in this gorgeous array of colour and costume, with their high white turbans, red flowing mantles, baggy blue trousers, and red saffian leather boots. The companies of the different regiments arrived with their bands of music playing until they had taken their places. After they had all arrived there came a silence, an uncanny silence, an obvious wait, every man standing to attention, awaiting a command which came not. It was a scorching cloudless day, and the quay at that hour must have seemed like the infernal regions to the heavily laden soldiers, standing in position for over an hour, in the blazing sunshine.

Finally a blast of trumpets — a shout of *garde à vous*, the band played the "Marseillaise," and down the steep zigzag incline came a large open car, containing the fossilized General, who had paid us a visit at Bel-Abbès.

In the midst of the troops he stopped, alighted, and talked to some of the officers in command for quite another hour, looking very fierce and dyspeptic. Then another blast of trumpets and a still louder playing of the "Marseillaise," and the General drove off.

The actual embarkment of the troops commenced; this took a considerable time, and just as the sun was about to set we steamed slowly out of the harbour bound for Marseilles.

Chapter 21

THE second class of the *Sidi Brahim* did not sport any luxuries whatever. The cabins and corridors were narrow and uncarpeted, with four berths in each cabin. The food was of the simplest: *hors d'oeuvres* à la Hôtel Continental Bel-Abbés, one meat dish with vegetable, and cheese, for luncheon; for dinner, about the same, only instead of the *hors d'oeuvres* a soup, and instead of the cheese some sweet cakes. There were no second helpings, everything was accurately measured out – small portions – the regular French *bout de chandelle* business. It was the food one might expect to get in a restaurant of the *petite bourgeoisie* of a provincial town. But of course the price was not at all *petite bourgeoisie*, and, in fact, considering it was a military transport and specially running for the convenience of the army fighting for *La Patrie*, one might have expected either lower fares or very excellent accommodation. But the same spirit prevailed all through France and Algiers: that the army must pay well, if there is no competition, and, in the case of this steamer, that it must pay doubly well. It was just the reverse in Italy, where every man thought he ought to help a soldier who was righting for his country, knowing he had little money and thinking of his own sons and relatives, hoping that they would be helped likewise. In France every one seemed to be thinking "this is wartime, we must make the best of it, we shall probably never see so many customers again, and certainly not these soldiers, let us make all we can." There is precious little sentiment about the lower class French when it comes to money! Some of the *sous-officiers* on the boat were quite nice chaps, mostly business-men who had been called to arms when the war broke out, altogether very different from those I had met in the Legion. They were talkative and sociable and pleasant. It was a great surprise to me that they treated me, a common soldier of the Legion, decently, but I think that was due to the fact that they really did not know I was a "Legionnaire" until after they got to know me and I told them. My uniform bore no particular sign to distinguish it from the regular uniform of the

"Campagne de France." I had merely a *One* at my collar. One of the officers, a *sous-lieutenant*, was quite an enthusiast about Germany and the Germans. He claimed that they were a marvellous people with a great culture, great men, and great systems. He admired their towns, their order and cleanliness, their administration and army, the discipline of their troops, their valour and heroism and what not. I had a word to say myself, and, aroused by his partiality, I was carried away in the other direction. Any way I gave him a few points as to what I thought of Germany and the Germans. I had had some experience with them in most spheres of life; I had lived amongst them for four years. I claimed that they have no culture at all – there is no period in their history which produced a creative culture which had a lasting influence on them or the world like the Renaissance in Italy, the times of Louis XIV and Louis XV in France, the Elizabethan period in England, or Ancient Rome or Greece, or the Arabic-Moorish culture. They are a wonderful scientific people, probably the most wonderful, but they have no creative faculties, they are not artists as a race. The flourishing period of German painting, the time of Dürer, Holbein and Cranach, is of the Netherlandish school, their Gothic architecture is of French origin, and in literature they have produced Goethe, Schiller, Lessing and Heine, hardly enough to bear comparison with the rich classical periods of France, England, Italy, Greece and Rome. All their other great writers are scientists, philosophers, historians, but not creative poets and dramatists, who go beyond the local spirit and have produced *Welt-Dichtung*.

They have a remarkable talent for assimilation, cribbing other peoples' ideas some call it, and they have a commendable spirit for education. In no country in the world are the best dramatists of the Western nations so often and so well produced as in the German theatre. Their versatility in translating, without losing the spirit or the finest points, is astonishing – this is probably due to the adaptability of their language. Ibsen, Shakespeare, Racine, Molière, Hamsun, D'Annunzio, Gorki, Bernard Shaw, Oscar Wilde, are as well known to the German theatre-goer as his Goethe, Schiller, Hofmannsthal or Hauptmann. Modern German architecture – surely architecture is a creative art – is beneath contempt.

I have never been in any place where the arts of other nations are so well represented in exhibitions as in Germany. In music they are remarkable – credit must be given to them for that; it is the only art in which they have excelled in creative ability and been of world influence. Of course I like to trace this genius to the great infusion of Slav and Jewish blood, for I believe the Teuton is sterile of imagination.

As to their cleanliness, it is very outward, and the idea of personal cleanliness is still in a very primitive state. And as to their administration, or rather their arbitrary bureaucracy, I found everything true in Prussia that is said in the traditional books on Russia, but which was not true of Russia.

I cannot rally any enthusiasm for their system of militarism, and their machine-like army, which involves the deprivation of individual liberty and development.

The *sous-lieutenant* thought I was *trop fort* – probably I was.

There was a Maréchal of African Chasseurs of the party, quite a young man, who realized the enormity of the Legion. "What? *you* are in the Legion – but every one must take you to be an assassin, thief, highway-robber, deserter, or bank forger!" I said that that was what I was generally taken for.

He told me about his life, how as a boy he would not study and wanted to become an officer. His father put him into a military academy, but still he would not study, until finally his father got impatient, took him out and said: "My son, if you want to become a soldier go and be one, but you will get no more help from me." Then he bucked up and worked his way from a common soldier to a Maréchal, although he had been degraded many times, "because," as he said, "I am not a good soldier, and am too fond of wine, women and song." He was on his way to Northern France to enter a school of *élève-officiers* and make his examination as an officer.

"You must land with me at Marseilles, otherwise the military guard at the dock will send you to the Fort, which is a horrible place, until you leave for Lyons, and then you will not be able to see anything of Marseilles."

I had never stopped at Marseilles and was anxious to see it, also I wanted to take a day's rest before recommencing my Legion life, which at Lyons wasn't likely to be much of an improvement on Bel-Abbès.

At night the *Sidi Brahim* showed no lights whatever. Dinner was served at twilight, and after that the porthole shutters were tightly closed and a small blue electric lamp was switched on, in order to see one's way to the cabin. The cabins were entirely without light, and it was necessary to undress in the dark. On deck there was not a single light anywhere;

guns on all sides and a gunner at each, ready for emergency; these were changed every few hours.

The following day, Sunday, the coast of Spain came into sight, and during the forenoon the Balearic Islands Iviza we passed quite closely. It was the finest crossing I have ever experienced in the Mediterranean; the sea was perfectly calm and the weather glorious, a cloudless sky, mild air and not a ripple on the indigo blue waters.

I had a look at the third class. The native troops were packed like sardines in barren bunks side by side. Each man made his bunk a perfect pigsty, what with eating, sleeping, and dressing in it, and many were seasick. The stench was insufferable. The first-class promenade deck was amidship, and our deck was on the poop, so that we saw nothing of the first-class passengers.

We were supposed to arrive in Marseilles the next forenoon, Monday, at eleven o'clock, but instead of that we arrived at about five, and were landed before 6 a.m.

The Maréchal took me under his protection and I landed without being asked any questions, but I kept in the Maréchal's wake until we were safely in a cab and driving to the Hôtel Splendide. He had many amusing things to tell me about the people of Marseilles and how proud they are of their town. They think there is no place on earth like it, and it is a common saying that if Paris had a Rue Cannebière it might be a little Marseilles. The Rue Cannebière is a wide business street in the centre of the town, the attraction of which I failed to see. The Maréchal and I spent a few hours together, after we had breakfasted and changed, seeing the most notable sights of the town: the Notre Dame de la Garde, the Palais de Longchamp, the Hôtel de Ville and the Vieux Port, and wound up by having a good lunch at Isnard's. He left by an afternoon train for Paris and I remained.

How the thoughts raced through my brain when I found myself alone and free to a certain extent! Could I escape? that was the question. I was on French soil, within eight hours of the Italian frontier. The greatest difficulty of getting out of Africa was overcome. If I had made my escape in Africa, I should have been compelled to travel into the interior, and get out via Tripoli; for it would have been next to impossible to leave any port under French domination without the necessary papers, unless I had succeeded in finding n Spanish tramp steamer or sailing vessel bound for Spain, and even that would have created suspicion, and the possibility of making a failure was too great a risk.

I was in soldier's uniform — I had no civilian clothes with me. I could have bought some, but Marseilles is not a big town and is a favourite place for deserters wishing to escape, so that every one is on the watch. I knew no one in Marseilles. Suspicion is easily aroused. I had my personal papers, but what explanation could I make that they were not stamped before leaving Algiers, considering that they had been stamped when I entered Tunis? My military pass had been sufficient. And if I had had them stamped they would have borne the military visé, which would have ruined them for all further eventualities. I could not go to the Commissionaire de Police and give satisfactory explanations in order to get my safe-conduct, which is necessary in France before it is possible to buy a railway ticket. Further, there was the possibility of creating suspicion at Lyons by my non-immediate arrival. Also the time was too short to make all the necessary preparations. Besides there was my valuable luggage at Bel-Abbès in pawn, so to speak. That might be confiscated and my private affairs gone into, and in that case I should have no loophole for a safe place to which to escape.

The end of my reflections brought me to the conclusion that it was not the moment — the risk of failure was too great, and I should not only have cut off any possibility of a future attempt of flight but have ruined my life. For I knew there was a limit to how long I could keep sane, and that if I remained in those vile surroundings much longer my energy and courage would be exhausted and I should either become a drunkard or thoroughly depraved like the rest. Whatever I was going to do, I should have to do carefully, and in such a manner that there would be next to no chance of failure — I must feel *certain* of success.

In the evening I took a look at the side streets of Marseilles, and wandered about as the spirit moved me. The streets were damp and muddy, the houses were grimy and cheerless, and the end of a typical Northern day in May, with grey skies, was not conducive to make Marseilles look any cheerier. I came to the docks, and by accident ran into the street where the "daughters of joy" can be bought at the price soldiers and sailors can afford to pay. It was a vile street, and I have never seen such outright vulgarity and indecency in manner, dress, voice, and speech except here, and at Hamburg.

I had always held the prejudicial opinion that what I had seen in Hamburg could only take place in Germany, and I had had a sneaking idea that French lowness of that kind would at least have a touch of good taste about it. I was mistaken – what I saw in Marseilles was almost worse than Hamburg.

I met two English soldiers who had arrived at that street in about the same manner as I had. We chatted – one was a born Frenchman who was attached to the British section as interpreter. He was horrified when he heard I was in the Legion, and told me that I ought to apply immediately for a position as interpreter, as they were greatly in demand, and that he would help me if he could. I thanked him and accepted his offer; we exchanged cards, and later I wrote him as he had told me to do, but he never replied, and I never heard of him again. Mazières was his name, a nice fellow. Probably the Military Censor confiscated my letter or his reply. The next day I left for Lyons.

Chapter 22

ARLES, Orange, Avignon – what memories! when I visited these places first, many many years before, I never thought that one day I should pass them as a soldier of the French Army. They were at that time my first taste of the southern part of Europe; I was on my way to the Riviera, and how I relished the mild cloudless days in early October after the London fogs! The bull-fight in the arena at Aries on a Sunday afternoon, the Roman theatre at Orange, the Papal Palace at Avignon and the Broken Bridge – these had meant to me the realization of my childhood dreams, and had intensified my love for history.

Now I was talking to an American merchant and his son, who had sold something or other to France, and had come over with it on the same boat to Cette, as there was no room to dock at Marseilles. Kindly but dull they were; they looked opulent, the war was throwing fortune into their arms. "Well – I hope you will come out of the war without any holes in your skin," the elder drawled in his twang, as he said good-bye to me at Aries. My next travelling companions were a dentist and his wife from Vienne, who deplored my foolishness in having entered the Legion, and wanted to know why I hadn't gone into the Ambulance or Flying Corps. What a difference from years ago!

I paid the supplement for second class, as I had noticed that the soldiers travelling third class were treated like cattle. Poor soldiers, fighting for their Government, leaving home and family to give their lives, or at best their health, for five sous a day – even then there was no equality. Because they had no money they received no respect.

Lyons with its bridges over the Rhone, its churches and St. Fourvière, came into sight. What future awaited me here? I lunched at the railway station restaurant and trotted into town looking for the Depot of the *Légion Etrangère*.

It had moved, and I was sent from pillar to post, until after seemingly endless peregrinations I arrived at the barracks, in a back street, which had been an old school building. I reported myself at the office.

"When did you leave Bel-Abbès?"

"On Thursday last."

"To-day is Tuesday. Where have you been in the meantime?"

"The steamer left Oran on Saturday."

"When did you arrive in Marseilles?"

"Yesterday."

"Yesterday? Where did you stop until to-day?"

"At an hotel in Marseilles."

"Hotel? Marseilles? at whose expense?"

"My own."

"Oh, all right."

And no further questions were asked. A sergeant-major entered: "From Bel-Abbès. What do the papers say from Algiers?"

"That he is to perfect his instructions and be sent to the front."

"Very well, he will go with the first detachment to Valbonne on Saturday. Show him the sergeant in charge of the dressing-room to change his clothes, and then the room of his squad."

The Depot was a large corner building in the slums of Lyons, four stories high, with a triangular courtyard. It was used for the offices of the headquarters of the Legion in France, and for the housing of *réformé* soldiers who expected to be discharged, or were waiting for a medical visit, or in transport to the front, or to Valbonne, the training camp within an hour of Lyons. Applications to enter the Legion were made here, and new outfits given to those going to the front.

On the third floor I was deprived of the *accoutrements* which had been given me at Bel-Abbès, including gun, knapsack, etc., and I received old worn-out things in exchange. Then in the basement my nice blue clothes were taken from me and I was given the foulest old rags which I had ever beheld in my life. They had not a semblance of decency, and had been worn by legions of soldiers, judging by the matriculation numbers. The cap was terrible, even the sergeants at the rapport complained about it; it was saturated with grease and entirely out of shape in consequence of the many disinfections. Its looks produced nausea, and it was loathsome to put on. The trousers were brown corduroy, and had been patched where the person who had worn them had stained them with his disease. The only things which were left me were the underclothes. Even the boots they wanted to change, but I called attention to the fact that they were my property. There was no pretence of a uniform here – no sash, no uniformly coloured trousers, the coat and the cap were the only signs of the soldier. The coats had dirty brass buttons, covered with verdigris, and buttons of other materials. The most detailed description will never suffice to give an adequate picture of the absolutely destitute appearance of these soldiers. No attempt was made to keep the clothes clean or to polish the boots.

Having been thus attired in the costume of a ragamuffin I was shown to my squad: a long room with eight windows facing the street and six windows facing the courtyard. The place looked barren. On each side there were some beds, and the rest was empty space. The corporal, a Frenchman, took me in hand. We went to an attic where there was a pile of raw boards and low stools. I dragged away three boards and a couple of stools to the room of the squad, and put up the boards with a stool under them at each end. Then we went to another attic and a dirty sack of straw was pulled down from a pile. That was deposited on the boards; then I received a dirty unwashed disinfected sleeping-bag made of linen, and a dirty blanket, and my bed was complete. The barracks of Bel-Abbès were a palace compared to this.

There were no exercises at the Depot, only a *rapport* twice a day and *corvées*. The chores were of all sorts: cleaning of dozens of guns and greasing them, greasing hundreds of boots of the filthiest kind in a mouldy damp cellar where no speck of daylight or breath of fresh air ever entered.

At these *corvées* I was continually reprimanded by my fellow-workers for working too quickly, and warned that the more I worked the more I had to do. The principle was to keep a man busy. A man never finished his work until it was 5 p.m., therefore it was no use spending unnecessary energy. New work was found always for the man who had finished, and the next job might be worse still.

The rooms were all more or less alike – a few nails on the walls to hang up one's things, but no shelf, and no table nor benches as at Bel-Abbès. The food was brought by the men on *corvée* to the room, dealt out by the corporal, and each man sat on his bed and swallowed his portion of slops from his tin plate. If anything the food was worse than at Bel-Abbès, though not quite so greasy and German.

My room companions were nearly all invalids – *réformé* or about to be *réformé*. There were some whose eyes were so sore and painful, from the effects of the poisonous gas at the front, they could hardly open them. Some had received cuts and wounds in the head, which, by the aid of the marvellous surgery of modern times, had been operated upon and healed. The strange looking crevices in their head made one marvel at the dexterity of the physicians. That a man with only a part of a head could walk about and appear perfectly healed seemed incredible; but to see them at close range and live in the same room with them proved that may be it would have been better if surgery had not been quite so advanced. They were all strange, to say the least, most of them were entirely unbalanced, had *idées fixes*, did unheard-of things at most unexpected moments, groaned in the night, yelled without any reason during the day, and then looked round in amazement as if it had been some one else. There was a tense feeling in the atmosphere, an alertness on the part of those not so afflicted, who were waiting for some mad outburst from one of the unfortunates.

After they were *réformé*, what use would they be to themselves or their families? A terrible burden, an uncertain unknown quantity, who could never be relied upon for a moment day or night for the rest of their lives! And the fact that they appeared sane to all superficial appearances made it worse and more dangerous.

Then there were those who had lost the use of their legs and arms, who had open sores in consequence of bullet wounds, which would not heal, and yet they had not got their discharge. Some had been lingering there for six and eight months and no help had come. The medical authorities had not yet arrived to give them their papers, or some other excuse was made. It was my opinion that the Government did not intend to let a single man go while the war lasted, and that the promises which were made had no value whatever. The days in this place were living nightmares, and the nights horrible deliriums. The disgust and loathing I had felt in Bel-Abbès at the awful depravity, beastliness, and filth turned here into horror. I did not know which was worse. The feeling of the necessity of escape became intensified.

The types and nationalities of the men were different from those in the Legion in Africa. Frenchmen, with something in their past to bring them here, Belgians, Bulgarians, Roumanians, French negroes, some Czechs, Swiss, Dutchmen, and any number of Jews from every one of these countries and Russia and Denmark. Most of them had been to the front, and some were to be sent to Valbonne for a "rest." Nearly all had been wounded. Not any one had any spirit left. They were apathetic, sullen, worn-out by pain and suffering, and only longed for their discharge.

There was usually an uncanny silence in the room when some one wasn't groaning or writhing in pain or doing some mad trick. But if any talked it was about his hope of getting away, or the latest successful deserter. Desertion was spoken of as an everyday event, and only praise and admiration were expressed for those who succeeded.

The hours were about the same as at Bel-Abbès, only that the *réveil* sounded at 6 o'clock, and the report was at 7. The second and last report was at 4 o'clock, and at 5 o'clock the soldiers were free until 9.30 p.m. Meals were at noon and at 5 p.m., and the morning *jus* at 6.30 a.m. Those who had no *corvées* sat on their beds all day doing nothing, some few read, and fewer still talked.

There was no discipline, and every one who knew the ropes did as he liked, but it took some time to learn the ropes.

The water arrangements were no better here than at Bel-Abbès – a few taps under a shed in the courtyard, and a scarcity of water, but the men kept themselves cleaner.

I managed to get out at noon for a half an hour on the quiet and go to a little restaurant to have my food. Two Italian sergeants, who were in the office, often closed an eye when I wanted to go out when it was really prohibited. They were the nicest chaps there, kind, tolerant and understanding, and several times they got me permissions to stay out late at night, which I should never have succeeded in getting alone from the other gruff, rude, hard, antipathetic officials, who treated every soldier as so much dirt under their feet.

Drink, though strictly forbidden, was brought into the barracks in goodly quantities, and drunkenness seemed to be just as prevalent here as at Bel-Abbès. In the evening if one chanced to meet a drunken soldier in the neighbouring slums, or a man in a brawl, it was sure to be a soldier from the Legion.

Chapter 23

ON the Saturday, following my arrival, about fifteen of us were marched off to the Gare des Brotteaux of Lyons at 7 a.m. to leave for Valbonne.

The only possible person to talk to in my room at Lyons was a young Bulgarian, Alexander Stojanoff. We had become friends the first few days. He had studied law in Geneva and Paris, had lived most of his life in Paris, and when the war broke out, his family having removed from Bulgaria to Roumania, owing to their pro-Ally sentiments, he had entered the Legion to show his own enthusiasm and loyalty for the French cause. He had been to the front, had been wounded several times, and finally received a wound on his right arm which would not heal. Although well built, he was not strong, and in spite of his healthy and fresh complexion I believe he was consumptive. He seemed to have plenty of money, which he received from his people in Roumania. He was only twenty-five years old and had shown great valour, which was rewarded by a *croix de guerre* with a palm. He was on his way to Valbonne for a "rest," since his arm did not permit him to return to the front. He did not want to go to Valbonne, told me it was a dreadful place, and the last time that he had been there, although not yet sufficiently trained, he went to the Colonel, fell at his feet, and implored him to send him to the front immediately, as he could not possibly endure the life at Valbonne any longer. The description he gave of Valbonne seemed incredible and I thought he was exaggerating, and that his imagination supplied the extravagances. He was a sensitive well-bred person, and naturally any decently brought up individual would revolt at what I had seen, but what he described was infinitely worse.

In the train he commenced to tell me his plans — what he would do in order to get away again from Valbonne. First he would try by fair means, and if they did not work he would try foul means, but under no circumstances would he stay.

We arrived at Valbonne at 9 a.m. in a drizzling spring rain. Valbonne is a village with two or three dozen houses, a few shops and restaurants, and some *estaminets*. The village lies on one side of the railway, the camp on the other. The camp is a huge place. From the station a fine avenue of old trees runs towards a large treeless field – but before reaching the field another avenue of trees crosses it, and on both sides of the avenues are interspersed the wooden shacks where the soldiers sleep, the offices of the-regiment, the kitchens and the canteens. Much green sward, but still more mud, especially in the open spaces where the soldiers assemble for the *rapport* and the *rassemblement*.

The wooden shacks are all of one model – low one-story affairs without any flooring inside; a shelf or slanting platform like a long stage, 2 1/2 feet above the ground, built along each side of the wall, served as flooring for the sacks of straw on which, with the same bedding as at Lyons, the soldiers could find their nightly repose! About a dozen men could be bedded on each platform. The centre of the two platforms was a mud path. Each shack was divided into about ten of these rooms, and the rooms were divided from each other by wooden partitions reaching half-way to the ceiling. Above the platform on the wall was a narrow shelf as at Bel-Abbès to deposit one's things. At the back was a window, at the front the door served as a window. At night a tiny petroleum lamp, suspended from a beam, pretended to give light.

The offices of the clerks and officers were only better in so far that they had flooring and sufficient daylight by way of decent windows, and at night a good petroleum lamp.

On our arrival we were marched to the front of such a wooden shack, which was the Commander's office, and waited *garde à vous* in the drizzling rain for about an hour and a half. Finally the Commander, a fine-looking old man, with a thick long beard, appeared in the doorway, looked us over, asked our names and nationalities, and then gave orders to the sergeant-major, assigning each man to his company and squad. By this time it was nearly eleven and we were thoroughly drenched.

After we had been shown our respective places it was time for food; and Stojanoff took me in hand and showed me about. He could not eat the regimental food either, and always dined out. We went to a canteen; they were wooden shacks with flooring; the front part was used as a shop where soldiers' requisites were sold, and the back part furnished with wooden tables and benches for a restaurant. The food was not prepared there but at the kitchen of the officers' mess, so that by the time it arrived it was cold. We had a *plat de jour* and some bread and wine and cheese. There was never any choice, the dish of the day was the only fare served. The bill was by no means cheap, though the portions were very small, dealt out by one of those economical, tight-mouthed, steely-eyed French women, who presided like a tin-god on wheels over the shop, and who, if one dared to complain, was ready with impertinences impossible to answer.

At the furthest end of the camp, facing it, and just across the road which formed the boundary line, stood a *café* which seemed like a temptation put there on purpose. There was no fence to enclose the camp, but a soldier was stationed there to see that no Legionary crossed the boundary and entered the *café* before 5 p.m., and to report any one who came out of it after 10 p.m. However, a cigar to a friendly sergeant or corporal worked wonders, and almost every hour of the day some soldiers were to be found here; only care had to be taken that no superior officer was in sight, for the position of the *café* was so exposed that it could be seen at a great distance. Here a greater variety of food could be obtained at a price no greater than the canteens, and without the impertinences of the presiding hyena, but with good-looking polite waitresses to attend to one's wishes.

At lunch we met Tolosa, a South American, who was very amiable and told me I must meet the other Americans in the camp, and he forthwith introduced me to them after we had finished our meal.

Casey was the first man I met; he was an artist from California, who had lived in Paris when the war broke out, and, carried away by enthusiasm, volunteered to go to the front at once and was accepted; Bouligny, a sergeant, was from New Orleans, of French descent and the first American who came over to enter the French Army; Attey was a would-be poet from Baltimore; Harvey a typical hayseed Yankee from Alabama; Sullivan was an Irish-American, and Becker, a Dutchman, who had lived all his life in America. Then there was a man whose name I have forgotten, who was born in Switzerland, but brought up in America. There were five or six other Americans, some of whom were in prison, and others before the Council of War and in the hospital at Lyons; I never met them while I was there. The regiment also boasted of an American nigger, but he wasn't introduced to me. They were all a jolly lot and immediately insisted upon treating to drinks. It was Saturday and there were no exercises in the afternoon, so the time was spent drinking. The canteens were open only from 11 to 1 o'clock and again after 5 p.m., so we stole into the *café*.

It did not take me long to realize that life was even worse here than at Bel-Abbès, and the Americans were very outspoken as to their opinion of the Legion and its rottenness. How to get away was the topic of conversation. They hoped and prayed America would enter the war so they could demand to be transferred to their own army; some had hopes of entering the Flying Corps or the Ambulance Department, and some hoped to escape. They all admitted being hopelessly demoralized in this den of filth and crime. And then they spoke of the "admirable" way some had deserted. One sergeant was mentioned, who has since written a book, who had many grievances and saw no justice forthcoming. He was at the front and broke his eye-glasses; he could not see without and had no prescription, so he asked to go to Paris to have his eyes re-examined and get new glasses. He received an eight days' permission and after a few days he wired for a further permission of eight days, which was granted. At the end of that time he did not return, and a few weeks later he was heard of as safely at home in America.

The night was horrible – the slanting platforms were like torture, no repose or relaxation was possible. I was either continually sliding down, or under the strain of trying to keep from sliding down, and keeping my feet on the straw sack. The place was infested with lice, fleas, bed-bugs and cockroaches; there were rats and mice besides which nibbled at everything, including one's underwear and handkerchiefs. The stench was overwhelming from these dozens of unwashed soldiers in this low narrow shack, with door and window tightly closed.

I had been assigned to a shack where I knew no one. The Americans were dispersed all over the camp, and Stojanoff was somewhere else too.

In the morning my shack companions trooped out and washed at the pump. One man had to pump while the other washed. There were no other conveniences for ablutions, except a bath shack where every eight or ten days a thin spray of water was turned on for five minutes for each man, which at the end of that time was turned off, ready or not.

Sunday morning was occupied with cleaning reviews – the straw sacks were aired in the sun, and the platforms and the muddy path in the centre of the shack were swept with a stump of a broom. There were no reviews here of clothes and *accoutrements*; it would not have been of any use, because everybody's stuff was so thoroughly worn-out and disreputable that no amount of cleaning would have altered appearances. As to the boots, no one made any attempt to keep them clean in these mud puddles.

I got a drunken old Legionnaire to do my *truc*, which here consisted only of polishing my gun and washing my towels. He struck after the first day – he wanted to see my money first.

Stojanoff had disappeared. He had forged a permission and gone to Lyons for Sunday.

The nigger who had come with us from Lyons, and who had just entered the Legion, disappeared in the night and was never heard of again.

Chapter 24

THE village of Valbonne has two streets, one running up from the railway station to a cross road, which is at the same time the highway to Lyons and Switzerland. The restaurants, shops and drinking places live on the soldiers. Another French regiment was stationed in our camp, so that there were several thousand soldiers who could be considered as customers of the villagers. The prices in the restaurants were absurdly high considering the bad food, the poor service, the soiled table linen, and the meagre portions, but there was no competition, so the soldiers had no choice and had to pay. It was nothing short of extortion, and these were the loyal patriotic French people with their cries and shouts of *Vive la France* and *Vive la Patrie*, who, when it came to money and profit, robbed their own compatriots and the very men who were fighting for them and their so-called *Liberté, Eglité, Fraternité*.

The camp was large and was really a town in itself. A big barn-like building of wood, containing some tables and chairs, was used during the day by the soldiers as a writing and reading-room, and on Sunday nights it was used for theatrical performances, given by some of the soldiers who had talent, for the amusement of their comrades. The programme consisted mostly of songs, juggling tricks and funny sketches. The French version of "It's a long way to Tipperary" struck me as the funniest, with the refrain of "Oh yes, oh yes" in English.

There were numerous canteens especially where only drinks were served. Beer was the principal beverage. The camp was not fenced in or roped off, but every one knew the boundary lines beyond which it was forbidden to go before 5 p.m. A guard was stationed at the entrance to the village, and at all important points of the frontier line, from which the main road could be reached or a *café*. Two guards were continually on duty at the railway station, one on each platform. No ticket was sold without showing a travel-permission from the Commander. Most of those without a permission used to walk to the next village and take a tram which started there for Lyons – others forged permissions. If they were caught it meant prison for eight days or more. Everything depended upon whether the corporal and sergeant of the squad were friendly or not. And again that depended upon whether you had money to lend them, cigars to give them, and if you were able to supply them otherwise with necessities. Valbonne was costlier than Bel-Abbès, for here lending meant never less than 40 sous, and usually 60 and 100 sous. And there were a goodly number to support, if one did not want to be imprisoned perpetually in that pigsty. Even the forged permissions were obtainable through the sergeants.

Casey was a very decent fellow, with an extraordinarily charming voice. He had been living many years in Paris and had won a reputation there and in America as an excellent painter. He deeply regretted his burst of enthusiasm in enlisting when the war broke out, and told me he was thoroughly broken up and had neither courage nor energy nor initiative left. The *régime* had crushed him, and he knew that if he ever got out of the Legion alive he would never be able to do another stroke of work. He had been to the front several times and was in camp now for a "rest." Of course it was no rest to be in camp, owing to the exercises, which were much more trying than being at the front, at least so every one told me. All the soldiers loathed Valbonne, and wished to be back at the front, where life was more endurable, and where there was no everlasting nagging by petty officers. Like all the rest he drank heavily – the only consolation, to forget for the moment the vile surroundings and the life. He had tried several times to enter the Flying Corps, for, as he said, it was better to be in the air than to crawl like a worm in the mud. But he had not succeeded, and did not think he would, for as time had gone on he had been punished with prison too often for intoxication and staying out beyond the hour of permission. On one occasion he had gone for an outing to a neighbouring village, had walked eight miles to get there, and, what with the walk and the week's exercises, he was so dog-tired he did not care what happened, went to an hotel and to a real bed, and slept the sleep of the just. Consequence, fourteen days' imprisonment.

Becker, the Dutchman, a very nice fellow, had often done the same – got a permission for two days, run up to Paris, and remained five days, which is the limit without being punished as a deserter.

Bouligny, the New Orleans man, was the first American to enter the Legion. He had set sail for France the day after war was declared. He was a good soldier and a very just fellow; he had become sergeant and was esteemed by every one. He always showed sympathy and understanding when one of his compatriots was in trouble, and tried to help as far as he could. I liked the way he defended the sergeant who had deserted, and who was attacked by his enemies in America as a "quitter" and a "coward" after he had published his book. Bouligny stood up for him, and wrote to the American papers that they could say what they liked about Morlae, but that he was a MAN, and every one who had known him at the front knew him to be one of their best fighters, and one of the most courageous men in the regiment. The papers published Bouligny's letters.

All the Americans had a very good reputation for courage and for being good fighters, but they were the devil for discipline and camp life. Most of them were nearly always in prison.

I had just arrived after a terrible row. Some of the Americans had gone to an inn in the next village the Sunday before, and one of them, who was very well to do, ordered drinks for everybody. The innkeeper, a typical Frenchman of the lowest class, seeing a soldier of the Legion, who has as bad a reputation in France as in Africa, and an American at that, refused to serve the drinks until he had paid for them. The American's blood was up.

"What, you don't think I can pay – you mean, dirty French skunk?" and he flashed out a thousand franc bill.

The innkeeper wasn't at all impressed, but told him he could pass off his forged banknotes on others, but not on him. And then there was a rough-house, and every one pitched in.

The innkeeper got hold of a crowbar and brained the American, and then the innkeeper was beaten nearly to death. After several bodies were lying about unconscious the gendarmes interfered – the American was taken to the hospital as dead, but recovered, and lived to be a hopeless invalid for life. The others were imprisoned, except the innkeeper, who went scotfree, and had to face *Concile de Guerre*. We never heard of any of them again or what happened – we knew only that the man in the hospital was condemned to *travaux publiques*, which is another term for hard labour for life.

Another American, with whom I came in contact a good deal, was Attey from Baltimore. He was a great reader of American newspapers and magazines and had written some poetry or was about to do so – I could not make out which. He used to talk literature, or rather American literature, by the hour, and was *au courant* with all the latest magazine and newspaper writers in America. He talked incessantly to any one who was willing to listen to him. He said his name was Attey, and that was his name in the company, but whenever a stranger came he had always another name for himself at the tip of his tongue. No one knew his real name. He had gone to the dogs, looked dirty, unwashed, unkempt, did not shave any more, and was only happy when he could raise a few sous for drink; and when he received any money from home or elsewhere he went on a spree until every penny was gone. He was only about twenty-five years old, and told us that he had had the spirit of adventure, was tired of home, and embarked on a cattle steamer for France and enlisted in the Legion. In his endless chatter he spoke often of England, and it seemed as if he must have lived in England for some time to be as conversant with it as he was.

Harvey from Alabama was a *minderwerthiger Mensch* who spoke in a long drawl — also a young chap — and no one could make head or tail of him. He seemed to have drifted into the Legion under mysterious circumstances. He told me a long story, which took him hours to tell, as to how he was stranded in Bordeaux, and went to see the American Consul, asking him to help him, who, after fumbling in his pockets for a long time, brought out six sous and gave them to him saying, “Here is the price of a plate of soup for you.”

Another story was that he left his wife and children in Alabama, because his wife thought he needed an ocean voyage, and then he met a chap on board the boat and they made a bet, and the end of it was that he enlisted in the Legion the day he arrived in Bordeaux. Bordeaux was the only town in France he knew, so he had been there and it was evidently also true that he had come from Bordeaux to Valbonne, but the rest of his stories did not hang together. He was obviously of a decent family, but he wasn't all there — something was wanting mentally. How they ever came to take him in the Legion, I could not understand.

Sullivan was the real typical Irish-American bully type, sarcastic, sneering, mean, cynical, domineering, and altogether *antipatico*. He used to publish letters in the Paris edition of the *New York Herald* about the Legion, and the hardships and his bravery. It was well known to his compatriots that he had a “graft” on some one in consequence of these letters. I could not connect these obviously untruthful letters (I used to read them, as I kept the paper) with his getting money, but the other men evidently knew what they were talking about, for they had known him for some time. Casey told me he was a rotter, and that he entered the Legion under a cloud, had had no money at all, and now he was getting money orders from all sorts of places, and it was evident he had a lot of money from the way he lived, and also he had a voluminous correspondence. All his talk in the papers, posing as a hero, wasn't true. Bouligny told me that whenever he went to the front he would hide in a trench and feign madness, and would not come out of the place for eighteen hours at a time, but that he feigned his madness so well that he had to be sent back to Valbonne repeatedly.

Bouligny was at Valbonne for training soldiers and for a rest. He was quite an engineer, and showed his men how to build trenches. I saw his work, which was splendid, but he could not finish it, as some superior officer, who was jealous of a mere sergeant's work, forbade him to go on, saying that the Government could not afford any extra expense.

Becker, the Dutchman, had also been to the front, and was now learning the mitrailleuse,* as he could not stand the ordinary soldier's existence any longer.

Neither Attey nor Harvey had been to the front.

I never came in contact with the American negro, as Bouligny, like a true Southerner, would not let him come near us. I saw very little of the American Swiss; he was a bit strange and kept very much to himself. Part of his chin had been shot away, and he told me that when he entered the Legion he wanted to die, but since he had been wounded he wanted to live.

Tolosa, the South American, was of our party. He was a rich young fellow, who had been living in Paris with a mistress, and, when the war broke out, he felt he ought to do his share, enlisted in the Legion, and regretted it ever since. His mistress used to come to Lyons, and he would run up without permission and spend a few days with her at the Terminus Hotel, and then return for two or three weeks in prison as punishment for his escapade, only to do the same thing over again as soon as he felt like it.

Altogether there were only a few *dozen* Americans in the Legion, and not 20,000 as some sensational journalists would have us believe before America dreamt of entering the war.

---

* machine-gun

Chapter 25

THE exercises at Valbonne were just as tedious and monotonous as at Bel-Abbès. In the morning *réveil* at 5, *rassemblement* at 5.30, and march to the field just beyond the last row of shacks.

The field was a wide plain, hilly here and there, with some shrubs in places; it stretched to the horizon from the further side of the camp; towards Lyons it was bordered by some houses and rows of trees, and towards Switzerland the snow-capped Alps were visible. How they beckoned me! The field was a rich green pasture with occasional mud-puddles, and owing to the dampness it was difficult to exercise on the sward, as the clods of earth and grass stuck to one's boots. The exercises consisted of the usual *demi-tour-à-droit, à gauche, à droit, un pas en avant, un pas à derrière, armes sur l'epaule, garde à vous*, no shooting, not once, and absolutely no instruction in anything that could be useful to defend one's life at the front.

I asked a friendly sergeant, a Belgian, whether we were never going to learn anything else, and what use it could possibly be at the front to present arms faultlessly, and not know how to shoot.

"No, you will never learn any more here."

"But what is going to happen at the front? The result of this training cannot help a man to defend the country."

"You will have to learn the rest there, and if you are not quick you will be just so much cannon fodder, which is what France needs most. Just look at all these men here – even if they were taught, they are no earthly good as soldiers. We take any one here – numbers are necessary. That Greek over there has been here eight months, and he has not yet learned the simplest elementary exercises, in spite of all the kicks and punishments he gets. He can't march nor keep in step. If we were not so hard up for men, do you think we would waste our time in trying to teach him, and feed and clothe him into the bargain?"

"But I want to know something before I am sent to the front."

"You won't learn it here, and if you make any complaint to a superior you will get yourself into trouble, and be no better off. What on earth did you come here for anyway?" And when I told him he said: "What an idea! You had better have stayed out of it."

The exercises lasted until 9.30 or 9.45 and then we marched back. The prisoners were treated better here than at Bel-Abbès; at the exercises they were allowed to play games like the rest. On cold mornings there was usually a running game, for about half an hour, before the exercises, in order to warm us up. The *rapport* was supposed to be at 10 a.m., but this was most unpunctual and sometimes we had to wait until 12 o'clock; it depended on the sergeant in charge. In fact there was no order whatever, nothing was punctual, neither the *rassemblement* nor the *rapport* nor the meals. But the soldiers were required to be ever ready at the sound of the whistle, so that no one could go out of hearing of his own camp centre. Each company had its own camp centre for its *rapport* and *rassemblement*, which was just outside their own shacks. After the report dinner was brought by the *garde de chambre* to the shack, dealt out on the bed-platform and eaten there. Nothing more dismal can be imagined than the sight of those soldiers standing and sitting on the straw sacks in that miserable dark damp shack swallowing their wretched food. At 1.30 another *rassemblement*, the same exercises until 4 o'clock, and then *rapport* until 5 p.m. At 5 o'clock supper, and free until 10 p.m. The only service which was punctual was the *appelle* at night, to see that every one was in his shack at that time. Even the *réveil* was not punctual, and, unless a man was self-disciplined and rose without the *réveil*, he had only about ten minutes in which to wash, dress, drink his *jus*, and get to the *rassemblement*. The slovenly way in which everything was done was most extraordinary. There was apparently no authority, no one person who was responsible; everything was shoved from one superior to another.

At the exercises I was again in the squad of *the jeunes soldats*. It seemed to me that a man could be a *jeune soldat* indefinitely according to the regiment's pleasure, for some had been there a year, and then suddenly were sent to the front. Evidently it depended upon the caprice of some superior who happened to think about it. The instructing sergeants were changed every few days, sometimes every day, so that there was no possibility of ascertaining if a man were making progress and was ready to enter his regular squad. Many of the sergeants varied in their methods of instruction, and often it happened that a sergeant told us just the reverse of what we had been taught the day before. To call attention to the fact that we had been taught differently produced a torrent of abuse for pretending to make any observation, and often punishment for disobedience. The next day we had to unlearn the method again with some one else.

The squad of the *jeunes soldats* consisted of Spaniards, Swiss, Belgians, Greeks, Czechs, Flems, Luxemburgers, Dutchmen, and some few Frenchmen. As at Bel-Abbès, most of them could not speak French, and in consequence innumerable punishments were dealt out for disobedience, because the poor devils could not understand the commands. The fury and rage into which some of those sergeants could fly defies description — there was something diabolical about it. Every fifty minutes there was a pause of ten minutes, but, if the sergeant felt specially devilish, he would make us exercise during the pause too. I don't remember all the names we were called, but some of them were camel, pig, ass, skunk, and a few others in the zoological dictionary which did not imply anything clean or clever.

The continual dampness and drizzling rain were very trying, and the inadequacy of the food in the morning, a cup of *jus* and a piece of bread as the only sustenance for hours of strenuous exercise, caused faintness and often dizziness among some of the men. The place where milk could be bought was just outside the boundary line, so it was impossible to buy it before 5 p.m., and no milk could be delivered for love or money by the milk people in the camp as they did not rise before 7 a.m. Sometimes, during the morning, a waggon would come across the exercise field selling beer in bottles at high prices. But this, taken on an empty stomach, was not conducive to taking any further interest in the exercises.

The men in my shack were a very disorderly lot — and churlish and sullen in disposition. My next neighbour was a Czech, who was a ladies' tailor in Paris, and being politically an Austrian subject, to evade the concentration camp had entered the Legion. He never murmured or had anything to say, he was quite apathetic. The man on my other side was French, an old Legionnaire who had been at Bel-Abbès. He was a bit dotty and talked to himself, and if he were asked a question he would repeat his answer two, three, four times until something else was said. It seemed that once wound up he had to go on talking. On Sundays he used to go out with a tin pail and gather snails in the fields and vineyards, which he sold to the restaurants and made six or eight francs that way. The corporal was a Corsican, with an impediment in his speech. He was a rough fellow until he smelt money and then he was lenient. He never borrowed less than one hundred sous. One man in my room from Flanders talked continually like an old washwoman, and commenced early in the morning to talk to the men in the next shack at the top of his voice in Flemish. He was a natural gossip and talked about everything he had heard and seen; nothing escaped him, no matter how unimportant.

Then there was a degraded sergeant, a Frenchman and old Legionnaire, who grumbled, complained and cursed all day long about the Legion. He had a sour face, and hadn't a good word to say for any one. He suspected every one of all sorts of special vices and was indignant about the subject, but in such a way that I could not help thinking that either he had a very prurient mind, or that it was an obsession with him. On one occasion he refused to obey some superior's command. He was ordered before the Captain:

"Why did you refuse to obey the sergeant-major's orders?"

"Because I will not obey any man who is in the habit of— ."

A Spaniard occupied the sack on the platform opposite to me. He was just a common, strong, well-built peasant, who had been spoilt probably by the slums of a big city, and was looked upon as a suspicious character and avoided by every one. But I found him all right, he wanted only decent treatment. He performed quite a number of chivalrous little services without the least ostentation, and I never found him to beg, steal, borrow, or toady to any one. He was genuine, and whatever his history, I felt convinced that if he had committed an act of violence, as was rumoured, it was in consequence of an environment over which he had no control. The filth of the place was most abhorrent, and my shack companions had not the remotest idea of the rudiments of elementary cleanliness; to come near them took one's breath away. Any animal, even a pig, has a smell which can be endured, but man, when dirty, is beyond endurance.

The mail department underwent the same censorship here as at Bel-Abbès. The regiment's post office, under the direction of the *waguemestre*, occupied a wooden shack by itself. The ordinary letters were dealt out at the *rapport*, but the names of the recipients of registered letters and money orders were posted up on a board in each camp centre. The soldier's sergeant had to go and sign first, and then after the money had passed through these officials' hands, the poor soldier received it – only to be borrowed from immediately.

My own experience was most painful. I was considered objectionable by the *waguemestre* for continually inquiring if there were no registered letters, which I knew had been sent. He cursed me, and finally, whenever I came, he disappeared and could not be found anywhere. I could do nothing – my registered letters did not arrive. At last it occurred to me to persuade the pretty girl at the village post-office not to deliver my telegrams or telegraphic money orders to the regiment, and telegraphed with immediate results. Many months later I found out that my bankers, who had declared the registered letters, had had them returned, with the remark, in the handwriting of that same *waguemestre* who swore nothing had arrived for me, that *militaire* is not allowed to receive value-declared letters, and on some he had written *inconnu*. Why he had taken such an obvious dislike to me I could not make out. I was invariably polite to every one of my superiors, even when they were rude to me. I had made it a point to avoid making bad blood, no matter at what sacrifice or humiliation, and took everything in good part. I needed the good-will of every one, and even if I did not get it, I certainly could not afford their ill-will, which might find explosion just at the wrong moment.

I was planning to get away. How did the nigger get away? And in uniform? And conspicuous on account of his colour?

Heavy munition trains rolled by incessantly on the railway tracks next to the camp. How I longed to be a passenger on one of them, bound for those distant Alps! But I had sense enough to know that that was not the way.

Chapter 26

THE next time I saw Stojanoff was in the infirmary. He had been to Lyons, had been to see the Colonel, and tried every means in his power not to have to stay at Valbonne. It was useless. Nothing could be done for him. He returned, without being caught with his forged permission, tore open his wound and reported ill. The doctor seeing the condition of the wound sent him to the infirmary.

"Here at least are beds to sleep on and the place is fairly clean," he said. "Only we don't get any food and I am nearly starved. All we get is milk and broth and bread."

A healthy soldier cannot stand such diet, and as soon as a man feels tolerably well he asks to leave the infirmary. That is what the authorities want. The system of starvation may prove to be a very good remedy for feigned illness, but it is certainly ruinous for the real invalids, who looked terrible, and were slowly wasting away from starvation.

The infirmary was the only stone house in the camp; one story high, primitive but clean in its furnishings, with a nice little garden at the back enclosed by a high stone wall, where the poor starved patients could take the air if well enough to move about. Visitors were allowed only twice a week, so that it was necessary for me to make friends with the attendant in order to have daily access to my friend, to whom I smuggled big sandwiches with cutlets and roast beef, which he devoured with a ravenous appetite.

"I am making my wound worse by rubbing an onion on it every night and morning, so that they will send me to the hospital at Lyons, and once there I shall find a way of escape. I cannot stay here or in the Legion any longer — it is insufferable. There is no chance of my being sent to the front again on account of my arm, and they will not *réformer* me."

I encouraged him to tell me more of his plans of escape, and confided to him that I had the same intention.

"Well, let us escape together," he said, and I agreed.

I came to see him every day, and we devised various plans of escape. The most possible one was to get a permission to go to Grenoble for two days, where his *fiancée* lived, change there, and with a real or forged civilian's safe-conduct go to Evians-les-Bains, on the French side of the Lake of Geneva, take a motor-boat and land somewhere on the Swiss side. He was going to telegraph for money and write his *fiancee* to wire him. We planned all details, and how to overcome difficulties that might present themselves.

What Stojanoff wrote to the *fiancee* I don't know, but a few days later, and not at all at the time that we had planned, a telegram arrived from her saying, "Come at once, aunt dying." He showed it to the doctor, but he would not give him permission. He went to the pretty girl at the village post office and told her to write on a telegraphic form, "Aunt dead." With this telegram in hand the doctor finally consented to give him the desired permission.

"I shall go to see my *fiancee* and talk over the plan with her, and have everything prepared. I shall be back in two days." And off he went.

I thought it was very unwise to ask for a permission, and risk not getting one a little later, when we really wanted it, for they might easily refuse a man who had had a permission very recently. And we were not ready then, for we were both waiting for money.

But he did not return in two days, nor in three days, nor in five days.

I went to the infirmary to inquire for him. The attendant looked at me suspiciously as if questioning me as to how much I knew.

"Hasn't Stojanoff returned?"

"He is not here."

"But I thought his permission is for two days only – did he get it prolonged?"

"He did not have any permission."

"But I saw it."

"He never had any permission, and he is not here."

"Do you know where he is?"

"No."

I could understand nothing. Had he changed his mind and thought it safer to escape alone? I wished him luck any way. A day or two later I saw his name on the money recipients' list. Surely he would not have gone without his money, though his *fiancee* might have supplied him with what he needed, but I knew he expected eight hundred francs, and I did not think he would let that go. It remained a mystery until about a week later I saw him marched off to prison.

What had happened I never found out, but I felt I had had a close shave.

While I was waiting for the registered letters which never came, Casey advised me to go to Lyons and ask the American Consul to cash me a cheque. The nights were so very dreadful – I could not sleep at all – the stench in the shack was suffocating, the vermin worried me so that my whole body became sore from scratching, the lack of water for intimate ablutions, the noise of the rats, the lumpy straw sack, the sloping platform from which I slid down continually, the filthy disinfected sleeping bag, and the thoughts that came to me at night which made me feel that my position was hopeless, the long hours, the restlessness, made me feel as if I would go mad; and in addition to all this waiting for money, not even able to pay for the few obtainable luxuries which made life endurable for a couple of hours of the day, I wanted a bed, I wanted a bath, I wanted to sit down at a decent clean table and eat decently served food. I was dog-tired, I wanted to sit alone in a room, if only for a few hours, without being disturbed, I wanted to write some letters at a table with blotter and decent paper, I wanted to get away, if only for some hours. I had to get away.

I applied for a twenty-four hours' permission to go to Lyons on Saturday night, and got it. I packed my little toilet case, Casey lent me the few sous it takes to go to Lyons, and I started. I arrived penniless, did not know if the Consul would cash me a cheque, did not know if I should raise any money at all the next day, Sunday, in a town where I did not know a soul; although knowing I had to return to camp the next night, without having the fare, yet I did not care, I was desperate, I had to have a rest and a decent meal, no matter what happened. I went to the Hôtel d'Angleterre, took a room, had a bath, and went down to dinner, as if I had as much money in my pocket as I wanted.

In the morning I made myself look as respectable as possible, and went to the American Consul. I did not find him at his office and finally discovered his hotel. I sent up a very courteous note asking him if I might speak to him as I could not come on week-days.

A big burly brutal-looking man came into the drawing-room where I was waiting. I rose to greet him.

"Well, what's your story?" he said in a hard sharp impatient voice. My breath was taken away. I did not find any words after that welcome. At last when I had collected myself I told him that my money had not come, and that I wanted to ask him if he would cash me a cheque on Rome.

"You an American?"

"Yes, I am."

"Show me your passport."

He looked it over very carefully, trying to find a flaw, but there happened to be none. It was in perfect condition and still valid. If I had been a soldier for three months I would not have had a passport at all, as a man is obliged to give up all his papers then to the regiment.

"Rome – who do you know in Rome?"

I mentioned some of our Embassy people.

"Well if you know Billy E—— I'll telegraph him, and if he is willing to take the responsibility, I'll cash your cheque. But I ain't no banker. In the meantime I can lend you 2.50 francs, which is all that is left in the American Benefit Fund, but you will have to come to the office with me to get it."

My throat was dry. The manners of the man were abominable, a rude, crude creature, who could not think of words harsh and insulting enough to cow me. I managed to screw up some courage:

"Oh, no, thank you, I could telegraph to Mr. E—— myself if it came to that. I am in need of 50 francs now at this moment, not to-morrow nor the next day, when very likely my money will have arrived."

He seemed relieved. "Well, you see how it is, Mr. What's-your-name, I ain't no banker, and when that stampede occurred at the outbreak of the war, and Americans wanted to get back, I was let in for 350 dollars, and I don't intend to be let in for another cent."

I bowed myself out, but there was a lump in my throat. What to do now? I went to the porter of the hotel – could he cash me a cheque? Very sorry, he could not. It was all this damned uniform.

I went to the Terminus Hotel, the best in Lyons – would they cash me a cheque for fifty francs? No, they would not. By this time I spat forth some of the venom that had been gathering all day at the treatment I had received in various places, because I was a soldier and in the Legion. Was this what I had come for, a stranger to fight for *La Belle France*; and in consequence was looked upon as if I were a highway-robber, thief, forger and what not, judging from the attitude and treatment I received from every one? Everywhere I was met with suspicion, lack of all courtesy and respect, and insulted in a thousand subtle ways. It was too much. If I were at that moment in Paris, in civilian clothes, there would not be a first-class hotel which would not cash me my cheque for the ridiculously small sum of 50 francs at once.

Somehow the porter of the Terminus had a little more intuition than the manager, and realized that he was not dealing with a man who was going to do him out of 50 francs. He said: "I don't like to take your cheque because it takes so long to get through, but I will lend you 50 francs, and you can return them to me when your money arrives – just give me a receipt for them."

I have never ceased feeling grateful to that porter, and naturally recompensed him for his kindness when my money arrived.

What I had gone through in those twelve hours was just the straw that broke the camel's back. My whole nature rebelled; here I was in a position where, in addition to the filth and disgusting surroundings, living among the dregs of human society, doing strenuous physical exercise at great expense to my purse, I was treated like a dog, a ruffian, a blackguard, an outcast. I would not stay another minute than was absolutely necessary. On my return to my hotel I made my plans, wrote letters, sent telegrams, and arranged matters in such a way that I could reasonably expect to leave in another week's time.

When I had returned to Valbonne I found that the permission on which I had gone to Lyons had been forged. This was serious. I could not afford to have anything against me when about to ask for a three days' permission. I was called to the office and fortunately was able to prove that I had received the permission in good faith from the sergeant on duty, who had neglected to get the Commander's signature.

The following day there was a call to arms – that is, several hundred men were to leave for the front at once. I was among those chosen. I did not think it could be possible – I had had no training worth the name, had only shot once in my life, and was still among the *jeunes soldats*. On enquiry I found that there was no mistake and that I must get ready. If Fate decided it like that there was nothing else to do, but I told the sergeant at the office that it was curious I should be sent when still so absolutely unfit to defend the country or my life. To my mental vision appeared the man with the chin shot away, the man with a crevice in his head who had fits of madness, the men who sat on their planks at Lyons holding their hands over their half-blinded eyes, the men with wounds which festered and made them useless, the men with legs and arms gone, and *yet they lived*. Death is great good fortune compared to any of these conditions.

"If every one had your good-will, and were like you, and knew even less, we would be all right. I might tell you you will never learn any more here."

We were lined up when we had packed our knapsacks for the Commander's inspection. I was about the third or fourth in the line. Each man was presented by the Captain and his record explained to the Commander. When my turn came he said: "This man has had no experience in shooting – in fact his training is not yet completed." The Commander ordered me out and to return to my shack.

Of the other Americans no one had been ordered to the front. However there were two Scotchmen and an English boy from Madagascar, whose names were on the list. One of the Scotchmen, Allen, had been a Berlitz school teacher at Bordeaux, and had enlisted when there was nothing more for him to do. The English boy was very fond of Allen, and Allen of him. They were inseparable, and when they heard that both their names were on the list they embraced each other, and were happy to go together to the front. Their joy was so sincere and real, and they were so completely oblivious to their surroundings, that some of those who saw them were justly envious of the devotion these two had for each other. It was undoubtedly the nicest and truest expression of feeling I had seen in the Legion.

One or two of the nicer chaps had told me that the front was all right if one had a good comrade. But where in that *mêlée* of all the dregs of humanity could a good comrade be found, who had a genuine feeling of friendship for any one? A case like Allen's was rare.

Chapter 27

THE week passed slowly. I used the sudden call to the front to further my cause to get permission to go to Paris for three or four days, saying that I wanted to settle my private affairs at my Embassy, in case I should be called again. I had applied for permission when I heard that the usual vacations had not been granted at Easter, and were to be given now in accordance with the orders from the Ministry of War. I was silent about the permission I had had at Bel-Abbès for Easter. I was told that my request could not be granted officially, as I had not been a soldier three months, and I had no right to get a permission for more than twenty-four hours; but the Captain would make an exception with me and give me two days' permission for Paris on his own account.

A day or two after the departure of the troops to the front a manoeuvre was announced. We had to be ready as usual, at 5.30 a.m., with full kit. Valbonne lies in a low plain, and in the early morning the dampness covers the earth and meadows like a wet thick sheet. Both the Legion and the French regiment encamped with us were to take part in the manoeuvre. We were lined up near the big *café*, just inside the camp boundary, and a horde of *élève-officiers* were apportioned to us, or rather we were apportioned to them. Most of them were educated young men, who, since the war commenced, had been given the privilege to study to be officers, not only to avoid being privates, but also to fill the enormous gaps caused by the killed and wounded officers at the front.

They divided us into squads of fourteen men each, and took complete charge. The manoeuvre was not for our training, but for the training of the *élève-officiers*. We knew nothing and were informed of nothing – our orders were simply to follow blindly.

For hours we stood in the damp grass until we were sopping wet – waiting for the *élève-officiers* to get their orders from the officers. Finally towards nine o'clock we were ready to march. Soon after we left camp our squads were scattered in different directions, and each schooling-officer took his squad in hand as if at the front.

On one occasion we came quite close to some shrubs and were to hide. *A genoux* was the order, but no one went down on their knees, again came the order *à genoux* but more emphatic, again no one moved, and the officer got impatient.

"Why don't you get on your knees?"

"Because the place is full of merde."

Our particular *élève-officier* was a very nice fellow, still young, but his grave and settled manner and long blonde beard made him look older than he was. He spoke English very well, and while we were marching we chatted. He was a professor from the University of Grenoble, and regretted infinitely the lack of talent and taste of the French to learn foreign languages.

"We think we can get along with French and that every educated person ought to know our language. This is not only very arrogant but we are making a great mistake. The Germans are wonderful about languages; next to the Russians they are the best linguists, and they always speak two or three languages. We would never have had this war if we had condescended to learn German, for then we might have learnt as much about their conditions as they learnt about ours."

He was extremely kind and showed me the map of our manoeuvre, the place we were bound for, the Cross of St. Maurice which we were to take and to which the enemy was retiring to hide, and where we were marching, and the different obstacles we had to overcome. It made it very interesting, and it was the only time that I really enjoyed any exercise I had ever done since I entered the Legion. My comrades were just as eager to see the map, and I could see that our squad did much better than the rest. To know what we were doing gave zest to our duty, and we were anxious to do our best. I think before the end of the manoeuvre every one liked our officer and we were sorry to see him go. Although his orders were given firmly, there was no peremptory intolerance about them. He realized if something was wrong, and had quick understanding either to help, or to follow his order by another which could overcome the difficulty; not like some, who gave orders and expected them to be executed even when it was a physical impossibility, and, when aware of the silliness of the situation, would fly into a blind fury and deal out punishments right and left – no redress being possible.

When we were thirsty we drank, and there was no investigation as to what it was we drank so that we risked our wine or cognac being poured on the ground. He shared our food and drink, and there wasn't anything we could not have done for him, he was so nice and fatherly to every one. He was like a brother or a friend, and our relation to him was what I have always heard the Italian soldiers' relation is to their officers. But all the time I had been in the Legion I had never come across such an officer – but then he wasn't of the Legion.

The day after the manoeuvre we saw a strange motorcar drive up to the camp filled with well-dressed young men and an officer with a photographic machine. A sergeant went about ordering all the Americans in the Legion to assemble.

We assembled, and as the only superior of the Americans was Bouligny, the sergeant, he took us in charge. A dapper good-looking young man stepped out of the automobile and said in an airy and familiar manner:

"Boys, you are to have your pictures taken by order of the Ministry of War. We want to show in America what the Americans are doing on the side of the Allies. It is propaganda work and we have already some very good pictures of the American Ambulance and Flying Corps. We want to show all the American activities."

No one seemed to care particularly, and we were marched off to the field where Bouligny had built his trenches.

"Look here, Bouligny," I said, "I am not going to have my picture taken, nor am I going to be in any cinematograph. I have come here as a soldier and not as a cinematograph actor, and no Ministry of War can compel me."

"You will make it very hard for yourself if that is your spirit – and you will have difficulty in getting on," he replied.

"I know that you, as sergeant, can order me to do this and I have to obey, and you can make lots of trouble for me if I disobey. Well, I am not going into this cinematograph show, nor will I have my picture taken, and I am perfectly prepared to take the consequences of disobedience. Do as you think fit."

Silence ensued and Bouligny was nice enough to pay no attention to me when the time came for the operator to work, and I had retired out of the field of vision.

They did very good work, this handful of Americans, and the young man who stage-managed the different scenes did remarkably well in giving the impression that a large company of Americans was doing service. The attacks on the trenches were particularly well done; then there were defence of the trenches, sudden exits and retirements, marches, exercises, attacks on the field, etc., and even a scene in bivouac.

The boys worked hard and hoped to get a treat afterwards – we stayed long overtime, in fact until it got too dark for the operator. The "southernness" of Bouligny had not permitted the nigger to be in any picture along with himself, and the negro understood and did not resent it.

I had several reasons for not wanting to be in this cinematograph show; the chief being that I did not care to have my photograph on record in the Legion, and then I didn't care for all this faked-up trench and war business, in order to make cheap propaganda for the French Government. Nor did I like the way we were forced into this – we should have been asked to begin with, and not ordered, since this was not part of our business, and then each man should have been told that he would earn so much for taking part. Nothing of the kind was done. I was sorry for the chaps because there wasn't one who wouldn't have been happy with a five franc piece, and since there were only twenty, it would have come to a hundred francs, or $20, or £4, in whichever currency you like. The dapper good-looking young man gave one of them a five franc piece to go and buy drinks for the lot, as he had to rush off and see if the operator couldn't still take the mitrailleuse which was working at the other end of the camp!

France had spent fabulous sums for propaganda abroad, and it would have been only decent to have offered those poor devils of soldiers, foreigners at that, serving her for purely altruistic reasons, a good dinner and a bottle of wine for their willingness, instead of which we arrived at the camp too late to get any dinner at all. And I don't believe that dapper young man was doing all his rushing work for nothing.

It is a great pity Italy did not make propaganda in America likewise – she who has done most to win the war. Advertisement pays in this world. It is not what one does that counts in our modern state of affairs, but what one is supposed to be doing. One of the results of France's propaganda in America was the liberality with which America treated France, and the lack of Italian propaganda, the very shoddy manner in which she treated Italy – Italy which is in much greater need than France, and in fact is worst off of all the Allies.

Chapter 28

I SAW more of Casey than of any one else. He was a very decent chap and a man of the world and thoroughly dependable. Over our drinks – we had many a drink together, when the guard could be bribed and no superior was in sight – we discussed the rottenness of the Legion and all that pertained to it. He confided in me and told me that since he could not get into the Flying Corps or the Ambulance he had decided to get out of the Legion by hook or crook, and had written home to California for the necessary money. "Not that I shall ever be any more good for anything, but I can't stand it any longer. I am broken completely – I shall never be able to do any more work."

It was useless to console him or contradict him – he was a broken man and he knew it.

"You'd better get out of this yourself before it is too late. You can do it still. Your health hasn't been impaired, and you have got your head all right. You're not a nervous and mental wreck as I am. There is no hope for me, even if I get out, and I don't know if I shall succeed, for I haven't any papers. When the war broke out not any of us had any papers, and since then all sorts of new regulations have come into force about passports. I doubt if I can get a passport. Anyway it will be very difficult for me to get out, and take a lot of money, and scheming, and help of others. Whereas it ought not to be difficult for you to get out when you like. You have all your papers – your passport is still good – you don't need much money – you have plain sailing. Besides you are not a soldier yet, under three months, so that if you don't succeed it doesn't matter, for they can't give you much of a punishment. But you would succeed if you wanted to get out – I know you would."

Then I opened my heart to him and told him all that I had planned, but that I meant to get out legitimately if possible. I wanted to see the Ambassador, and see if he could not use his influence with the Ministry of War to get me into the Ambulance or the Red Cross, or to get me released altogether – for flying I have no taste – and if I did not succeed

I meant to get out any way, and certainly not return here. He approved of my decision and gave me all the advice possible, how to go about it in Paris, and addresses of some of his friends, who might be useful.

Somehow my decision reacted on him and made him buck up – he too wanted to get out immediately. He wrote to his *fiancée* in Paris, and asked her to come down to Lyons with his civilian clothes, two safe-conducts and two return tickets. He asked for a four days' leave to get married. The military authorities have never been known to refuse a permission for this purpose, and once in Paris and he would see what he could do. What happened I don't know as I left before his permission had been granted. I only knew that he had much difficulty about it.

His Captain was a nasty person, very stiff, and correct and unbending; he walked like a sissy and gave a haughty cold stare to every one within a radius of ten metres. Casey was an impulsive true Bohemian, and together with his charming expressive voice he used his hands when talking. The Captain commanded him to his office to ask him about this marriage. Casey saluted and commenced to explain, and in talking in his natural manner he moved his hands whenever emphasis required it. The Captain, sitting at his desk like a stick, thundered "Garde à vous!" and Casey straightened out like the stone effigies we were supposed to resemble when this order was commanded. "Now continue," said the Captain. But it was quite impossible for Casey to keep standing in that ridiculous manner without unbending and tell the Captain in a cold-blooded way about his intimate affairs and why he wanted to get married now, so his hand came up again and he said, "Mon capitaine, you see it is like this ...."

"Garde à vous!" And after the salute, "Now continue."

"Mon capitaine, you see ..." and off he went falling again into his natural attitude.

"Garde à vous!"

After this had happened about ten times the Captain ordered him out, and Casey never had his say while I was there.

Knowing he had to talk naturally, or not at all, he made his request in writing to the Commander just as I was leaving.

Casey had fought valiantly from the beginning of the war, had given up his art, his position, to fight for a country to which he owed only some hospitality, for it had not given him his living; he had spent his good American dollars, and this was the treatment accorded him by some *kiek in die Luft* Legionnaire officer.

I had asked for Monday and Tuesday on which to go to Paris, knowing that Sunday I should be free any way, so that I had really three days from Sunday, after the *rapport* at 10 a.m., until the *réveil* at 6 a.m. on Wednesday.

Soldiers could only travel on certain trains, and to have tried to travel on any others but those prescribed would have been useless, as neither the ticket office would sell a ticket nor the sergeant would let a man pass except at the time mentioned on the permission.

I had left my small valise at the hotel in Lyons the week previous, in order not to appear to leave with too many things for two days. So that I had only to pack the remainder of my personal effects into the *musette*, and when I departed I looked like any other soldier going on a holiday. I had received my money, paid all my debts in the camp, telegraphed the money for my hotel bill to Bel-Abbès, ordered my luggage there to be sent to a friend, and after another few drinks with Casey at the next village (he was going to meet his *fiancee* a village or two beyond), I returned to Valbonne to take my train for Lyons.

At Lyons I got my bag and went to the station. I paid for my ticket and my money was refused. In the provinces of France there was the same system of paper money issued by the Chamber of Commerce of a town as in Algiers. Oran money was no good in Algiers and vice versa. Here my Marseilles money was refused as this was Lyons. And there is no place to change it, even if one loses a few sous by it – it is simply worthless, and one loses the money. I don't know any other Western civilized country where such a silly system exists.

I was just in time for the I p.m. train for Paris, and although I did not know what my fate was going to be, still I felt I was going one step forward towards my release from that terrible Legion, and all that my status as a Legionnaire meant.

Towards evening the train filled up and third-class passengers were pushed into our second-class compartment, and among them a few French soldiers who were returning to the front. Their heads were covered with scars. The conductor came along, saw their permits and military passes, and said in a most insolent tone: "What are you doing here? This is second class. What do you mean by this?" The poor fellows were quite abashed and murmured some excuse that third class was full.

"Third class full – well, if third class is full you ought to take the military train. Anyway you have no business on this train – you must get out at the next station." He did not say a word to the civilians, who travelled second class on third-class tickets. The big bully of a guard ought to have been at the front himself, and left this soft job to an older man, or one who was physically unfit, instead of maltreating the men who were fighting for him and his country. But the lower class French can never forget the power of money. They were soldiers, and I was a soldier – we were travelling on a train for which the ticket office had sold us tickets – nothing was said to me; the difference was they were third class, and I was second.

The train arrived late in Paris; it must have been nearly midnight. Of course there were no porters at the Gare de Lyon. If one attempted to address a uniformed person, under the impression that this might be a porter willing to carry some parcels, a look of contempt, a shrug of the shoulders, hands in trousers pockets, but no answer.

I saw one English lady speak to a man who was unmistakably a porter.

"What do you want?" he asked her.

"I would like you to carry my luggage and call me a taxi."

"Would you? Well, you can carry your own luggage, and as to taxis I believe you will have to walk. You are English, aren't you – don't think that we are going to fight much longer – you can do it alone – but we have had enough of this war." And he turned his back on her and walked off.

Outside the station not a taxi in sight. The streets pitch dark, and only at great intervals a lighted lantern, which, in consequence of the black reflector over it, sheds its light into its own immediate vicinity only. It was impossible to see any one's face and you could not see a man until he was quite close to you. As I heard later anything and everything was done in this enveloping darkness, and spooning couples no longer sought shelter in the woods, the streets being just as safe.

I walked for several blocks and hailed every taxi I heard. The drivers were insolent and most lordly.

"Where are you going?"

"Rue Cambon."

"Oh no, I am not going that way," and off he drove.

Another one: "Rue Cambon! At the other end of the world! Are you alone? If you can't find another passenger, who is going in the same direction and also pays full night fare and a good *pourboire*, I can't take you." And the next moment he was gone.

It seemed to be the custom, as there were so few taxis, for a driver to crowd as many passengers as possible into his taxi, charge each one full fare, and if he could not get several fares he would not drive. No use calling a policeman, there weren't any. And if there had been, it was too dark to find one. Besides there weren't any laws or regulations about anything as far as I could make out.

Finally I hailed one who was willing to take me – he had several passengers inside, and took each one home first. When I had entered my hotel and told the porter to pay him I heard an ungodly row going on outside; he had been paid full night fare, and would not budge until he had five francs *pourboire*.

Bath – bed – and bliss.

Chapter 29

NEXT morning I rose early and for the last time put on those vile disinfected rags. I bought a ready-made suit, which I ordered to be altered to fit me and be sent to my hotel by 11 a.m. Then a shoe shop, the Bon Marché for shirts, collars, ties and gloves, a hat shop, and by twelve o'clock the transformation had taken place. I was in civilian clothes and felt again like a decent human being, who had a right to go wherever he chose without being subject to insult. I packed, paid my bill, had a taxi called, and departed for the Gare St. Lazare. But on my way through the Rue Auber I apparently changed my mind, and ordered the driver to take me to an hotel in the Rue de Rivoli, where I was well known. Having arrived I paid him, and saw him drive off. So much of any trace of having worn a uniform was behind me.

At the hotel I asked for a friend of mine, who always lived there, and who I knew had just sailed for America.

"Not here – oh that is too bad – then I have come all the way from Rome for nothing. I must return in a day or two."

I told the porter that I had lost my French passport, and that I must get a *billet de séjour*. He sent a chasseur with me to the *Commissionaire de Police*, and the Sojourn Ticket was obtained without any difficulty, on the strength of my regular American passport.

What a wonderful feeling it was to be again independent and to stand for the value of one's face, so to speak. Everything seemed possible.

Tuesday morning I went to the American Embassy, after I had written the necessary letters and telegrams, in case I should not achieve what I wanted through legitimate appeal. One letter I sent to the Commander of the regiment at Valbonne saying that my business prevented me from returning before Friday (this was the five days' limit without being a deserter), and as there was no time to ask his permission, and my business was urgent, I took the law in my own hands and was willing to suffer the consequences on my return for transgressing upon the *règlement*. That would quiet the Legion for the moment.

My visit to the Embassy was a farce. Could I see the Ambassador? I sent in my card. A secretary came out to tell me that the Ambassador was ill and would I state my business? I did so and was referred to the Military Attaché.

"That's the way it is – you come over here and do all sorts of foolish things without consulting us, and then you expect us to get you out of a scrape. I can't understand why you are in civilian clothes – you ought to be in uniform. Do you know that you are likely to be arrested at any moment for not being in uniform?"

"If I can't apply to the representative of my own country when I am in trouble, whether this is caused through my own foolishness or not, to whom am I to apply? And who is going to arrest me driving about in taxis and living at an hotel where they have known me for years, and know nothing of my having been in the Legion, unless you are going to report me?"

"Well, we can't help you. The Ambassador certainly would not, even if he could. I can't give you any advice at all. You'll have to stick to it. Besides I don't know that you haven't lost your nationality, according to the new law, for having entered a foreign army, and in that case I don't know why you come here. Of course no American ought to enter the Legion, and no gentleman ought to put himself in the position of a common soldier. You should have thought of all that before."

Coaxing, persuading, pleading were of no avail – he was as hard as nails.

There was no time to be lost. I saw I had come to the wrong place, and was up against a stone wall. I had to act quickly.

I jumped into my taxi and drove immediately to the American Consulate to have my passport vised for departure, before the Military Attaché and Consul might accidentally meet and talk over the day's events. >From there to the Italian Embassy to obtain the *visa* necessary for entering Italy, and then back to the hotel, where I told the porter to get me my ticket and sleeper and safe-conduct for Italy for two days ahead.

"For Italy," he said, "I can't get you a safe conduct. You must go to the Prefecture, and deposit your passport for eight days, before you can get permission to leave the country."

This was a serious blow which I had not bargained for, but this was not the moment to appear undecided or nervous or to dally.

"All right," I said, "I will go to the Prefecture at once. Send one of your men with me, have him tip the ushers, so I don't have to wait, and promise ample tips if my passport gets through in less than a week."

At the Prefecture I did not have to leave my passport, but show it only. My declarations were written down, and I was promised the permit to leave the country as soon as all the necessary investigations were made.

This was very risky – I could not afford a moment's delay, still I had to chance it. I employed Wednesday in going to see my most influential Parisian acquaintances, who had no idea of my escapade, to have them use their influence at the Prefecture to get me my permit to leave at once, telling them that my presence in Italy at that moment was most urgently wanted by my affairs. I was promised every possible help, which I had every reason to believe was going to be effective – among my friends was the editor and proprietor of one of the leading Parisian newspapers.

Thursday I spent waiting for results.

Friday I was getting nervous. My time was up to be back at the Legion. They might possibly wait until Saturday before making any enquiries, especially as they had my veracious sounding letter. And it would take them some time to find out what had become of me. At the Legion I had given my address as the hotel in the Rue Cambon, where I was not known, and where I had left immediately; and to the Commander I had given the same address when writing.

I ordered the porter to get me a ticket for Nice, and a safe-conduct, telling him that I would wait for my permit where it was sunny and lovely, instead of in Paris, where it was cold and foggy and rainy, and that he was to send me the permit to Nice.

In spite of my anxiety I thoroughly enjoyed every minute of my liberty in Paris. To sit down at a well-set table and have proper service and decent food, and not have to salute every superior uniform of every nationality and ask permission to be allowed to sit down and eat and drink in the same place, to be able to go to an American bar and order cocktails and whiskies and sodas, to go about irrespective of hours, what privileges! All the things one is accustomed to do become privileges after one has been deprived of them for a long time. The luxury of a good bed, the cleanliness and care of a first-class hotel, the feeling of wearing clean clothes, the comfort of breakfast in bed, and lounging over the *New York Herald* – I felt I was suddenly transported from a pigsty to paradise. Prunier's, Voisin's, Hôtel Meurice, and a few other of my favourite restaurants – each meal was a feast, and it seemed as if I had never been in the Legion, as if it had been a bad nightmare only.

Paris wasn't the same – it wasn't as of yore by any means, and just a bit gloomier than when I had been there six months before. Instead of taxis, elegant broughams, carriages and cars going up and down the Rue de la Paix and the Rue de Rivoli, there was a steady stream of Red Cross motors with wounded, with officers, with nurses. The shops looked sad and forlorn, the streets empty, the people looked serious, every second person was in mourning, and mourning was written on the faces of those who did not wear it. At night all was dark, the restaurants were difficult to find, not a ray of light emanated from window or doorway, as all blinds had to be drawn by order of the police. The few taxis which were about were driven by crippled young men. Parts of the big hotels were turned into hospitals. There was a feeling of depression everywhere, and the heavy muggy air did not help matters. One had the impression that every one expected the worst to happen, as if one were in a doomed city. It was ghastly.

On one occasion I got a bit of a fright. In an American bar I met a man I had met six months ago: "Why, how do you do? I heard you had entered the army. I quite expected to see you in khaki next."

"What rot," I replied, "who could have told you that? Besides I am an American and they would not take me in the British Army."

The conversations I overheard in some of the American bars in Paris among the British, French and Belgian officers were most astounding. The nationalities seldom mixed, and if they did, it was only to exchange the most polite courtesies which on their face were insincere. The British thought the French were not doing all they could, and that they themselves were doing all the work. The French thought that the British only talked big and did not do anything, that they were really fighting to save Great Britain, and that the British always got other people to fight their battles for them. The Belgians did not have much to say, except that they thought that neither the British nor the French were doing all they could. And of course the British never forgot to say that if it had not been for them the Germans would have been in Paris long ago. As to the Italians, they were not mentioned – evidently they did not count. And the Americans were so ashamed of Mr. Wilson and his antiwar attitude, at a time when every Anglo-Saxon and Latin heart was filled with righteous indignation, that they lay very low.

I burnt all my military papers and all correspondence which bore my address at the Legion, packed my filthy uniform and the rest of the

Legion's rotten rags into a pasteboard box, and left it with the porter telling him that a friend of mine would call for it. I paid my bill, drove to the Gare de Lyon, and took my seat in the first-class compartment of the night express for Nice.

I was a bit nervous at the station — I might meet some one from Lyons, or an officer might enter my compartment who remembered me. Still I was not a deserter yet, and could say I was on my way to Valbonne, since the train passed Lyons, and as to my civilian clothes I could plead ignorance, and say I had to make some private visits.

The minutes seemed hours until the train finally steamed out of the station into the dark night. This was only the first stage of my journey. Would I succeed or would chance play me some ironic trick?

Chapter 30

I WAS filled with doubts and apprehensions during the night. What if an officer, who knew me, should happen to pass my compartment? I drew the blinds on the corridor side where I had taken a seat. When you pass a compartment the person furthest from you, that is the one on the window side, catches your eye first. You do not go out of your way to look in and see who is sitting in the corners on the corridor side – you do not make the effort – as long as you see there is no seat for you.

At every stop during the night my heart was in my mouth. Would I succeed? Very early in the morning we steamed into the Gare Pérrache of Lyons. What if some of my officers should be leaving by that train to go South, or had come to meet an arriving friend? I put something on my seat to show that it was occupied and vanished into the *cabinet de toilette* to wash up. I took good care to spend all the time of that long stop at Lyons washing, and did not come out until I felt the train moving. I knew that in my compartment all seats were taken to beyond Marseilles, so I was safe not to see a new arrival in it.

I thought over the past and the narrow escapes of the last few days – the unkind Military Attache, the man in the bar, the detectives who stood around the Italian Embassy, the Consul who was going to ask a lot of questions, and was interrupted by a telephone message of a sweet nature, which made him smile and fall into musing, instead of continuing the questions, the *billet de séjour*, the questions asked at the Prefecture, and all the dozens of little incidents which might easily have led me into a trap by an unwise word, not to mention the possibility of being recognized by some one. It was dangerous ground I had trodden and now would the rest be passed over as smoothly?

What if they were on my track now? It was Saturday – I was not in my place – they would make an effort to trace me. At that moment they might be wiring to Paris. If they were lucky they could trace me that day and – no, not at Marseilles, but by the time I would get to Cannes they might have wired to look for me in the train. At Nice certainly some might have been ordered to arrest me.

Before noon we reached Marseilles – another fit of funk. Some one might recognize me here who had seen me a few weeks ago in uniform. Then again the words of Casey occurred to me: "They don't look for deserters in first-class railway carriages or the best hotels – they pick them up when they are shelterless in the streets." I spent the interminable wait at Marseilles in the toilet room also.

Then came St. Raphael. St. Raphael had many memories: when I was quite a boy I had been very ill there, and during my convalescence I took long drives along the beautiful shore dotted with charming villas and gardens. How delicious had been the scent of the mimosa overhanging the garden walls, how quiet the air, with only the noise of the insects buzzing in the warm sunshine, how aromatic the rich odour of the tall pines, and how gorgeous the ever-changing colours of the little rocky island in the blue waters of the bay! I had been coming back to life again after a close knowledge of pain and delirium and the brink of death. I wondered whether the cottage by the sea where Gounod wrote his Romeo and Juliette, with its pretty arbour, had had to make way for some big hotel or rich man's villa.

But St. Raphael had a more real importance to me at that moment. Acharock, the sergeant from Bel-Abbès, was stationed here now with a French regiment. I should like to have seen him and greeted him, but I knew that was impossible, in fact I dreaded seeing him. What if by chance he had come to the train looking for a friend? I could not have explained. I did not know him well enough to expect him to understand. I did not dare to show my face – it would be fatal.

Nothing happened. By the time the train arrived in Cannes I quite expected, after my imagination had been working without interruption or sleep for eighteen hours, to see some one come in and say "please step this way." Some of my fellow-passengers got out – who would enter now? I scrutinized every face, wondering if it were a detective looking for me. Inward prayers went up to Heaven incessantly.

Nice next. Should I get out at Nice or not? I had contemplated getting out at Nice in order not to look suspicious, and go where I said I was going, and then next day I would go over to Monte Carlo to spend the day, and, just by the way, walk over to Mentone. Besides I thought it might look suspicious to go to Mentone at once, so near the frontier. It was hopeless to wait for the permit to leave France from Paris; it might not come for days, and it might discover me, if they made enquiries, or rather if the Legion followed me up. What should I do? I was funky of getting out at Nice. I might have been tracked, and if so I should be taken at Nice, where they could reasonably expect me on account of my ticket and safe-conduct, and they would wait for me at the exit, where I had to give up both. Whereas if I stayed in the train they might think I had got out on the way and would arrive later. It would give me time, this little confusion on their part, if things were as I imagined them.

I went to the dining-car and asked an English-speaking waiter, who had been very attentive at lunch (I thought it better to ask him than the conductor, who on a later occasion might remember my question), if I could go on to Mentone by paying the difference of my fare between Nice and Mentone on the train mentioned? Also, that my safe-conduct said Nice.

"Oh, it doesn't matter. Of course you can go on without getting out – just give the guard a tip."

"But shall I have difficulty at Mentone on account of my safe-conduct at the station?"

"No, I don't think so. You are there and they won't send you back to Nice. You will have to register at the Police when you get there – that's all – but you would have to do that any way."

That decided me. I sweated blood when the train got into Nice, and remained in that condition until, after what seemed to me an endless halt, it pulled out again. I had stayed in my corner never budging. The compartment had emptied at Nice. I was alone. The conductor came round – he had been only once before, at Cannes. Between Paris and Cannes no one had been asked to show their tickets. I paid the supplementary fare with a great deal of nonchalance, gave him a tip, and was asked no questions.

Beaulieu, Monte Carlo, Roquebrunne – how I remembered all these delightful places and the long walking tours I had taken up into the mountains and woods in my youth. I knew every square of the landscape, every turn of the road, every path in the woods and the mountains.

Finally Mentone. The last time I had been there I had seen the aged Empress Eugénie, who travelled under the name of Comtesse de Pierrefonds, arrive with her suite, on her way to her villa at Cap Martin.

Hardly any one got out – the crowd of passengers had dwindled to an infinitesimal number – a few remained in the train going on to Italy. Would they make difficulty about my safe-conduct? But, as the waiter had said, I was there, and they would not send a first-class passenger back. At least I felt that at Mentone they could not have been notified yet. Things would not go as quick as that.

I got out, and somehow there was some confusion at the gate, so I went to the cloak-room and deposited my bag and hold-all first. That took some time, and when I was ready to depart the man at the gate had vanished and I passed out through the station without giving up either my ticket or safe-conduct. Now not even the station people could answer if I had arrived or not.

Although my luggage was trifling in weight I thought it best not to carry it, in order to attract as little attention as possible, for a traveller at this season of the year, the end of May, was unusual. Besides it would give me more freedom in looking for an hotel.

In the Avenue de la Gare I entered a *café* and had something to drink, and casually enquired how the war was affecting business. Nearly all the big hotels were closed, and only the smaller ones were open. They did not tell me that most of them were closed because the proprietors were Germans. Of the first-class hotels only the Bellevue was open, and that was at Mentone-Garavan, the east bay of Mentone beyond the small harbour.

I would go to the best hotel, not only because I would like it better, but principally because in small hotels people are likely to be more suspicious and more fearful of the law, and very precise in everything to do with the authorities, of which they stand in holy horror. To them it would seem unusual for an English or American civilian traveller to be there at that time of the year, and they could see from the tip of my nose that I wasn't choosing their third-rate hotels from choice.

How bleak and empty the streets of Mentone looked that late warm afternoon in May – most of the shops were closed – the hotels I used to stop at in years gone by were closed too, some turned into convalescent hospitals for soldiers and officers.

I walked the entire length of the town to the East Bay, beyond the Hôtel des Anglais, to the Hôtel Bellevue, which is wonderfully situated with a beautiful garden overlooking the sea.

Yes, I could have a room if I did not stay long, as they were about to close up for the summer.

"I want to stay a couple of days only. I am waiting for my permit to return to Italy from Paris, and I thought I would rather wait here in the sunshine than in gloomy Paris."

The proprietor, a perfectly delightful jolly good-natured Englishman, said: "But Italy is over there, you can see the frontier from here; of course we are glad to have you, but I don't see that there is anything to prevent you from walking over that bridge without that permit, if you have your passport."

That was exactly what I had been thinking all the time but I did not say so.

"Well, I might try. It is a good idea. I am in a hurry to get back, besides I haven't much clothes with me. I ran up to Paris for a few days only and did not know about that eight-day passport law."

"You try anyway," he said.

I washed and made myself look tidy, gave my linen to be washed immediately, as I had not much, to be ready next morning, and sauntered along the sea-front reviewing the situation before dinner.

There was no time to lose. At any moment they might find out my whereabouts and the game would be up.

How would I get into Italy? And even then I would be safe for a few days only, for, according to the new agreement between the Allies, deserters were extraditable immediately. I should have to hurry after I got into Italy and get my papers ready for Spain.

But I wasn't in Italy yet. There was the Bridge of St. Louis, which separates the French Republic from the Kingdom of Italy, as it says on the sign-posts. Would I get over that? There are guards there. I knew the way across the mountains up at Grimaldi. I might get over that way; there were not such grand officials there as on the highroad, who knew all about the new permit for leaving France. After all my papers were in order for Italy. I might say I was just taking a stroll up there in the mountains, and accidentally get over the frontier, and once over, the Italian Carabinier! aren't going to make any trouble. Again, wouldn't it look suspicious to be up there in the mountains in war-time? But then I should have no luggage — just my cane. All the pros and cons presented themselves. How would it be to take a boat and go for a row in this lovely calm weather, and just accidentally be landed on the other side of the Bay? It was so near. In the morning I would investigate the port and have a drink in an *osteria*, where the fishermen assembled, and see if some fisherman wouldn't offer to take me out for a row.

I took a walk in the direction of the port to take a bird's-eye view of the boats there and the place where the fishermen assembled. Then I sauntered back, and there, lo and behold, on the sea-front came an Italian Finanziere — what was he doing in Mentone? Evidently it was not difficult for the people living along here to cross over and see each other. He was a friendly looking person and wished me a *buona sera*. I returned the salute and asked him in Italian what he was doing there. "Oh, I am just out for a walk."

"Is it so easy to cross over the frontier?"

"Yes, I often take a walk over here. I am stationed in the Dogana just on the other side. You could take a walk into Italy if you wanted to."

"No, I don't think so. I am stopping here to wait for my permit to leave France."

"Have you your passport?"

I replied, "Yes."

"Well then you could take a walk on that side – but wait, I'll ask that French guard over there – he is a friend of mine."

He sped across the street and returned after a few moments.

"Yes, that's right, you must have that permit, but I think you could walk over any way if you wanted to."

We went to have a drink together. He was a Neapolitan and we talked Naples and the neighbourhood. He told me how dull the life was here, and that he did not care for the French, nor for the people of Liguria, and that he longed to be back in his Bella Napoli. Then we talked about the war, and he told me of the deserters who were caught by the dozen daily, especially up in the mountains. Deserters from Italy to France and from France to Italy.

We became friends, and before we parted he said: "Come and see me to-morrow, Sunday afternoon, if you have nothing better to do – I am up there in that big house over the bridge; that is our barracks. We have lunch about eleven in the morning, so come about twelve or twelve-thirty – our lunch isn't up to much – and we will go to have something to eat together at a *trattoria* I know, where the wine is good."

I promised I would.

"If they ask you at the Frontier show your passport, and just say you are going for a walk to see me," and he gave me his name. "They know me, and tell them you are returning. You must return then too, but if your permit doesn't come soon I'll see that you get over all right, bag and baggage. Trust me."

I accompanied him a little way and we parted with an *arivederci domani.*

It was getting dark – and I returned to the hotel for dinner.

My conversation with the Finanziere had bucked me up wonderfully. It seemed as if the man had been sent to me from God.

Chapter 31

I WAS very tired and as the night wore on I was getting more tired – I could not sleep. New doubts and apprehensions arose – what if I could not get over the frontier – what if they refused me or became suspicious – what if they had my name already on record? But then that wasn't likely; it might be noted down at a regular frontier railway station, but not on this lonely country road. However, I could not dally any longer – I had to do something, and if one thing did not succeed, I had to attempt another immediately, before the entire frontier line was put on guard. I had to take some guard unawares and get over – unless I got over by boat towards dusk. Once in Italy I would be all right. I know the people and like them and they like me. I can get along with an Italian always.

Towards the small hours I fell asleep and woke up at sunrise a bit refreshed. I made plans and unmade them – the hours until my coffee came were endless. I asked for my linen – it wasn't ready. I took a walk and had another look at the port. I hung round the pier and watched the fishermen and the boatmen, but French people of that class are not so sociable as Italians. The French see in a gentleman a natural enemy, or a thing to be treated obsequiously, whereas the Italians look upon any man as a friend, providing he is natural and *simpatico*, and he accepts your treating him as an equal with graciousness and with a debonair manner.

No one spoke – there was no way of opening a conversation. An Italian looks into your eyes and reads more than words can express, and then if he likes your looks he speaks naturally, as if he had known you for ages. I made several attempts to talk; the French are different – they answered, and then silence. No one offered me a boat, and I wasn't going to ask for one, in order not to arouse suspicion. I wandered away, for it was too early to go to the wine shop close by.

I took a walk up to the cemetery, which Maupassant described as the saddest and most beautiful he had seen, where among a profusion of roses rest so many young. What a glorious coast – the view from the cemetery is superb – and yet I never felt well on the French side. I always had the feeling that I wasn't at home. The stilted atmosphere of a fashionable health resort, the cared-for houses, the immaculate streets, in fact Parisian life on the Riviera – it was all so very artificial to me. I preferred the Italian side with the old houses and villas standing in neglected gardens – the picturesque-ness of the narrow streets – the churches in the small villages with their indigenous atmosphere and customs, and where Parisian life had not entered. The stranger was a guest there among a natural people who were the same as they had always been, and who made him feel that their home was at his disposal. The habitations on the Italian side are a part of the coast, whereas on the French side everything looks imported, theatrical, unreal – it really doesn't belong there, and therefore it is very bad taste.

By ten o'clock I was again at the port and took a glass of wine at the *osteria* – but I was looked at askance. I would never have attracted attention in an *osteria* of the same kind in Italy. Here I did. I took another walk along the pier but made no friends. When I turned I noticed I was being followed. This would not do at all. I must give the impression that I had just sauntered down here by accident. I directed my steps towards the other front, the West Bay. I was not anxious to be followed and have enquiries made at the hotel. I must get rid of this person who was following – he must lose me.

I came to the market, and pretended to be most interested in the barter that went on, buying and selling vegetables and fruits. I stood about and watched, amused, and this gave me a chance to see what kind of a person was following me, without his knowing I had noticed him. He was the real French detective type – you can't miss him. No detective in the world is quite so clumsily got up as a French detective, and the marvellous part is that he is so cocksure of himself – he thinks he looks like a gentleman; in reality he looks like a bounder dressed up as one.

Then I walked through the main street, and looked at the shop windows, then up the hill towards the cemetery, where the old town of Mentone winds itself in narrow streets around the crowning point, the cathedral. These streets I knew well, and once in them I walked quickly. The detective wasn't young and the climb would take the breath out of him before long. At first I eluded him, then I lost him altogether in that labyrinth of streets and alleys. I descended a road on the other side, through the woods, and finally reached my hotel from the hill behind it.

The boat escape plan was off – I saw that that wasn't the way. There was nothing else to do but to brave it out at the frontier, and if I did not succeed there, to return and go up the valley and climb up to Belinda and Grimaldi, and cross there. There would be ample time – by twelve o'clock I would be at the frontier – if that failed, I had all the long afternoon to do my climb and descend on the other side before dark.

My linen was ready. I changed and packed all my things together, so that in case I did not return they would be ready for shipment. I did not take anything with me but my papers, so that in case I was searched no impression would be given that I was doing anything else but taking a walk. Even extra collars, socks, handkerchiefs, comb and such like, which one can put in one's pockets, might look as if flight was intended. I walked out of the hotel with just gloves and cane in hand. I did not say what my plan was, not knowing if I would succeed. If I did not, they would see me back, and if I did I would write, send a cheque, and give orders about my luggage.

My heart was in my mouth – this would not do at all. I had better take a good stiff drink to steady me. At a *cafe* I had a whisky, and, with a Havanna in my mouth, I sallied forth as if nothing in the world fascinated me so much as the blue waters of the Mediterranean and the glorious panorama of the Maritime Alps.

Towards the bridge... I downed every thought of doubt and hesitation, and tried to wipe out completely all the hideous imaginings and apprehensions of the last few days. This was no time to think or worry, but the time for action, and above all a perfectly calm and tranquil exterior, in manner, voice, and speech.

It was difficult with a heart full of conflicting emotions – but it had to be done – it was a convict's life I was escaping from – I could never return to it – rather death than that.

Pont St. Louis – what a beautiful name. Would I remember it as beautiful? The Maritime Alps at this point fall abruptly into the sea, and there is just the narrow road hewn into the rock which runs along the coast, but the line of the frontier is marked by the rocks opening like a cleft – a deep gorge down which torrents of waters rush during the rainy season, and the bridge that crosses this gorge is the Pont St. Louis.

I walked on to the bridge, ignoring the guard house on the French side, as if I did not know anything about it.

"Hey there," and a very black-haired, black-moustached French guard in blue uniform appeared at the door.

I stopped and turned surprised.

"Where are you going?"

"I am going up there to see my friend Agostino Faresi of the Finanze – why?"

"Your friend? How do you know such a person as that?"

"Why shouldn't I know him? I have friends in all classes of society. I knew him in Naples, where I used to live."

"Have you your papers?"

"Yes," and I produced my passport.

"But to go across you must have a special permit to leave France."

"Oh yes, I know that – that is what I am waiting for now. I am stopping at the Bellevue. But I just want to go up there and see my friend – I shall be back in an hour or so."

He looked at my papers again – looked them all over – he could not find any fault with them, and then he looked at me in a surly lowering way with his black eyes, as if trying to pierce my soul. He held the passport for a moment – looked down as if hesitating and contemplating if he should let me pass or not – then he folded the passport very deliberately – all this seemed to take ages, and a thousand thoughts rushed through my brain while waiting for the verdict – then he gave it back to me and said:

"You can go, but you must return soon."

"Oh yes, I shan't be long."

On the Italian side of the bridge there is no guard house, but half-way up the hill, beyond a curve, out of sight of the bridge, there is a small guard house for Carabinieri. It was empty – the door closed – no guard in sight. I passed on – passed an *osteria* – a jolly looking *carabiniere* jumped out at me.

"Your passport."

"Yes, certainly – but I am just going up there to see my friend Agostino Faresi of the Finanze, and am returning shortly."

"Oh that's all right, but I had better stamp your passport, so that you will have no difficulty in case you should be asked for your papers."

He wasn't surprised I knew a Finanziere. He took my passport, walked back to the guard house, opened it, stamped it, and I asked him if I owed him anything. No, there was no charge. I offered him a cigar, we chatted, passed the time of day, and I walked on.

At the top of the hill, after another curve of the road, again within sight of the Pont St. Louis, was the Customs House or barracks of the Finanze. I asked for my friend. He had seen me and was just coming down the stairs to meet me. We shook hands and trotted for about a half-mile to the *trattoria* he spoke of, and regaled ourselves with a good lunch and wine.

"Let us go to Ventimiglia together," he said, "and spend the afternoon there and go to a cinematograph; but I shall have to ask my Maréchal first, as that is beyond the boundary where we can go."

I agreed and we walked back to the barracks. He went upstairs to ask and was down in a minute. "The Maréchal asks you to come up."

I went – another attack of palpitation of the heart. What would come now? Wasn't I safe yet?

"You know Faresi from Naples," said a very severe looking official.

"Yes," I replied as firmly as possible.

"You want to go and spend the afternoon in Ventimiglia with him?"

"Yes, if you will allow him to come."

"Have you your papers?"

"Yes, here is my passport."

He looked it over carefully. "Your papers are in perfect order, but Faresi can't leave here to-day. I have other work for him."

"I am sorry," and I bowed myself out. Faresi wanted to come with me, but the Marshal stopped him: "Faresi, you stay here, I have to talk to you."

Faresi winked to me and motioned me to wait downstairs. I bade the Marshal good-bye and left.

There is a rickety omnibus that runs from the Customs House to Ventimiglia once in the afternoon. Faresi and I had planned to take that.

I waited five minutes, ten minutes, a quarter of an hour – the omnibus came and departed, but Faresi did not appear. Should I wait longer? This was a chance, and there were a good many miles along the winding coast road to Ventimiglia. I rushed after the omnibus.

Ventimiglia is the frontier railway station for both countries. I wanted to get out of Ventimiglia as quickly as I got into it. After I descended from the omnibus I walked straight to the beach and sauntered along in the direction of Bordighera, as if I were taking a constitutional. Ventimiglia is full of detectives like all frontier places. When I had passed the last houses of the town I struck inland to the main road, and waited for the tramway "Ventimiglia-Bordighera," and in less than an hour I was in Bordighera.

So far so well. I did not feel safe yet, although the worst was over long ago. It was probably only the prolonged feeling of insecurity which made me still feel that I was not yet safe.

At Bordighera I went to an hotel and asked for a whisky and soda – I needed it. I sat down and wrote to the hotel in Mentone explaining the situation, that I had succeeded in passing the frontier, and gave instructions about my baggage. Then I wrote to a friend of mine in Paris to call at the hotel there and ask for the box I had left with the porter, to address it, and send it by post to the Commander of the Foreign Legion at Valbonne.

That done I took the five o'clock express in the afternoon and awoke blissfully next morning in Rome.

There is nothing more to tell except that I received my necessary *visas* in Rome, and a few days later sailed from Naples for Spain.

THE END

About Maurice Magnus

by D. H. Lawrence

On a dark, wet, wintry evening in November, 1919, I arrived in Florence, having just got back to Italy for the first time since 1914. My wife was in Germany, gone to see her mother, also for the first time since that fatal year 1914. We were poor; who was going to bother to publish me and to pay for my writings, in 1918 and 1919? I landed in Italy with nine pounds in my pocket and about twelve pounds lying in the bank in London. Nothing more. My wife, I hoped, would arrive in Florence with two or three pounds remaining. We should have to go very softly, if we were to house ourselves in Italy for the winter. But after the desperate weariness of the war, one could not bother.

So I had written to N—— D—— [Norman Douglas]; to get me a cheap room somewhere in Florence, and to leave a note at Cook's. I deposited my bit of luggage at the station, and walked to Cook's in the Via Tornabuoni. Florence was strange to me: seemed grim and dark and rather awful on the cold November evening. There was a note from D——, who has never left me in the lurch. I went down the Lung' Arno to the address he gave.

I had just passed the end of the Ponte Vecchio, and was watching the first lights of evening and the last light of day on the swollen river as I walked, when I heard D——'s voice:

"Isn't that Lawrence? Why of course it is, of course it is, beard and all! Well, how are you, eh? You got my note? Well now, my dear boy, you just go on to the Cavelotti – straight ahead, straight ahead – you've got the number. There's a room for you there. We shall be there in half an hour. Oh, let me introduce you to M—— "

This essay appeared as the "Introduction" to the 1924 edition of the *Memoirs*.

I had unconsciously seen the two men approaching, D—— tall and portly, the other man rather short and strutting. They were both buttoned up in their overcoats, and both had rather curly little hats. But D—— was decidedly shabby and a gentleman, with his wicked red face and tufted eyebrows. The other man was almost smart, all in grey, and he looked at first sight like an actor-manager, common. There was a touch of down-on-his-luck about him too. He looked at me, buttoned up in my old thick overcoat, and with my beard bushy and raggy because of my horror of entering a strange barber's shop, and he greeted me in a rather fastidious voice, and a little patronizingly. I forgot to say I was carrying a small hand-bag. But I realized at once that I ought, in this little grey-sparrow man's eyes – he stuck his front out tubbily, like a bird, and his legs seemed to perch behind him, as a bird's do – I ought to be in a cab. But I wasn't. He eyed me in that shrewd and rather impertinent way of the world of actor-managers: cosmopolitan, knocking shabbily round the world.

He looked a man of about forty, spruce and youngish in his deportment, very pink-faced, and very clean, very natty, very alert, like a sparrow painted to resemble a tom-tit. He was just the kind of man I had never met: little smart man of the shabby world, very much on the spot, don't you know.

"How much does it cost?" I asked D——, meaning the room.

"Oh, my dear fellow, a trifle. Ten francs a day. Third rate, tenth rate, but not bad at the price. Pension terms of course – everything included – except wine."

"Oh no, not at all bad for the money," said M——. "Well now, shall we be moving? You want the post-office, D—— ?" His voice was precise and a little mincing, and it had an odd high squeak.

"I do," said D——.

"Well then come down here—— " M—— turned to a dark little alley.

"Not at all," said D——. "We turn down by the bridge."

"This is quicker," said M——. He had a twang rather than an accent in his speech – not definitely American.

He knew all the short cuts of Florence. Afterwards I found that he knew all the short cuts in all the big towns of Europe.

I went on to the Cavelotti and waited in an awful plush and gilt drawing-room, and was given at last a cup of weird muddy brown slush called tea, and a bit of weird brown mush called jam on some bits of bread. Then I was taken to my room. It was far off, on the third floor of the big, ancient, deserted Florentine house. There I had a big and lonely, stone-comfortless room looking on to the river. Fortunately it was not very cold inside, and I didn't care. The adventure of being back in Florence again after the years of war made one indifferent.

After an hour or so someone tapped. It was D—— coming in with his grandiose air – now a bit shabby, but still very courtly.

"Why here you are – miles and miles from human habitation! I *told* her to put you on the second floor, where we are. What does she mean by it? Ring that bell. Ring it."

"No," said I, "I'm all right here."

"What!" cried D——. "In this Spitzbergen! Where's that bell?"

"Don't ring it," said I, who have a horror of chambermaids and explanations.

"Not ring it! Well you're a man, you are! Come on then. Come on down to my room. Come on. Have you had some tea – filthy muck they call tea here? I never drink it."

I went down to D—— 's room on the lower floor. It was a littered mass of books and type-writer and papers: D—— was just finishing his novel. M—— was resting on the bed, in his shirt sleeves: a tubby, fresh-faced little man in a suit of grey, faced cloth bound at the edges with grey silk braid. He had light blue eyes, tired underneath, and crisp, curly, dark brown hair just grey at the temples. But everything was neat and even finicking about his person.

"Sit down! Sit down!" said D——, wheeling up a chair. "Have a whisky?"

"Whisky!" said I.

"Twenty-four francs a bottle – and a find at that," moaned D——. I must tell that the exchange was then about forty-five lire to the pound.

"Oh N——," said M——, "I didn't tell you. I was offered a bottle of 1913 Black and White for twenty-eight lire."

"Did you buy it?",

"No. It's your turn to buy a bottle."

"Twenty-eight francs – my dear fellow!" said D——, cocking up his eyebrows. "I shall have to starve myself to do it."

"Oh no you won't, you'll eat here just the same," said M——.

"Yes, and I'm starved to death. Starved to death by the muck – the absolute muck they call food here. I can't face twenty-eight francs, my dear chap – can't be done, on my honour."

"Well look here, N——. We'll both buy a bottle. And you can get the one at twenty-two, and I'll buy the one at twenty-eight."

So it always was, M—— indulged D——, and spoilt him in every way. And of course D—— wasn't grateful. *Au contraire!* And M——'s pale blue smallish round eyes, in his cockatoo-pink face, would harden to indignation occasionally.

The room was dreadful. D—— never opened the windows: didn't believe in opening windows. He believed that a certain amount of nitrogen – I should say a great amount – is beneficial. The queer smell of a bedroom which is slept in, worked in, lived in, smoked in, and in which men drink their whiskies, was something new to me. But I didn't care. One had got away from the war.

We drank our whiskies before dinner. M—— was rather yellow under the eyes, and irritable; even his pink fattish face went yellowish.

"Look here," said D——. "Didn't you say there was a turkey for dinner? What? Have you been to the kitchen to see what they're doing to it?"

"Yes," said M—— testily. "I forced them to prepare it to roast."

"With chestnuts – stuffed with chestnuts?" said D——.

"They *said* so," said M——.

"Oh but go down and see that they're doing it. Yes, you've got to keep your eye on them, got to. The most awful howlers if you don't. You go now and see what they're up to." D—— used his most irresistible grand manner.

"It's too late," persisted M——, testy.

"It's *never* too late. You just run down and absolutely prevent them from boiling that bird in the old soup-water," said D——. "If you need force, fetch me."

M—— went. He was a great epicure, and knew how things should be cooked. But of course his irruptions into the kitchen roused considerable resentment, and he was getting quaky. However, he went. He came back to say the turkey was being roasted, but without chestnuts.

"What did I tell you! What did I tell you!" cried D——. "They are absolute—— ! If you don't hold them by the neck while they peel the chestnuts, they'll stuff the bird with old boots, to save themselves trouble. Of course you should have gone down sooner, M——."

Dinner was always late, so the whisky was usually two whiskies. Then we went down, and were merry in spite of all things. That is, D—— always grumbled about the food. There was one unfortunate youth who was boots and porter and waiter and all. He brought the big dish to D——, and D—— always poked and pushed among the portions, and grumbled frantically, sotto voce, in Italian to the youth Beppo, getting into a nervous frenzy. Then M—— called the waiter to himself, picked the nicest bits off the dish and gave them to D——, then helped himself.

The food was not good, but with D—— it was an obsession. With the waiter he was terrible – "Cos' è? Zuppa? Grazie. No, niente per me. *No – No!* – Quest' acqua sporca non bevo io. I don't drink this dirty water. What—— What's that in it – a piece of dish clout? Oh holy Dio, I can't eat another thing this evening——"

And he yelled for more bread – bread being war-rations and very limited in supply – so M—— in nervous distress gave him his piece, and D—— threw the crumb part on the floor, anywhere, and called for another litre. We always drank heavy dark red wine at three francs a litre. D—— drank two-thirds, M—— drank least. He loved his liquors, and did not care for wine. We were noisy and unabashed at table. The old Danish ladies at the other end of the room, and the rather impecunious young Duca and family not far off were not supposed to understand English. The Italians rather liked the noise, and the young signorina with the high-up yellow hair eyed us with profound interest. On we sailed, gay and noisy, D—— telling witty anecdotes and grumbling wildly and only half whimsically about the food. We sat on till most people had finished – then went up to more whisky – one more perhaps – in M——'s room.

When I came down in the morning I was called into M——'s room. He was like a little pontiff in a blue kimono-shaped dressing-gown with a broad border of reddish purple: the blue was a soft mid-blue, the material a dull silk. So he minced about, in demi-toilette. His room was very clean and neat, and slightly perfumed with essences. On his dressing-table stood many cut-glass bottles and silver-topped bottles with essences and pomades and powders, and heaven knows what. A very elegant little prayer book lay by his bed – and a life of St. Benedict. For M—— was a Roman Catholic convert. All he had was expensive and finicking: thick leather silver-studded suit-cases standing near the wall, trouser-stretcher all nice, hair-brushes and clothes-brush with old ivory backs. I wondered over him and his niceties and little pomposities. He was a new bird to me.

For he wasn't at all just the common person he looked. He was queer and sensitive as a woman with D——, and patient and fastidious. And yet he *was* common, his very accent was common, and D—— despised him.

And M—— rather despised me because I did not spend money. I paid for a third of the wine we drank at dinner, and bought the third bottle of whisky we had during M——'s stay. After all, he only stayed three days. But I would not spend for myself. I had no money to spend, since I knew I must live and my wife must live.

"Oh," said M——. "Why, that's the very time to spend money, when you've got none. If you've got none, why try to save it? That's been my philosophy all my life; when you've got no money, you may just as well spend it. If you've got a good deal, that's the time to look after it." Then he laughed his queer little laugh, rather squeaky. These were his exact words.

"Precisely," said D——. "Spend when you've nothing to spend, my boy. Spent *hard* then."

"No," said I. "If I can help it, I will never let myself be penniless while I live. I mistrust the world too much."

"But if you're going to live in fear of the world," said M——, "what's the good of living at all? Might as well die."

I think I give his words almost verbatim. He had a certain impatience of me and of my presence. Yet we had some jolly times – mostly in one or other of their bedrooms, drinking a whisky and talking. We drank a bottle a day – I had very little, preferring the wine at lunch and dinner, which seemed delicious after the war famine. D—— would bring up the remains of the second litre in the evening, to go on with before the coffee came.

I arrived in Florence on the Wednesday or Thursday evening; I think Thursday. M—— was due to leave for Rome on the Saturday. I asked D—— who M—— was. "Oh, you never know what he's at. He was manager for Isadora Duncan for a long time – knows all the capitals of Europe: St. Petersburg, Moscow, Tiflis, Constantinople, Berlin, Paris – knows them as you and I know Florence. He's been mostly in that line – theatrical. Then a journalist. He edited the *Roman Review* till the war killed it. Oh, a many-sided sort of fellow,"

"But how do you know him?" said I.

"I met him in Capri years and years ago – oh, sixteen years ago – and clean forgot all about him till somebody came to me one day in Rome and said: You're N—— D——. *I* didn't know who he was. But he'd never forgotten me. Seems to be smitten by me, somehow or other. All the better for me, ha-ha! – if he *likes* to run round for me. My dear fellow, I wouldn't prevent him, if it amuses him. Not for worlds."

And that was how it was. M—— ran D——'s errands, forced the other man to go to the tailor, to the dentist, and was almost a guardian angel to him.

"Look here!" cried D——. "I *can't* go to that damned tailor. Let the thing wait, I can't go."

"Oh yes. Now look here N——, if you don't get it done now while I'm here you'll never get it done. I made the appointment for three o'clock—— "

"To hell with you! Details! Details! I can't stand it, I tell you."

D—— chafed and kicked, but went.

"A little fussy fellow," he said. "Oh yes, fussing about like a woman. Fussy, you know, fussy. I *can't stand* these fussy—— " And D—— went off into improprieties.

Well, M—— ran round and arranged D——'s affairs and settled his little bills, and was so benevolent, and so impatient and nettled at the ungrateful way in which the benevolence was accepted. And D—— despised him all the time as a little busybody and an inferior. And I there between them just wondered. It seemed to me M—— would get very irritable and nervous at midday and before dinner, yellow round the eyes and played out. He wanted his whisky. He was tired after running round on a thousand errands and quests which I never understood. He always took his morning coffee at dawn, and was out to early Mass and pushing his affairs before eight o'clock in the morning. But what his affairs were I still do not know. Mass is all I am certain of.

However, it was his birthday on the Sunday, and D—— would not let him go. He had once said he would give a dinner for his birthday, and this he was not allowed to forget. It seemed to me M—— rather wanted to get out of it. But D—— was determined to have that dinner.

"You aren't going before you've given us that hare, don't you imagine it, my boy. I've got the smell of that hare in my imagination, and I've damned well got to set my teeth in it. Don't you imagine you're going without having produced that hare."

So poor M——, rather a victim, had to consent. We discussed what we should eat. It was decided the hare should have truffles, and a dish of champignons, and cauliflower, and zabaioni – and I forget what else. It was to be on Saturday evening. And M—— would leave on Sunday for Rome.

Early on the Saturday morning he went out, with the first daylight, to the old market, to get the hare and the mushrooms. He went himself because he was a connoisseur.

On the Saturday afternoon D—— took me wandering round to buy a birthday present.

"I shall have to buy him something – have to – have to—— " he said fretfully. He only wanted to spend about five francs. We trailed over the Ponte Vecchio, looking at the jewellers' booths there. It was before the foreigners had come back, and things were still rather dusty and almost at pre-war prices. But we could see nothing for five francs except the little saint-medals. D—— wanted to buy one of those. It seemed to me infra dig. So at last coming down to the Mercato Nuovo we saw little bowls of Volterra marble, a natural amber colour, for four francs.

"Look, buy one of those," I said to D——, "and he can put his pins or studs or any trifle in, as he needs."

So we went in and bought one of the little bowls of Volterra marble.

M—— seemed so touched and pleased with the gift.

"Thank you a thousand times, N——," he said. "That's charming! That's exactly what I want."

The dinner was quite a success, and, poorly fed as we were at the pension, we stuffed ourselves tight on the mushrooms and the hare and the zabaioni, and drank ourselves tight with the good red wine which swung in its straw flask in the silver swing on the table. A flask has two and a quarter litres. We were four persons, and we drank almost two flasks. D—— made the waiter measure the remaining half-litre and take it off the bill. But good, good food, and cost about twelve francs a head the whole dinner.

Well, next day was nothing but bags and suit-cases in M——'s room, and the misery of departure with luggage. He went on the midnight train to Rome: first class.

"I always travel first class," he said, "and I always shall, while I can buy the ticket. Why should I go second? It's beastly enough to travel at all."

"My dear fellow, I came up third the last time I came from Rome," said D——. "Oh, not bad, not bad. Damned fatiguing journey anyhow."

So the little outsider was gone, and I was rather glad. I don't think he liked me. Yet one day he said to me at table:

"How lovely your hair is – such a lovely colour! What do you dye it with?"

I laughed, thinking he was laughing too. But no, he meant it.

"It's got no particular colour at all," I said, "so I couldn't dye it that!"

"It's a lovely colour," he said. And I think he didn't believe me, that I didn't dye it. It puzzled me, and it puzzles me still.

But he was gone. D—— moved into M——'s room, and asked me to come down to the room he himself was vacating. But I preferred to stay upstairs.

M—— was a fervent Catholic, taking the religion alas, rather unctuously. He had entered the Church only a few years before. But he had a bishop for a god-father, and seemed to be very intimate with the upper clergy. He was very pleased and proud because he was a constant guest at the famous old monastery south of Rome. He talked of becoming a monk; a monk in that aristocratic and well-bred order. But he had not even begun his theological studies: or any studies of any sort. And D—— said he only chose the Benedictines because they lived better than any of the others.

But I had said to M——, that when my wife came and we moved south, I would like to visit the monastery some time, if I might. "Certainly," he said. "Come when I am there. I shall be there in about a month's time. Do come! Do be sure and come. It's a wonderful place – oh, wonderful. It will make a great impression on you. Do come. Do come. And I will tell Don Bernardo, who is my *greatest* friend, and who is guest-master, about you. So that if you wish to go when I am not there, write to Don Bernardo. But do come when I am there."

My wife and I were due to go into the mountains south of Rome, and stay there some months. Then I was to visit the big, noble monastery that stands on a bluff hill like a fortress crowning a great precipice, above the little town and the plain between the mountains. But it was so icy cold and snowy among the mountains, it was unbearable. We fled south again, to Naples, and to, Capri. Passing, I saw the monastery crouching there above, world-famous, but it was impossible to call then.

I wrote and told M—— of my move. In Capri I had an answer from him. It had a wistful tone – and I don't know what made me think that he was in trouble, in monetary difficulty. But I felt it acutely – a kind of appeal. Yet he said nothing direct. And he wrote from an expensive hotel in Anzio, on the sea near Rome.

At the moment I had just received twenty pounds unexpected and joyful from America – a gift too. I hesitated for some time, because I felt unsure. Yet the curious appeal came out of the letter, though nothing was said. And I felt also I owed M—— that dinner, and I didn't want to owe him anything, since he despised me a little for being careful. So partly out of revenge, perhaps, and partly because I felt the strange wistfulness of him appealing to me, I sent him five pounds, saying perhaps I was mistaken in imagining him very hard up, but if so, he wasn't to be offended.

It is strange to me even now, how I knew he was appealing to me. Because it was all as vague as I say. Yet I felt it so strongly. He replied: "Your cheque has saved my life. Since I last saw you I have fallen down an abyss. But I will tell you when I see you. I shall be at the monastery in three days. Do come – and come alone." I have forgotten to say that he was a rabid woman-hater.

This was just after Christmas. I thought his "saved my life" and "fallen down an abyss" was just the American touch of "very, very——." I wondered what on earth the abyss could be, and I decided it must be that he had lost his money or his hopes. It seemed to me that some of his old buoyant assurance came out again in this letter. But he was now very friendly, urging me to come to the monastery, and treating me with a curious little tenderness and protectiveness. He had a queer delicacy of his own, varying with a bounce and a commonness. He was a common little bounder. And then he had this curious delicacy and tenderness and wistfulness.

I put off going north. I had another letter urging me – and it seemed to me that, rather assuredly, he was expecting more money. Rather cockily, as if he had a right to it. And that made me not want to give him any. Besides, as my wife said, what right had I to give away the little money we had, and we there stranded in the south of Italy with no resources if once we were spent up. And I have always been determined never to come to my last shilling – if I have to reduce my spending almost to nothingness. I have always been determined to keep a few pounds between me and the world.

I did not send any money. But I wanted to go to the monastery, so wrote and said I would come for two days. I always remember getting up in the black dark of the January morning, and making a little coffee on the spirit-lamp, and watching the clock, the big-faced, blue old clock on the campanile in the piazza in Capri, to see I wasn't late. The electric light in the piazza lit up the face of the campanile. And we were then, a stone's throw away, high in the Palazzo Ferraro, opposite the bubbly roof of the little duomo. Strange dark winter morning, with the open sea beyond the roofs, seen through the side window, and the thin line of the lights of Naples twinkling far, far off.

At ten minutes to six I went down the smelly dark stone stairs of the old palazzo, out into the street. A few people were already hastening up the street to the terrace that looks over the sea to the bay of Naples. It was dark and cold. We slid down in the funicular to the shore, then in little boats were rowed out over the dark sea to the steamer that lay there showing her lights and hooting.

It was three long hours across the sea to Naples, with dawn coming slowly in the east, beyond Ischia, and flushing into lovely colour as our steamer pottered along the peninsula, calling at Massa and Sorrento and Piano. I always loved hanging over the side and watching the people come out in boats from the little places of the shore, that rose steep and beautiful. I love the movement of these watery Neapolitan people, and the naïve trustful way they clamber in and out the boats, and their softness, and their dark eyes. But when the steamer leaves the peninsula and begins to make away round Vesuvius to Naples, one is already tired, and cold, cold, cold in the wind that comes piercing from the snow-crests away there along Italy. Cold, and reduced to a kind of stony apathy by the time we come to the mole in Naples, at ten o'clock – or twenty past ten.

We were rather late, and I missed the train. I had to wait till two o'clock. And Naples is a hopeless town to spend three hours in. However, time passes. I remember I was calculating in my mind whether they had given me the right change at the ticket-window. They hadn't – and I hadn't counted in time. Thinking of this, I got in the Rome train. I had been there ten minutes when I heard a trumpet blow.

"Is this the Rome train?" I asked my fellow-traveller.

"Si."

"The express?"

"No, it is the slow train."

"It leaves?"

"At ten past two."

I almost jumped through the window. I flew down the platform.

"The diretto!" I cried to a porter.

"Parte! Eccolo la!" he said, pointing to a big train moving inevitably away.

I flew with wild feet across the various railway lines and seized the end of the train as it travelled. I had caught it. Perhaps if I had missed it fate would have been different. So I sat still for about three hours. Then I had arrived.

There is a long drive up the hill from the station to the monastery. The driver talked to me. It was evident he bore the monks no good will.

"Formerly," he said, "if you went up to the monastery you got a glass of wine and a plate of maccaroni. But now they kick you out of the door."

"Do they?" I said. "It is hard to believe."

"They kick you out of the gate," he vociferated.

We twisted up and up the wild hillside, past the old castle of the town, past the last villa, between trees and rocks. We saw no one. The whole hill belongs to the monastery. At last at twilight we turned the corner of the oak wood and saw the monastery like a huge square fortress-palace of the sixteenth century crowning the near distance. Yes, and there was M—— just stepping through the huge old gateway and hastening down the slope to where the carriage must stop. He was bareheaded, and walking with his perky, busy little stride, seemed very much at home in the place. He looked up to me with a tender, intimate look as I got down from the carriage. Then he took my hand.

"So *very* glad to see you," he said. "I'm so *pleased* you've come."

And he looked into my eyes with that wistful, watchful tenderness rather like a woman who isn't quite sure of her lover. He had a certain charm in his manner; and an odd pompous touch with it at this moment, welcoming his guest at the gate of the vast monastery which reared above us from its buttresses in the rock, was rather becoming. His face was still pink, his eyes pale blue and sharp, but he looked greyer at the temples.

"Give me your bag," he said. "Yes do – and come along. Don Bernardo is just at Evensong, but he'll be here in a little while. Well now, tell me all the news."

"Wait," I said. "Lend me five francs to finish paying the driver – he has no change."

"Certainly, certainly," he said, giving the five francs. I had no news, – so asked him his.

"Oh, I have none either," he said. "Very short of money, that of course is *no* news." And he laughed his little laugh. "I'm so glad to be here," he continued. "The peace, and the rhythm of the life is so *beautiful!* I'm sure you'll love it."

We went up the slope under the big, tunnel-like entrance and were in the grassy courtyard, with the arched walk on the far sides, and one or two trees. It was like a grassy cloister, but still busy. Black monks were standing chatting, an old peasant was just driving two sheep from the cloister grass, and an old monk was darting into the little post-office which one recognized by the shield with the national arms over the doorway. From under the far arches came an old peasant carrying a two-handed saw.

And there was Don Bernardo, a tall monk in a black, well-shaped gown, young, good-looking, gentle, hastening forward with a quick smile. He was about my age, and his manner seemed fresh and subdued, as if he were still a student. One felt one was at college with one's college mates.

We went up the narrow stair and into the long, old, naked white corridor, high and arched. Don Bernardo had got the key of my room: two keys, one for the dark antechamber, one for the bedroom. A charming and elegant bedroom, with an engraving of English landscape, and outside the net curtain a balcony looking down on the garden, a narrow strip beneath the walls, and beyond, the clustered buildings of the farm, and the oak woods and arable fields of the hill summit: and beyond again, the gulf where the world's valley was, and all the mountains that stand in Italy on the plains as if God had just put them down ready made. The sun had already sunk, the snow on the mountains was full of a rosy glow, the valleys were full of shadow. One heard, far below, the trains shunting, the world clinking in the cold air. "Isn't it wonderful! Ah, the most wonderful place on earth!" said M——. "What now could you wish better than to end your days here? The peace, the beauty, the eternity of it." He paused and sighed. Then he put his hand on Don Bernardo's arm and smiled at him with that odd, rather wistful smirking tenderness that made him such a quaint creature in my eyes.

"But I'm going to enter the order. You're going to let me be a monk and be one of you, aren't you, Don Bernardo?"

"We will see," smiled Don Bernardo. "When you have begun your studies."

"It will take me two years," said M——. "I shall have to go to the college in Rome. When I have got the money for the fees——" He talked away, like a boy planning a new rôle.

"But I'm sure Lawrence would like to drink a cup of tea," said Don Bernardo. He spoke English as if it were his native language. "Shall I tell them to make it in the kitchen, or shall we go to your room?"

"Oh, we'll go to my room. How thoughtless of me! Do forgive me, won't you?" said M——, laying his hand gently on my arm. "I'm so awfully sorry, you know. But we get so excited and enchanted when we talk of the monastery. But come along, come along, it will be ready in a moment on the spirit-lamp."

We went down to the end of the high, white, naked corridor. M—— had a quite sumptuous room, with a curtained bed in one part, and under the window his writing-desk with papers and photographs, and nearby a sofa and an easy table, making a little sitting-room, while the bed and toilet things, pomades and bottles were all in the distance, in the shadow. Night was fallen. From the window one saw the world far below, like a pool the flat plain, a deep pool of darkness with little twinkling lights, and rows and bunches of light that were the railway station.

I drank my tea, M—— drank a little liqueur, Don Bernardo in his black winter robe sat and talked with us. At least he did very little talking. But he listened and smiled and put in a word or two as we talked, seated round the table on which stood the green-shaded electric lamp.

The monastery was cold as the tomb. Couched there on the top of its hill, it is not much below the winter snow-line. Now by the end of January all the summer heat is soaked out of the vast, ponderous stone walls, and they become masses of coldness cloaking around. There is no heating apparatus whatsoever – none. Save the fire in the kitchen, for cooking, nothing. Dead, silent, stone cold everywhere.

At seven we went down to dinner. Capri in the daytime was hot, so I had brought only a thin old dust-coat. M—— therefore made me wear a big coat of his own, a coat made of thick, smooth black cloth, and lined with black sealskin, and having a collar of silky black sealskin. I can still remember the feel of the silky fur. It was queer to have him helping me solicitously into this coat, and buttoning it at the throat for me.

"Yes, it's a beautiful coat. Of course!" he said. "I hope you find it warm."

"Wonderful," said I. "I feel as warm as a millionaire."

"I'm so glad you do," he laughed.

"You don't mind my wearing your grand coat?" I said.

"Of course not! Of course not! It's a pleasure to me if it will keep you warm. We don't want to die of cold in the monastery, do we? That's one of the mortifications we will do our best to avoid. What? Don't you think? Yes, I think this coldness is going almost too far. I had that coat made in New York fifteen years ago. Of course in Italy—— " he said It'ly – "I've never worn it, so it is as good as new. And it's a beautiful coat, fur and cloth of the very best. *And* the tailor." He laughed a little, self-approving laugh. He liked to give the impression that he dealt with the *best* shops, don't you know, and stayed in the *best* hotels, etc. I grinned inside the coat, detesting best hotels, best shops, and best overcoats. So off we went, he in his grey overcoat and I in my sealskin millionaire monster, down the dim corridor to the guests' refectory. It was a bare room with a long white table. M—— and I sat at the near end. Further down was another man, perhaps the father of one of the boy students. There is a college attached to the monastery.

We sat in the icy room, muffled up in our overcoats. A lay-brother with a bulging forehead and queer, fixed eyes waited on us. He might easily have come from an old Italian picture. One of the adoring peasants. The food was abundant – but alas, it had got cold in the long cold transit from the kitchen. And it was roughly cooked, even if it was quite wholesome. Poor M—— did not eat much, but nervously nibbled his bread. I could tell the meals were a trial to him. He could not bear the cold food in that icy, empty refectory. And his tisickyness offended the lay-brothers. I could see that his little pomposities and his "superior" behaviour and his long stay made them have that old monastic grudge against him, silent but very obstinate and effectual – the same now as six hundred years ago. We had a decanter of good red wine – but he did not care for much wine. He was glad to be peeling the cold orange which was dessert.

After dinner he took me down to see the church, creeping like two thieves down the dimness of the great, prison-cold white corridors, on the cold flag floors.

Stone cold: the monks must have invented the term. These monks were at Compline. So we went by our two secret little selves into the tall dense nearly-darkness of the church. M——, knowing his way about here as in the cities, led me, poor wondering worldling, by the arm through the gulfs of the tomb-like place. He found the electric light switches inside the church, and stealthily made me a light as we went. We looked at the lily marble of the great floor, at the pillars, at the Benvenuto Cellini casket, at the really lovely pillars and slabs of different coloured marbles, all coloured marbles, yellow and grey and rose and green and lily white, veined and mottled and splashed: lovely, lovely stones— And Benvenuto had used pieces of lapis lazuli, blue as cornflowers. Yes, yes, all very rich and wonderful.

We tiptoed about the dark church stealthily, from altar to altar, and M—— whispered ecstasies in my ear. Each time we passed before an altar, whether the high altar or the side chapels, he did a wonderful reverence, which he must have practised for hours, bowing waxily down and sinking till his one knee touched the pavement, then rising like a flower that rises and unfolds again, till he had skipped to my side and was playing cicerone once more. Always in his grey overcoat, and in whispers: me in the big black overcoat, millionairish. So we crept into the chancel and examined all the queer fat babies of the choir stalls, carved in wood and rolling on their little backs between monk's place and monk's place – queer things for the chanting monks to have between them, these shiny, polished, dark brown fat babies, all different, and all jolly and lusty. We looked at everything in the church – and then at everything in the ancient room at the side where surplices hang and monks can wash their hands.

Then we went down to the crypt, where the modern mosaics glow in wonderful colours, and sometimes in fascinating little fantastic trees and birds. But it was rather like a scene in the theatre, with M—— for the wizard and myself a sort of Parsifal in the New York coat. He switched on the lights, the gold mosaic of the vaulting glittered and bowed, the blue mosaic glowed out, the holy of holies gleamed theatrically, the stiff mosaic figures posed around us. To tell the truth I was glad to get back to the normal human room and sit on a sofa huddled in my overcoat, and look at photographs which M—— showed me: photographs of everywhere in Europe. Then he showed me a wonderful photograph of a picture of a lovely lady – asked me what I thought of it, and seemed to expect me to be struck to bits by the beauty. His almost sanctimonious expectation made me tell the truth, that I thought it just a bit cheap, trivial. And then he said, dramatic:

"That's my mother."

It looked so unlike anybody's mother, much less M——'s, that I was startled. I realized that she was his great stunt, and that I had put my foot in it. So I just held my tongue. Then I said, for I felt he was going to be silent forever:

"There are so few portraits, unless by the really great artists, that aren't a bit cheap. She must have been a beautiful woman."

"Yes, she *was*," he said curtly. And we dropped the subject.

He locked all his drawers *very* carefully, and kept the keys on a chain. He seemed to give the impression that he had a great many secrets, perhaps dangerous ones, locked up in the drawers of his writing-table there. And I always wonder what the secrets can be, that are able to be kept so tight under lock and key.

Don Bernardo tapped and entered. We all sat round and sipped a funny liqueur which I didn't like. M—— lamented that the bottle was finished. I asked him to order another and let me pay for it. So he said he would tell the postman to bring it up next day from the town. Don Bernardo sipped his tiny glass with the rest of us, and he told me, briefly, his story – and we talked politics till nearly midnight. Then I came out of the black overcoat and we went to bed.

In the morning a fat, smiling, nice old lay-brother brought me my water. It was a sunny day. I looked down on the farm cluster and the brown fields and the sere oak woods of the hill-crown, and the rocks and bushes savagely bordering it round. Beyond, the mountains with their snow were blue-glistery with sunshine, and seemed quite near, but across a sort of gulf. All was still and sunny. And the poignant grip of the past, the grandiose, violent past of the Middle Ages, when blood was strong and unquenched and life was flamboyant with splendours and horrible miseries, took hold of me till I could hardly bear it. It was really agony to me to be in the monastery and to see the old farm and the bullocks slowly working in the fields below, and the black pigs rooting among weeds, and to see a monk sitting on a parapet in the sun, and an old, old man in skin sandals and white bunched, swathed legs come driving an ass slowly to the monastery gate, slowly, with all that lingering nonchalance and wildness of the Middle Ages, and yet to know that I was myself, child of the present. It was so strange from M——'s window to look down on the plain and see the white road going straight past a mountain that stood like a loaf of sugar, the river meandering in loops, and the railway with glistening lines making a long black swoop across the flat and into the hills. To see trains come steaming, with white smoke flying. To see the station like a little harbour where trucks like shipping stood anchored in rows in the black bay of railway. To see trains stop in the station and tiny people swarming like flies! To see all this from the monastery, where the Middle Ages live on in a sort of agony, like Tithonus, and cannot die, this was almost a violation to my soul, made almost a wound.

Immediately after coffee we went down to Mass. It was celebrated in a small crypt chapel underground, because that was warmer. The twenty or so monks sat in their stalls, one monk officiating at the altar. It was quiet and simple, the monks sang sweetly and well, there was no organ. It seemed soon to pass by. M—— and I sat near the door. He was very devoted and scrupulous in his going up and down. I was an outsider. But it was pleasant – not too sacred. One felt the monks were very human in their likes and their jealousies. It was rather like a group of dons in the dons' room at Cambridge, a cluster of professors in any college. But during Mass they, of course, just sang their responses. Only I could »ell some watched the officiating monk rather with ridicule – he was one of the ultra-punctilious sort, just like a don. And some boomed their responses with a grain of defiance against some brother monk who had earned dislike. It was human, and more like a university than anything. We went to Mass every morning, but I did not go to Evensong.

After Mass M—— took me round and showed me everything of the vast monastery. We went into the Bramante Courtyard, all stone, with its great well in the centre, and the colonnades of arches going round, full of sunshine, gay and Renaissance, a little bit ornate but still so jolly and gay, sunny pale stone waiting for the lively people, with the great flight of pale steps sweeping up to the doors of the church, waiting for gentlemen in scarlet trunk-hose, slender red legs, and ladies in brocade gowns, and page-boys with fluffed, golden hair. Splendid, sunny, gay Bramante Courtyard of lively stone. But empty. Empty of life. The gay red-legged gentry dead forever. And when pilgrimages do come and throng in, it is horrible artisan excursions from the great town, and the sordidness of industrialism.

We climbed the little watchtower that is now an observatory, and saw the vague and unshaven Don Giovanni among all his dust and instruments. M—— was very familiar and friendly, chattering in his quaint Italian, which was more wrong than any Italian I have ever heard spoken; very familiar and friendly, and a tiny bit deferential to the monks, and yet, and yet – rather patronizing. His little pomposity and patronizing tone coloured even his deferential yearning to be admitted to the monastery. The monks were rather brief with him. They no doubt have their likes and dislikes greatly intensified by the monastic life.

We stood on the summit of the tower and looked at the world below: the town, the castle, the white roads coming straight as judgment out of the mountains north, from Rome, and piercing into the mountains south, toward Naples, traversing the flat, flat plain. Roads, railway, river, streams, a world in accurate and lively detail, with mountains sticking up abruptly and rockily, as the old painters painted it. I think there is no way of painting Italian landscape except that way – that started with Lorenzetti and ended with the sixteenth century.

We looked at the ancient cell away under the monastery, where all the sanctity started. We looked at the big library that belongs to the State, and at the smaller library that belongs still to the abbot. I was tired, cold, and sick among the books and illuminations. I could not bear it any more. I felt I must be outside, in the sun, and see the world below, and the way out.

That evening I said to M—— :

"And what was the abyss, then?"

"Oh well, you know," he said, "it was a cheque which I made out at Anzio. There should have been money to meet it, in my bank in New York. But it appears the money had never been paid in by the people that owed it me. So there was I in a very nasty hole, an unmet cheque, and no money at all in Italy. I really had to escape here. It is an *absolute* secret that I am here, and it must be, till I can get this business settled. Of course I've written to America about it. But as you see, I'm in a very nasty hole. That five francs I gave you for the driver was the last penny I had in the world: absolutely the last penny. I haven't even anything to buy a cigarette or a stamp." And he laughed chirpily, as if it were a joke. But he didn't really think it a joke. Nor was it a joke.

I had come with only two hundred lire in my pocket, as I was waiting to change some money at the bank. Of this two hundred I had one hundred left or one hundred and twenty-five. I should need a hundred to get home. I could only give M— the twenty-five, for the bottle of drink. He was rather crestfallen. But I didn't want to give him money this time: because he expected it.

However, we talked about his plans: how he was to earn something. He told me what he had written. And I cast over in my mind where he might get something published in London, wrote a couple of letters on his account, told him where I thought he had best send his material. There wasn't a great deal of hope, for his smaller journalistic articles seemed to me very self-conscious and poor. He had one about the monastery, which I thought he might sell because of the photographs.

That evening he first showed me the Legion manuscript. He had got it rather raggedly typed out. He had a type-writer, but felt he ought to have somebody to do his typing for him, as he hated it and did it unwillingly. That evening and when I went to bed and when I woke in the morning I read this manuscript. It did not seem very good – vague and diffuse where it shouldn't have been – lacking in sharp detail and definite event. And yet there was something in it that made me want it done properly. So we talked about it, and discussed it carefully, and he unwillingly promised to tackle it again. He was curious, always talking about his work, even always working, but never *properly* doing anything.

We walked out in the afternoon through the woods and across the rocky bit of moorland which covers most of the hill-top. We were going to the ruined convent which lies on the other brow of the monastery hill, abandoned and sad among the rocks and heath and thorny bushes. It was sunny and warm. A barefoot little boy was tending a cow and three goats and a pony, a barefoot little girl had five geese in charge. We came to the convent and looked in. The further part of the courtyard was still entire, the place was a sort of farm, two rooms occupied by a peasant-farmer. We climbed about the ruins. Some creature was crying – crying, crying, crying with a strange, inhuman persistence, leaving off and crying again. We listened and listened – the sharp, poignant crying. Almost it might have been a sharp-voiced baby. We scrambled about, looking. And at last outside a little cave-like place found a blind black puppy crawling miserably on the floor, unable to walk, and crying incessantly. We put it back in the little cave-like shed, and went away. The place was deserted save for the crying puppy.

On the road outside however was a man, a peasant, just drawing up to the arched convent gateway with an ass under a load of brushwood.

He was thin and black and dirty. He took off his hat, and we told him of the puppy. He said the bitch-mother had gone off with his son with the sheep. Yes, she had been gone all day. Yes, she would be back at sunset. No, the puppy had not drunk all day. Yes, the little beast cried, but the mother would come back to him.

They were the old-world peasants still about the monastery, with the hard, small bony heads and deep-lined faces and utterly blank minds, crying their speech as crows cry, and living their lives as lizards among the rocks, blindly going on with the little job in hand, the present moment, cut off from all past and future, and having no idea and no sustained emotion, only that eternal will-to-live which makes a tortoise wake up once more in spring, and makes a grasshopper whistle on in the moonlight nights even of November. Only these peasants don't whistle much. The whistlers go to America. It is the hard, static, unhoping souls that persist in the old life. And still they stand back, as one passes them in the corridors of the great monastery, they press themselves back against the whitewashed walls of the still place, and drop their heads, as if some mystery were passing by, some God-mystery, the higher beings, which they must not look closely upon. So also this old peasant – he was not old, but deep-lined like a gnarled bough. He stood with his hat down in his hands as we spoke to him and answered the short, hard, insentient answers, as a tree might speak.

"The monks keep their peasants humble," I said to M——.

"Of course!" he said. "Don't you think they are quite right? Don't you think they should be humble?" And he bridled like a little turkey-cock on his hind legs.

"Well," I said, "if there's any occasion for humility, I do."

"Don't you think there is occasion?" he cried. "If there's one thing worse than another, it's this *equality* that has come into the world. Do you believe in it yourself?"

"No," I said. "I don't believe in equality. But the problem is, wherein does superiority lie."

"Oh," chirped M—— complacently. "It lies in many things. It lies in birth and in upbringing and so on, but it is chiefly in *mind*. Don't you think? Of course I don't mean that the physical qualities aren't *charming*. They are, and nobody appreciates them more than I do. Some of the peasants are *beautiful* creatures, perfectly beautiful. But that passes. And the mind endures."

I did not answer. M—— was not a man one talked far with. But I thought to myself, I *could* not accept M——'s superiority to the peasant. If I had really to live always under the same roof with either one of them, I would have chosen the peasant. If I had had to choose, I would have chosen the peasant. Not because the peasant was wonderful and stored with mystic qualities. No, I don't give much for the wonderful mystic qualities in peasants. Money is their mystery of mysteries, absolutely. No, if I chose the peasant it would be for what he *lacked* rather than for what he had. He lacked that complacent mentality that M—— was so proud of, he lacked all the trivial trash of glib talk and more glib thought, all the conceit of our shallow consciousness. For his mindlessness I would have chosen the peasant: and for his strong blood-presence. M—— wearied me with his facility and his readiness to rush into speech, and for the exhaustive nature of his presence. As if he had no strong blood in him to sustain him, only this modern parasitic lymph which cries for sympathy all the, time.

"Don't you think yourself that you are superior to that peasant?" he asked me, rather ironically. He half expected me to say no.

"Yes, I do," I replied. "But I think most middle-class, most so-called educated people are inferior to the peasant. I do that."

"Of course," said M—— readily. "In their *hypocrisy*——" He was great against hypocrisy – especially the English sort.

"And if I think myself superior to the peasant, it is only that I feel myself like the growing tip, or one of the growing tips of the tree, and him like a piece of the hard, fixed tissue of the branch or trunk. We're part of the same tree: and it's the same sap," said I.

"Why, exactly! Exactly!" cried M——. "Of course! The Church would teach the same doctrine. We are all one in Christ – but between our souls and our duties there are great differences."

It is terrible to be agreed with, especially by a man like M——. All that one says, and means, turns to nothing.

"Yes," I persisted. "But it seems to me the so-called culture, education, the so-called leaders and leading-classes to-day, are only parasites – like a great flourishing bush of parasitic consciousness flourishing on top of the tree of life, and sapping it. The consciousness of to-day doesn't rise from the roots. It is just parasitic in the veins of life. And the middle and upper classes are just parasitic upon the body of life which still remains in the lower classes."

"What!" said M—— acidly. "Do you believe in the democratic lower classes?"

"Not a bit," said I.

"I should think not, indeed!" he cried complacently.

"No, I don't believe the lower classes can ever make life whole again, till they *do* become humble, like the old peasants, and yield themselves to real leaders. But not to great negators like Lloyd George or Lenin or Briand."

"Of course! of course!" he cried. "What you need is the Church in power again. The Church has a place for everybody."

"You don't think the Church belongs to the past?" I asked.

"Indeed I don't, or I shouldn't be here. No," he said sententiously, "the Church is eternal. It puts people in their proper place. It puts women down into *their* proper place, which is the first thing to be done——"

He had a great dislike of women, and was very acid about them. Not because of their sins, but because of their virtues: their economies, their philanthropies, their spiritualities. Oh, how he loathed women. He had been married, but the marriage had not been a success. He smarted still. Perhaps his wife had despised him, and he had not *quite* been able to defeat her contempt.

So, he loathed women, and wished for a world of men. "They talk about love between men and women," he said. "Why it's all a *fraud*. The woman is just taking all and giving nothing, and feeling sanctified about it. All she tries to do is to thwart a man in whatever he is doing. No, I have found my life in my *friendships*. Physical relationships are very attractive, of course, and one tries to keep them as decent and all that as one can. But one knows they will pass and be finished. But one's *mental* friendships last for ever."

"With me, on the contrary," said I. "If there is no profound blood-sympathy, I know the mental friendship is trash. If there is real, deep blood response, I will stick to that if I have to betray all the mental sympathies I ever made, or all the lasting spiritual loves I ever felt."

He looked at me, and his face seemed to fall. Round the eyes he was yellow and tired and nervous. He watched me for some time.

"Oh!" he said, in a queer tone, rather cold. "Well, my experience has been the opposite."

We were silent for some time,

"And you," I said, "even if you do manage to do all your studies and enter the monastery, do you think you will be satisfied?"

"If I can be so fortunate, I do really," he said. "Do you doubt it?"

"Yes," I said. "Your nature is worldly, more worldly than mine. Yet I should die if I had to stay up here."

"Why?" he asked, curiously.

"Oh, I don't know. The past, the past. The beautiful, the wonderful past, it seems to prey on my heart, I can't bear it."

He watched me closely.

"Really!" he said stoutly. "Do you feel like that? But don't you think it is a far preferable life up here than down there? Don't you think the past is far preferable to the future, with all this *socialismo* and these *communisti* and so on?"

We were seated, in the sunny afternoon, on the wild hill-top high above the world. Across the stretch of pale, dry, standing thistles that peopled the waste ground, and beyond the rocks was the ruined convent. Rocks rose behind us, the summit. Away on the left were the woods which hid us from the great monastery. This was the mountain top, the last foothold of the old world. Below we could see the plain, the straight white road, straight as a thought, and the more flexible black railway with the railway station. There swarmed the *ferrovieri* like ants. There was democracy, industrialism, socialism, the red flag of the communists and the red, white and green tricolor of the fascist! That was another world. And how bitter, how barren a world! Barren like the black cinder-track of the railway, with its two steel lines.

And here above, sitting with the little stretch of pale, dry thistles around us, our back to a warm rock, we were in the Middle Ages. Both worlds were agony to me. But here, on the mountain top was worst: The past, the poignancy of the not-quite-dead past.

"I think one's got to go through with the life down there – get somewhere beyond it. One can't go back," I said to him.

"But do you call the monastery going back?" he said. "I don't. The peace, the eternity, the concern with things that matter. I consider it the happiest fate that could happen to me. Of course it means putting physical things aside. But when you've done that – why, it seems to me perfect."

"No," I said. "You're too worldly."

"But the monastery is worldly too. We're not Trappists. Why the monastery is one of the centres of the world – one of the most active centres."

"Maybe. But that impersonal activity, with the blood suppressed and going sour – no, it's too late. It is too abstract – political maybe ——"

"I'm sorry you think so," he said, rising. "I don't."

"Well," I said. "You'll never be a monk here, M——. You see if you are."

"You don't think I shall?" he replied, turning to me. And there was a catch of relief in his voice. Really, the monastic state must have been like going to prison for him.

"You haven't a vocation," I said.

"I may not *seem* to have, but I hope I actually have."

"You haven't."

"Of course, if you're so sure," he laughed, putting his hand on my arm.

He seemed to understand so much, round about the questions that trouble one deepest. But the quick of the question he never felt. He had no real middle, no real centre bit to him. Yet, round and round about all the questions, he was so intelligent and sensitive.

We went slowly back. The peaks of those Italian mountains in the sunset, the extinguishing twinkle of the plain away below, as the sun declined and grew yellow; the intensely powerful mediaeval spirit lingering on this wild hill summit, all the wonder of the mediaeval past; and then the huge mossy stones in the wintry wood, that was once a sacred grove; the ancient path through the wood, that led from temple to temple on the hill summit, before Christ was born; and then the great Cyclopean wall one passes at the bend of the road, built even before the pagan temples; all this overcame me so powerfully this afternoon, that I was almost speechless. That hill-top must have been one of man's intense sacred places for three thousand years. And men die generation after generation, races die, but the new cult finds root in the old sacred place, and the quick spot of earth dies very slowly. Yet at last it too dies. But this quick spot is still not quite dead. The great monastery couchant there, half empty, but also not quite dead. And M—— and I walking across as the sun set yellow and the cold of the snow came into the air, back home to the monastery! And I feeling as if my heart had once more broken: I don't know why. And he feeling his fear of life, that haunted him, and his fear of his own self and its consequences, that never left him for long. And he seemed to walk close to me, very close. And we had neither of us anything more to say.

Don Bernardo was looking for us as we came up under the archway, he hatless in the cold evening, his black dress swinging voluminous. There were letters for M——. There was a small cheque for him from America – about fifty dollars – from some newspaper in the Middle West that had printed one of his articles. He had to talk with Don Bernardo about this.

I decided to go back the next day. I could not stay any longer. M—— was very disappointed, and begged me to remain. "I thought you would stay a week at least," he said. "Do stay over Sunday. Oh do!" But I couldn't,

I didn't want to. I could see that his days were a torture to him – the long, cold days in that vast quiet building, with the strange and exhausting silence in the air, and the sense of the past preying on one, and the sense of the silent, suppressed scheming struggle of life going on still in the sacred place.

It was a cloudy morning. In the green courtyard the big Don Anselmo had just caught the little Don Lorenzo round the waist and was swinging him over a bush, like lads before school. The Prior was just hurrying somewhere, following his long fine nose. He bade me goodbye; pleasant, warm, jolly, with a touch of wistfulness in his deafness. I parted with real regret from Don Bernardo.

M—— was coming with me down the hill – not down the carriage road, but down the wide old paved path that swoops so wonderfully from the top of the hill to the bottom. It feels thousands of years old. M—— was quiet and friendly. We met Don Vincenzo, he who has the care of the land and crops, coming slowly, slowly uphill in his black cassock, treading slowly with his great thick boots. He was reading a little book. He saluted us as we passed. Lower down a strapping girl was watching three merino sheep among the bushes. One sheep came on its exquisite slender legs to smell of me, with that insatiable curiosity of a pecora. Her nose was silken and elegant as she reached it to sniff at me, and the yearning, wondering, inquisitive look in her eyes, made me realize that the Lamb of God must have been such a sheep as this.

M—— was miserable at my going. Not so much at my going, as at being left alone up there. We came to the foot of the hill, on to the town highroad. So we went into a little cave of a wine-kitchen to drink a glass of wine. M—— chatted a little with the young woman. He chatted with everybody. She eyed us closely – and asked if we were from the monastery. We said we were. She seemed to have a little lurking antagonism round her nose, at the mention of the monastery. M—— paid for the wine – a franc. So we went out on the highroad, to part.

"Look," I said. "I can only give you twenty lire, because I shall need the rest for the journey—— "

But he wouldn't take them. He looked at me wistfully. Then I went on down to the station, he turned away uphill. It was market in the town, and there were clusters of bullocks, and women cooking a little meal at a brazier under the trees, and goods spread out on the floor to sell, and sacks of beans and corn standing open, clustered round the trunks of the mulberry trees, and wagons with their shafts on the ground. The old peasants in their brown homespun frieze and skin sandals were watching for the world. And there again was the Middle Ages.

It began to rain, however. Suddenly it began to pour with rain, and my coat was wet through, and my trouser-legs. The train from Rome was late – I hoped not very late, or I should miss the boat. She came at last: and was full. I had to stand in the corridor. Then the man came to say dinner was served, so I luckily got a place and had my meal too. Sitting there in the dining-car, among the fat Neapolitans eating their macaroni, with the big glass windows steamed opaque and the rain beating outside, I let myself be carried away, away from the monastery, away from M——, away from everything.

At Naples there was a bit of sunshine again, and I had time to go on foot to the Immacolatella, where the little steamer lay. There on the steamer I sat in a bit of sunshine, and felt that again the world had come to an end for me, and again my heart was broken. The steamer seemed to be making its way away from the old world, that had come to another end in me.

It was after this I decided to go to Sicily. In February, only a few days after my return from the monastery, I was on the steamer for Palermo, and at dawn looking out on the wonderful coast of Sicily. Sicily, tall, forever rising up to her gem-like summits, all golden in dawn, and always glamorous, always hovering as if inaccessible, and yet so near, so distinct. Sicily unknown to me, and amethystine-glamorous in the Mediterranean dawn: like the dawn of our day, the wonder-morning of our epoch.

I had various letters from M——. He had told me to go to Girgenti. But I arrived in Girgenti when there was a strike of sulphur-miners, and they threw stones. So I did not want to live in Girgenti. M—— hated Taormina – he had been everywhere, tried everywhere, and was not, I found, in any good odour in most places. He wrote however saying he hoped I would like it. And later he sent the Legion manuscript. I thought it was good, and told him so. It was offered to publishers in London, but rejected.

In early April I went with my wife to Syracuse for a few days: lovely, lovely days, with the purple anemones blowing in the Sicilian fields, and Adonis-blood red on the little ledges, and the corn rising strong and green in the magical, malarial places, and Etna flowing now to the northward, still with her crown of snow. The lovely, lovely journey from Catania to Syracuse, in spring, winding round the blueness of that sea, where the tall pink asphodel was dying, and the yellow asphodel like a lily showing her silk. Lovely, lovely Sicily, the dawn-place, Europe's dawn, with Odysseus pushing his ship out of the shadows into the blue. Whatever had died for me, Sicily had then not died: dawn-lovely Sicily, and the Ionian sea.

We came back, and the world was lovely: our own house above the almond trees, and the sea in the cove below. Calabria glimmering like a changing opal away to the left, across the blue, bright straits, and all the great blueness of the lovely dawn-sea in front, where the sun rose with a splendour like trumpets every morning, and me rejoicing like a madness in this dawn, day-dawn, life-dawn, the dawn which is Greece, which is me.

Well, into this lyricism suddenly crept the serpent. It was a lovely morning, still early. I heard a noise on the stairs from the lower terrace, and went to look. M—— on the stairs, looking up at me with a frightened face.

"Why!" I said. "Is it you?"

"Yes," he replied. "A terrible thing has happened."

He waited on the stairs, and I went down. Rather unwillingly, because I detest terrible things, and the people to whom they happen. So we leaned on the creeper-covered rail of the terrace, under festoons of creamy bignonia flowers, and looked at the pale blue, ethereal sea.

"What terrible thing!" said I.

"When did you get back?" said he.

"Last evening."

"Oh! I came before. The contadini said they thought you would come yesterday evening. I've been here several days."

"Where are you staying?"

"At the San Domenico."

The San Domenico being then the most expensive hotel here, I thought he must have money. But I knew he wanted something of me.

"And are you staying some time?"

He paused a moment, and looked round cautiously.

"Is your wife there?" he asked, sotto voce.

"Yes, she's upstairs."

"Is there anyone who can hear?"

"No – only old Grazia down below, and she can't understand anyhow."

"Well," he said, stammering. "Let me tell you what's happened. I had to escape from the monastery. Don Bernardo had a telephone message from the town below, that the carabinieri were looking for an Americano – my name—— Of course you can guess how I felt, up there! Awful! Well—— ! I had to fly at a moment's notice. I just put two shirts in a handbag and went. I slipped down a path – or rather, it isn't a path – down the back of the hill. Ten minutes after Don Bernardo had the message I was running down the hill."

"But what did they want you for?" I asked dismayed.

"Well," he faltered. "I told you about the cheque at Anzio, didn't I? Well, it seems the hotel people applied to the police. Anyhow," he added hastily, "I couldn't let myself be arrested up there, could I? So awful for the monastery!"

"Did they know then that you were in trouble?" I asked.

"Don Bernardo knew I had no money," he said. "Of course he had to know. Yes – he knew I was in *difficulty*. But, of course, he didn't know – well – *everything*." He laughed a little, comical laugh over the *everything*, as if he was just a little bit naughtily proud of it: most ruefully also.

"No," he continued, "that's what I'm most afraid of – that they'll find out everything at the monastery. Of course it's *dreadful* – the Americano, been staying there for months, and everything so nice and –, well you know how they are, they imagine every American is a millionaire, if not a multi-millionaire. And suddenly to be wanted by the police! Of course it's *dreadful!* Anything rather than a scandal at the monastery – anything. Oh, how awful it was! I can tell you, in that quarter of an hour, I sweated blood. Don Bernardo lent me two hundred lire of the monastery money – which he'd no business to do. And I escaped down the back of the hill, I walked to the next station up the line, and took the next train – the slow train – a few stations up towards Rome. And there I changed and caught the diretto for Sicily. I came straight to you—— Of course I was in *agony*: imagine it! I spent most of the time as far as Naples in the lavatory." He laughed his little jerky laugh.

"What class did you travel?"

"Second. All through the night. I arrived more dead than alive, not having had a meal for two days – only some sandwich stuff I bought on the platform."

"When did you come then?"

"I arrived on Saturday evening. I came out here on Sunday morning, and they told me you were away. Of course, imagine what it's like! I'm in torture every minute, in torture, of course. Why just imagine!" And he laughed his little laugh.

"But how much money have you got?"

"Oh – I've just got twenty-five francs and five soldi." He laughed as if it was rather a naughty joke.

"But," I said, "if you've got no money, why do you go to the San Domenico? How much do you pay there?"

"Fifty lire a day. Of course it's *ruinous* — "

"But at the Bristol you only pay twenty-five – and at Fichera's only twenty."

"Yes, I know you do," he said. "But I stayed at the Bristol once, and I loathed the place. Such an offensive manager. And I couldn't touch the food at Fichera's."

"But who's going to pay for the San Domenico, then?" I asked.

"Well, I thought," he said, "you know all those manuscripts of mine? Well, you think they're some good, don't you? Well, I thought if I made them over to you, and you did what you could with them and just kept me going till I can get a new start – or till I can get away— "

I looked across the sea: the lovely morning-blue sea towards Greece.

"Where do you want to get away to?" I said.

"To Egypt. I know a man in Alexandria who owns newspapers there. I'm sure if I could get over there he'd give me an editorship or something. And of course money will come. I've written to — , who was my *greatest* friend, in London. He will send me something — "

"And what else do you expect?"

"Oh, my article on the monastery was accepted by *Land and Water* – thanks to you and your kindness, of course. I thought if I might stay very quietly with you, for a time, and write some things I'm wanting to do, and collect a little money – and then get away to Egypt — "

He looked up into my face, as if he were trying all he could on me. First thing I knew was that I could not have him in the house with me: and even if I could have done it, my wife never could.

"You've got a lovely place here, perfectly beautiful," he said. "Of course, if it had to be Taormina, you've chosen far the best place here. I like this side so much better than the Etna side. Etna always there and people raving about it gets on my nerves. And a *charming* house, *charming*."

He looked round the loggia and along the other terrace.

"Is it all yours?" he said.

"We don't use the ground floor. Come in here."

So we went into the salotto.

"Oh, what a beautiful room," he cried. "But perfectly palatial. Charming! Charming! *Much* the nicest house in Taormina."

"No," I said, "as a house it isn't very grand, though I like it for myself. It's just what I want. And I love the situation. But I'll go and tell my wife you are here."

"Will you?" he said, bridling nervously. "Of course I've never met your wife." And he laughed the nervous, naughty, jokey little laugh.

I left him, and ran upstairs to the kitchen. There was my wife, with wide eyes. She had been listening to catch the conversation. But M——'s voice was too hushed.

"M—— !" said I softly. "The carabinieri wanted to arrest him at the monastery, so he has escaped here, and wants me to be responsible for him."

"Arrest him what for?"

"Debts, I suppose. Will you come down and speak to him?"

M—— of course was very charming with my wife. He kissed her hand humbly, in the correct German fashion, and spoke with an air of reverence that infallibly gets a woman.

"Such a beautiful place you have here," he said, glancing through the open doors of the room, at the sea beyond. "So clever of you to find it."

"Lawrence found it," said she. "Well, and you are in all kinds of difficulty!"

"Yes, isn't it terrible!" he said, laughing as if it were a joke – rather a wry joke. "I felt dreadful at the monastery. So dreadful for them, if there was any sort of scandal. And after I'd been so well received there – and so much the Signor Americano —— Dreadful, don't you think?" He laughed again, like a naughty boy.

We had an engagement to lunch that morning. My wife was dressed, so I went to get ready. Then we told M—— we must go out, and he accompanied us to the village. I gave him just the hundred francs I had in my pocket, and he said could he come and see me that evening? I asked him to come next morning.

"You're so awfully kind," he said, simpering a little.

But by this time I wasn't feeling kind.

"He's quite nice," said my wife. "But he's rather an impossible little person. And you'll see, he'll be a nuisance. Whatever do you pick up such dreadful people for?"

"Nay," I said. "You can't accuse me of picking up dreadful people. He's the first. And even he isn't dreadful."

The next morning came a letter from Don Bernardo addressed to me, but only enclosing a letter to M——. So he was using my address. At ten o'clock he punctually appeared: slipping in as if to avoid notice. My wife would not see him, so I took him out on the terrace again.

"Isn't it beautiful here!" he said. "Oh, so beautiful! If only I had my peace of mind. Of course I sweat blood every time anybody comes through the door. You are splendidly private out here."

"Yes," I said. "But M——, there isn't a room for you in the house. There isn't a spare room anyway. You'd better think of getting something cheaper in the village."

"But what can I get?" he snapped.

That rather took my breath away. Myself, I had never been near the San Domenico hotel. I knew I simply could not afford it.

"What made you go to the San Domenico in the first place?" I said. "The most expensive hotel in the place!"

"Oh, I'd stayed there for two months, and they knew me, and I knew they'd ask no questions. I knew they wouldn't ask for a deposit or anything."

"But nobody dreams of asking for a deposit," I said.

"Anyhow I shan't take my meals there. I shall just take coffee in the morning. I've had to eat there so far, because I was starved to death, and had no money to go out. But I had two meals in that little restaurant yesterday; disgusting food."

"And how much did that cost?"

"Oh fourteen francs and fifteen francs, with a quarter of wine – and such a poor meal!"

Now I was annoyed, knowing that I myself should have bought bread and cheese for one franc, and eaten it in my room. But also I realized that the modern creed says, if you sponge, sponge thoroughly: and also that every man has a "right to live," and that if he can manage to live well, no matter at whose expense, all credit to him. This is the kind of talk one accepts in one's slipshod moments; now it was actually tried on me, I didn't like it at all.

"But who's going to pay your bill at the San Domenico?" I said.

"I thought you'd advance me the money on those manuscripts."

"It's no good talking about the money on the manuscripts," I said. "I should have to give it to you. And as a matter of fact, I've got just sixty pounds in the bank in England, and about fifteen hundred lire here. My wife and I have got to live on that. We don't spend as much in a week as you spend in three days at the San Domenico. It's no good your thinking I can advance money on the manuscripts. I can't. If I was rich, I'd give you money. But I've got no money, and never have had any. Have you nobody you can go to?"

"I'm waiting to hear from ——. When I go back into the village, I'll telegraph to him," replied M——, a little crestfallen. "Of course I'm in torture night and day, or I wouldn't appeal to you like this. I know it's unpleasant for you —— " and he put his hand on my arm and looked up beseechingly. "But what am I to do?"

"You must get out of the San Domenico," I said. "That's the first thing."

"Yes," he said, a little piqued now. "I know it is. I'm going to ask Pancrazio Melenga to let me have a room in his house. He knows me quite well – he's an awfully nice fellow. He'll do *anything* for me – *anything*. I was just going there yesterday afternoon when you were coming from Timeo. He was out, so I left word with his wife, who is a charming little person. If he has a room to spare, I know he will let me have it. And he's a *splendid* cook —— splendid. By far the nicest food in Taormina."

"Well," I said. "If you settle with Melenga, I will pay your bill at the San Domenico, but I can't do any more. I simply can't."

"But what am I to *do*?" he snapped.

"I don't know," I said. "You must think."

"I came here," he said, "thinking you would help me. What am I to do, if you won't? I shouldn't have come to Taormina at all, save for you. Don't be unkind to me – don't speak so coldly to me —— " He put his hand on my arm, and looked up at me with tears swimming in his eyes. Then he turned aside his face, overcome with tears. I looked away at the Ionian sea, feeling my blood turn to ice and the sea go black. I loathe scenes such as this.

"Did you telegraph to —— ?" I said.

"Yes. I have no answer yet. I hope you don't mind – I gave your address for a reply."

"Oh," I said. "There's a letter for you from Don Bernardo."

He went pale. I was angry at his having used my address in this manner.

"Nothing further has happened at the monastery," he said. "They rang up from the Questura, from the police station, and Don Bernardo answered that the Americano had left for Rome. Of course I did take the train for Rome. And Don Bernardo wanted me to go to Rome. He advised me to do so. I didn't tell him I was here till I had got here. He thought I should have had more resources in Rome, and of course I should. I should certainly have gone there, if it hadn't been for *you here*——"

Well, I was getting tired and angry. I would not give him any more money at the moment. I promised, if he would leave the hotel I would pay his bill, but he must leave it at once. He went off to settle with Melenga. He asked again if he could come in the afternoon: I said I was going out.

He came nevertheless while I was out. This time my wife found him on the stairs. She was for hating him, of course. So she stood immovable on the top stair, and he stood two stairs lower, and he kissed her hand in utter humility. And he pleaded with her, and as he looked up to her on the stairs the tears ran down his face and he trembled with distress. And her spine crept up and down with distaste and discomfort. But he broke into a few phrases of touching German, and I know he broke down her reserve and she promised him all he wanted. This part she would never confess, though. Only she was shivering with revulsion and excitement and even a sense of power, when I came home.

That was why M—— appeared more impertinent than ever, next morning. He had arranged to go to Melenga's house the following day, and to pay ten francs a day for his room, his meals extra. So that was something. He made a long tale about not eating any of his meals in the hotel now, but pretending he was invited out, and eating in the little restaurants where the food was so bad. And he had now only fifteen lire left in his pocket. But I was cold, and wouldn't give him any more. I said I would give him money next day, for his bill.

He had now another request, and a new tone.

"Won't you do *one more* thing for me?" he said. "Oh do! Do do this one thing for me. I want you to go to the monastery and bring away my important papers and some clothes and my important trinkets. I have made a list of the things here – and where you'll find them in my writing-table and in the chest of drawers. I don't think you'll have any trouble. Don Bernardo has the keys. He will open everything for you. And I beg you, *in the name of God*, don't let anybody else see the things. Not even Don Bernardo. Don't, whatever you do, let him see the papers and manuscripts you are bringing. If he sees them, there's an end to me at the monastery. I can *never* go back there. I am ruined in their eyes for ever. As it is – although Don Bernardo is the best person in the world and my dearest friend, still – you know what people are – especially monks. A little curious, don't you know, a little inquisitive. Well, let us hope for the best as far as that goes. But you will do this for me, won't you? I shall be so eternally grateful."

Now a journey to the monastery meant a terrible twenty hours in the train each way – all that awful journey through Calabria to Naples and northwards. It meant mixing myself up in this man's affairs. It meant appearing as his accomplice at the monastery. It meant travelling with all his "compromising" papers and his valuables. And all this time, I never knew what mischiefs he had really been up to, and I didn't trust him, not for one single second. He would tell me nothing save that Anzio hotel cheque. I knew that wasn't all, by any means. So I mistrusted him. And with a feeling of utter mistrust goes a feeling of contempt and dislike—— And finally, it would have cost me at least ten pounds sterling, which I simply did not want to spend in waste.

"I don't want to do that," I said.

"Why not?" he asked, sharp, looking green. He had planned it all out.

"No, I don't want to."

"Oh, but I *can't* remain here as I am. I've got no *clothes* – I've got nothing to *wear*. I *must* have my things from the monastery. What can I do? What can I do? I came to you, if it hadn't been for you I should have gone to Rome. I came to you – Oh yes, you *will* go. You *will* go, won't you? You *will* go to the monastery for my things?" And again he put his hand on my arm, and the tears began to fall from his upturned eyes. I turned my head aside. Never had the Ionian sea looked so sickening to me.

"I don't *want* to," said I.

"But you *will!* You will! You *will* go to the monastery for me, won't you? Everything else is no good if you won't. I've nothing to wear. I haven't got my manuscripts to work on, I can't do the things I am doing. Here I live in a sweat of anxiety. I try to work, and I can't settle. I can't do anything. It's dreadful. I shan't have a minute's peace till I have got those things from the monastery, till I know they can't get at my private papers. You will do this for me! You will, won't you? Please do! Oh please do!" And again tears.

And I with my bowels full of bitterness, loathing the thought of that journey there and back, on such an errand. Yet not quite sure that I ought to refuse. And he pleaded and struggled, and tried to bully me with tears and entreaty and reproach, to do his will. And I couldn't quite refuse. But neither could I agree.

At last I said:

"I don't want to go, and I tell you. I won't promise to go. And I won't say that I will not go. I won't say until to-morrow. To-morrow I will tell you. Don't come to the house. I will be in the Corso at ten o'clock."

"I didn't doubt for a minute you would do this for me," he said. "Otherwise I should never have come to Taormina." As if he had done me an honour in coming to Taormina; and as if I had betrayed *him*.

"Well," I said. "If you make these messes you'll have to get out of them yourself. I don't know why you are *in* such a mess."

"Any man may make a mistake," he said sharply, as if correcting me.

"Yes, a *mistake!*" said I. "If it's a question of a mistake."

So once more he went, humbly, beseechingly, and yet, one could not help but feel, with all that terrible insolence of the humble. It is the humble, the wistful, the would-be-loving souls to-day who bully us with their charity-demanding insolence. They just make up their minds, these needful sympathetic souls, that one is there to do their will. Very good.

I decided in the day I would *not* go. Without reasoning it out, I knew I *really* didn't want to go. I plainly didn't want it. So I wouldn't go.

The morning came again hot and lovely. I set off to the village. But there was M—— watching for me on the path beyond the valley. He came forward and took my hand warmly, clingingly. I turned back, to remain in the country. We talked for a minute of his leaving the hotel – he was going that afternoon, he had asked for his bill. But he was waiting for the other answer.

"And I have decided," I said, "I won't go to the monastery."

"You won't." He looked at me. I saw how yellow he was round the eyes, and yellow under his reddish skin.

"No," I said.

And it was final. He knew it. We went some way in silence. I turned in at the garden gate. It was a lovely, lovely morning of hot sun. Butterflies were flapping over the rosemary hedges and over a few little red poppies, the young vines smelt sweet in flower, very sweet, the corn was tall and green, and there were still some wild, rose-red gladiolus flowers among the watery green of the wheat. M—— had accepted my refusal. I expected him to be angry. But no, he seemed quieter, wistfuller, and he seemed almost to love me for having refused him. I stood at a bend in the path. The sea was heavenly blue, rising up beyond the vines and olive leaves, lustrous pale lacquer blue as only the Ionian sea can be. Away at the brook below the women were washing, and one could hear the chock-chock-chock of linen beaten against the stones. I felt M—— then an intolerable weight and like a clot of dirt over everything.

"May I come in?" he said to me.

"No," I said. "Don't come to the house. My wife doesn't want it."

Even that he accepted without any offence, and seemed only to like me better for it. That was a puzzle to me. I told him I would leave a letter and a cheque for him at the bank in the Corso that afternoon.

I did so, writing a cheque for a few pounds, enough to cover his bill and leave a hundred lire or so over, and a letter to say I could *not* do any more, and I didn't want to see him any more.

So, there was an end of it for a moment. Yet I felt him looming in the village, waiting. I had rashly said I would go to tea with him to the villa of one of the Englishmen resident here, whose acquaintance I had not made. Alas, M—— kept me to the promise. As I came home he appealed to me again. He was rather insolent. What good to him, he said, were the few pounds I had given him? He had got a hundred and fifty lire left. What good was that? I realized it really was not a solution, and said nothing. Then he spoke of his plans for getting to Egypt. The fare, he had found out, was thirty-five pounds. And where were thirty-five pounds coming from? Not from me.

I spent a week avoiding him, wondering what on earth the poor devil was doing, and yet *determined* he should not be a parasite on me. If I could have given him fifty pounds and sent him to Egypt to be a parasite on somebody else, I would have done so. Which is what we call charity. However, I couldn't.

My wife chafed, crying: "What have you done! We shall have him on our hands all our life. We can't let him starve. It is degrading, degrading, to have him hanging on to us."

"Yes," I said. "He must starve or work or something. I am not God who is responsible for him."

M—— was determined not to lose his status as a gentleman. In a way I sympathized with him. He would never be out at elbows. That is your modern rogue. He will not degenerate outwardly. Certain standards of a gentleman he *would* keep up: he would be well-dressed, he would be lavish with borrowed money, he would be as far as possible honourable in his small transactions of daily life. Well, very good. I sympathized with him to a certain degree. If he could find his own way out, well and good. Myself, I was not his way out.

Ten days passed. It was hot and I was going about the terrace in pyjamas and a big old straw hat, when suddenly, a Sicilian, handsome, in the prime of life, and in his best black suit, smiling at me and taking off his hat!

And could he speak to me. I threw away my straw hat, and we went into the salotto. He handed me a note.

"Il Signor M—— mi ha dato questa lettera per Lei!" he began, and I knew what was coming. Melenga had been a waiter in good hotels, had saved money, built himself a fine house which he let to foreigners. He was a pleasant fellow, and at his best now, because he was in a rage. I must repeat M——'s letter from memory – "Dear Lawrence, would you do me another kindness. *Land and Water* sent a cheque for seven guineas for the article on the monastery, and Don Bernardo forwarded this to me under Melenga's name. But unfortunately he made a mistake, and put Orazio instead of Pancrazio, so the post office would not deliver the letter, and have returned it to the monastery. This morning Melenga insulted me, and I cannot stay in his house another minute. Will you be so kind as to advance me these seven guineas, and I shall leave Taormina at once, for Malta."

I asked Melenga what had happened, and read him the letter. He was handsome in his rage, lifting his brows and suddenly smiling:

"Ma senta, Signore! Signor M—— has been in my house for ten days, and lived well, and eaten well, and drunk well, and I have not seen a single penny of his money. I go out in the morning and buy all the things, all he wants, and my wife cooks it, and he is very pleased, very pleased, has never eaten such good food in his life, and everything is splendid, splendid. And he never pays a penny. Not a penny. Says he is waiting for money from England, from America, from India. But the money never comes. And I am a poor man, signore, I have a wife and child to keep. I have already spent three hundred lire for this Signor M——, and I never see a penny of it back. And he says the money is coming, it is coming —— But when? He never says he has got no money. He says he is expecting. To-morrow – always to-morrow. It will come to-night, it will come to-morrow. This makes me in a rage. Till at last this morning I said to him I would bring nothing in, and he shouldn't have not so much as a drop of coffee in my house until he paid for it. It displeases me, Signore, to say such a thing. I have known Signor M—— for many years, and he has always had money, and always been pleasant, molto bravo, and also generous with his money. Si, lo so! And my wife, poverina, she cries and says if the man has no money he must eat. But he doesn't say he has no money. He says always it is coming, it is coming, to-day, to-morrow, to-day, to-morrow. E non viene mai niente. And this enrages me, Signore. So I said that to him this morning. And he said he wouldn't stay in my house, and that I had insulted him, and he sends me this letter to you, signore, and says you will send him the money. Ecco come!"

Between his rage he smiled at me. One thing however I could see: he was not going to lose his money, M—— or no M——.

"Is it true that a letter came which the post would not deliver?" I asked him.

"Si signore, e vero. It came yesterday, addressed to me. And why, signore, why do his letters come addressed in my name? Why? Unless he has done something—— ?"

He looked at me enquiringly. I felt already mixed up in shady affairs.

"Yes," I said, "there is something. But I don't know exactly what. I don't ask, because I don't want to know in these affairs. It is better not to know."

"Gia! Gia! Molto meglio, signore. There will be something. There will be something happened that he had to escape from that monastery. And it will be some affair of the police."

"Yes, I think so," said I. "Money and the police. Probably debts. I don't ask. He is only an acquaintance of mine, not a friend."

"Sure it will be an affair of the police," he said with a grimace. "If not, why does he use my name! Why don't his letters come in his own name? Do you believe, signore, that he has any money? Do you think this money will come?"

"I'm sure he's *got* no money," I said. "Whether anybody will send him any I don't know."

The man watched me attentively.

"He's got nothing?" he said.

"No. At the present he's got nothing."

Then Pancrazio exploded on the sofa.

"Allora! Well then! Well then, why does he come to my house, why does he come and take a room in my house, and ask me to buy food, good food as for a gentleman who can pay, and a flask of wine, and everything, if he has no money. If he has no money, why does he come to Taormina? It is many years that he has been in Italy — ten years, fifteen years. And he has no money. Where has he had his money from before? Where?"

"From his writing, I suppose."

"Well then why doesn't he get money for his writing now? He writes. He writes, he works, he says it is for the big newspapers."

"It is difficult to sell things."

"Heh! then why doesn't he live on what he made before? He hasn't a soldo. He hasn't a penny – But how! How did he pay his bill at the San Domenico?"

"I had to lend him the money for that. He really hadn't a penny."

"You! You! Well then, he has been in Italy all these years. How is it he has nobody that he can ask for a hundred lire or two? Why does he come to you? Why? Why has he nobody in Rome, in Florence, anywhere?"

"I wonder that myself."

"Sicuro! He's been all these years here. And why doesn't he speak proper Italian? After all these years, and speaks all upside-down, it isn't Italian, an ugly confusion. Why? Why? He passes for a signore, for a man of education. And he comes to take the bread out of my mouth. And I have a wife and child, I am a poor man, I have nothing to eat myself if everything goes to a mezzo-signore like him. Nothing! He owes me now three hundred lire. But he will not leave my house, he will not leave Taormina till he has paid. I will go to the Prefettura, I will go to the Questura, to the police. I will not be swindled by such a mezzo-signore. What does he want to do? If he has no money, what does he want to do?"

"To go to Egypt where he says he can earn some," I replied briefly. But I was feeling bitter in the mouth. When the man called M—— a mezzo-signore, a half-gentleman, it was so true. And at the same time it was so cruel, and so rude. And Melenga – there I sat in my pyjamas and sandals – probably he would be calling me also a mezzo-signore, or a quarto-signore even. He was a Sicilian who feels he is being done out of his money – and that is saying everything.

"To Egypt! And who will pay for him to go? Who will give him money? But he must pay me first. He must pay me first."

"He says," I said, "that in the letter which went back to the monastery there was a cheque for seven pounds – some six hundred lire – and he asks me to send him this money, and when the letter is returned again I shall have the cheque that is in it."

Melenga watched me.

"Six hundred lire——" he said.

"Yes."

"Oh well then. If he pays me, he can stay——" he said; he almost added: "till the six hundred is finished." But he left it unspoken.

"But am I going to send the money? Am I sure that what he says is true?"

"I think it is true. I think it is true," said he. "The letter *did* come."

I thought for a while.

"First," I said, "I will write and ask him if it is quite true, and to give me a guarantee."

"Very well," said Melenga.

I wrote to M——, saying that if he could assure me that what he said about the seven guineas was quite correct, and if he would give me a note to the editor of *Land and Water*, saying that the cheque was to be paid to me, I would send the seven guineas.

Melenga was back in another half-hour. He brought a note which began:

"Dear Lawrence, I seem to be living in an atmosphere of suspicion. First Melenga this morning, and now you—— " Those are the exact opening words. He went on to say that of course his word was true, and he enclosed a note to the editor, saying the seven guineas were to be transferred to me. He asked me please to send the money, as he could not stay another night at Melenga's house, but would leave for Catania, where, by the sale of some trinkets, he hoped to make some money and to see once more about a passage to Egypt. He had been to Catania once already – travelling *third class!* – but had failed to find any cargo boat that would take him to Alexandria. He would get away now to Malta. His things were being sent down to Syracuse from the monastery.

I wrote and said I hoped he would get safely away, and enclosed the cheque.

"This will be for six hundred lire," said Melenga.

"Yes," said I.

"Eh, va bene! If he pays the three hundred lire, he can stop in my house for thirty lire a day."

"He says he won't sleep in your house again."

"Ma! Let us see. If he likes to stay. He has always been a bravo signore. I have always liked him quite well. If he wishes to stay and pay me thirty lire a day——"

The man smiled at me rather greenly.

"I'm afraid he is offended," said I.

"Eh, va bene! Ma senta, signore. When he was here before – you know I have this house of mine to let. And you know the English signorina goes away in the summer. Oh, very well. Says M——, he writes for a newspaper, he owns a newspaper, I don't know what, in Rome. He will put in an advertisement advertising my villa. And so I shall get somebody to take it. Very well. And he put in the advertisement. He sent me the paper and

I saw it there. But no one came to take my villa. Va bene! But after a year, in the January, that is, came a bill for me for twenty-two lire to pay for it. Yes, I had to pay the twenty-two lire, for nothing – for the advertisement which Signore M—— put in the paper."

"Bah!" said I.

He shook hands with me and left. The next day he came after me in the street and said that M—— had departed the previous evening for Catania. As a matter of fact the post brought me a note of thanks from Catania. M—— was never indecent, and one could never dismiss him just as a scoundrel. He was not. He was one of these modern parasites who just assume their right to live and live well, leaving the payment to anybody who can, will, or must pay. The end is inevitably swindling.

There came also a letter from Rome, addressed to me. I opened it unthinking. It was for M——, from an Italian lawyer, stating that enquiry had been made about the writ against M——, and that it was for *qualche affaro di truffa*, some affair of swindling: that the lawyer had seen this, that and the other person, but nothing could be done. He regretted, etc. etc. I forwarded this letter to M—— at Syracuse, and hoped to God it was ended. Ah, I breathed free now he had gone.

But no. A friend who was with us dearly wanted to go to Malta. It is only about eighteen hours' journey from Taormina – easier than going to Naples. So our friend invited us to take the trip with her, as her guests. This was rather jolly. I calculated that M——, who had been gone a week or so, would easily have got to Malta. I had had a friendly letter from him from Syracuse, thanking me for the one I had forwarded, and enclosing an I.O.U. for the various sums of money he had had.

So, on a hot, hot Thursday, we were sitting in the train again running south, the four and a half hours journey to Syracuse. And M—— dwindled now into the past. If we should see him! But no, it was impossible. After all the wretchedness of that affair we were in holiday spirits.

The train ran into Syracuse station. We sat on, to go the few yards further into the port. A tout climbed on the foot-board: were we going to Malta? Well, we couldn't. There was a strike of the steamers, we couldn't go. When would the steamer go? Who knows? Perhaps to-morrow.

We got down crestfallen. What should we do? There stood the express train about to start off back northwards. We could be home again that evening. But no, it would be too much of a fiasco. We let the train go, and trailed off into the town, to the Grand Hotel, which is an old Italian place just opposite the port. It is rather a dreary hotel – and many bloodstains of squashed mosquitoes on the bedroom walls. Ah, vile mosquitoes!

However, nothing to be done. Syracuse port is fascinating too, a tiny port with the little Sicilian ships having the slanting eyes painted on the prow, to see the way, and a coal boat from Cardiff, and one American and two Scandinavian steamers – no more. But there were two torpedo boats in the harbour, and it was like a festa, a strange, lousy festa.

Beautiful the round harbour where the Athenian ships came. And wonderful, beyond, the long sinuous sky-line of the long flat-topped table-land hills which run along the southern coast, so different from the peaky, pointed, bunched effect of many-tipped Sicily in the north. The sun went down behind that lovely, sinuous sky-line, the harbour water was gold and red, the people promenaded in thick streams under the pomegranate trees and hibiscus trees. Arabs in white burnouses and fat Turks in red fezzes and black alpaca long coats strolled also – waiting for the steamer.

Next day it was very hot. We went to the consul and the steamer agency. There was real hope that the brute of a steamer might actually sail that night. So we stayed on, and wandered round the town on the island, the old solid town, and sat in the church looking at the grand Greek columns embedded there in the walls.

When I came in to lunch the porter said there was a letter for me. Impossible! said I. But he brought me a note. Yes. M—— ! He was staying at the other hotel along the front. "Dear Lawrence, I saw you this morning, all three of you walking down the Via Nazionale, but you would not look at me. I have got my visés and everything ready. The strike of the steamboats has delayed me here. I am sweating blood. I have a last request to make of you. Can you let me have ninety lire, to make up what I need for my hotel bill? If I cannot have this I am lost. I hoped to find you at the hotel but the porter said you were out. I am at the Casa Politi, passing every half-hour in agony. If you can be so kind as to stretch your generosity to this last loan, of course I shall be eternally grateful. I can pay you back once I get to Malta——"

Well, here was a blow! The worst was that he thought I had cut him – a thing I wouldn't have done. So after luncheon behold me going through the terrific sun of that harbour front of Syracuse, an enormous and powerful sun, to the Casa Politi. The porter recognized roe and looked enquiringly. M—— was out, and I said I would call again at four o'clock.

It happened we were in the town eating ices at four, so I didn't get to his hotel till half-past. He was out – gone to look for me. So I left a note saying I had not seen him in the Via Nazionale, that I had called twice, and that I should be in the Grand Hotel in the evening.

When we came in at seven, M—— in the hall, sitting the picture of misery and endurance. He took my hand in both his, and bowed to the women, who nodded and went upstairs. He and I went and sat in the empty lounge. Then he told me the trials he had had – how his luggage had come, and the station had charged him eighteen lire a day for deposit – how he had had to wait on at the hotel because of the ship – how he had tried to sell his trinkets, and had to-day parted with his opal sleeve-links – so that now he only wanted seventy, not ninety lire. I gave him a hundred note, and he looked into my eyes, his own eyes swimming with tears, and he said he was sweating blood.

Well, the steamer went that night. She was due to leave at ten. We went on board after dinner. We were going second class. And so, for once, was M——. It was only an eight hours' crossing, yet, in spite of all the blood he had sweated, he would not go third class. In a way I admired him for sticking to his principles. I should have gone third myself, out of shame of spending somebody else's money. He would not give way to such weakness. He knew that as far as the world goes, you're a first-class gentleman if you have a first-class ticket; if you have a third, no gentleman at all. It behoved him to be a gentleman. I understood his point, but the women were indignant. And I was just rather tired of him and his gentlemanliness.

It amused me very much to lean on the rail of the upper deck and watch the people coming on board – first going into the little customs house with their baggage, then scuffling up the gangway on board. The tall Arabs in their ghostly white woollen robes came carrying their sacks: they were going on to Tripoli. The fat Turk in his fez and long black alpaca coat with white drawers underneath came beaming up to the second class. There was a great row in the customs house: and then, simply running like a beetle with rage, there came on board a little Maltese or Greek fellow, followed by a tall lantern-jawed fellow: both seedy-looking scoundrels suckled in scoundrelism. They raved and nearly threw their arms away into the sea, talking wildly in some weird language with the fat Turk, who listened solemnly, away below on the deck. Then they rushed to somebody else. Of course, we were dying with curiosity. Thank heaven I heard men talking in Italian. It appears the two seedy fellows were trying to smuggle silver coin in small sacks and rolls out of the country. They were detected. But they declared they had a right to take it away, as it was foreign specie, English florins and half-crowns, and South American dollars and Spanish money. The customs-officers however detained the lot. The little enraged beetle of a fellow ran back and forth from the ship to the customs, from the customs to the ship, afraid to go without his money, afraid the ship would go without him.

At five minutes to ten, there came M—— : very smart in his little grey overcoat and grey curly hat, walking very smart and erect and genteel, and followed by a porter with a barrow of luggage. They went into the customs, M—— in his grey suède gloves passing rapidly and smartly in, like the grandest gentleman on earth, and with his grey suède hands throwing open his luggage for inspection. From on board we could see the interior of the little customs shed.

Yes, he was through. Brisk, smart, superb, like the grandest little gentleman on earth, strutting because he Was late, he crossed the bit of flagged pavement and came up the gangway, haughty as you can wish. The carabinieri were lounging by the foot of the gangway, fooling with one another. The little gentleman passed them with his nose in the air, came quickly on board, followed by his porter, and in a moment disappeared. After about five minutes the porter reappeared – a red-haired fellow, I knew him – he even saluted me from below, the brute. But M—— lay in hiding.

I trembled for him at every unusual stir. There on the quay stood the English consul with his bull-dog, and various elegant young officers with yellow on their uniforms, talking to elegant young Italian ladies in black hats with stiff ospreys and bunchy furs, and gangs of porters and hotel people and onlookers. Then came a tramp-tramp-tramp of a squad of soldiers in red fezzes and baggy grey trousers. Instead of coming on board they camped on the quay. I wondered if all these had come for poor M——. But apparently not.

So the time passed, till nearly midnight, when one of the elegant young lieutenants began to call the names of the soldiers: and the soldiers answered: and one after another filed on board with their kit. So, they were on board, on their way to Africa.

Now somebody called out – and the visitors began to leave the boat. Barefooted sailors and a boy ran to raise the gangway. The last visitor or official with a bunch of papers stepped off the gangway. People on shore began to wave handkerchiefs. The red-fezzed soldiers leaned like so many flower-pots over the lower rail. There was a calling of farewells. The ship was fading into the harbour, the people on shore seemed smaller, under the lamp, in the deep night – without one's knowing why.

So, we passed out of the harbour, passed the glittering lights of Ortygia, past the two lighthouses, into the open Mediterranean. The noise of a ship in the open sea! It was a still night, with stars, only a bit chill. And the ship churned through the water.

Suddenly, like a revenant, appeared M—— near us, leaning on the rail and looking back at the lights of Syracuse sinking already forlorn and little on the low darkness. I went to him.

"Well," he said, with his little smirk of a laugh. "Good-bye Italy!"

"Not a sad farewell either," said I.

"No, my word, not this time," he said. "But what an awful long time we were starting! A brutta mezz'ora for me, indeed. Oh, my word, I begin to breathe free for the first time since I left the monastery! How awful it's been! But of course, in Malta, I shall be all right. Don Bernardo has written to his friends there. They'll have everything ready for me that I want, and I can pay you back the money you so kindly lent me."

We talked for some time, leaning on the inner rail of the upper deck.

"Oh," he said, "there's Commander So-and-so, of the British fleet. He's stationed in Malta. I made his acquaintance in the hotel. I hope we're going to be great friends in Malta. I hope I shall have an opportunity to introduce you to him. Well, I suppose you will want to be joining your ladies. So long, then. Oh, for to-morrow morning! I never longed so hard to be in the British Empire ——" He laughed, and strutted away.

In a few minutes we three, leaning on the rail of the second-class upper deck, saw our little friend large as life on the first-class deck, smoking a cigar and chatting in an absolutely first-class-ticket manner with the above mentioned Commander. He pointed us out to the Commander, and we felt the first-class passengers were looking across at us second-class passengers with pleasant interest. The women went behind a canvas heap to laugh, I hid my face under my hat-brim to grin and watch. Larger than any first-class ticketer leaned our little friend on the first-class rail, and whiffed at his cigar. So *dégagé* and so genteel he could be. Only I noticed he wilted a little when the officers of the ship came near.

He was still on the first-class deck when we went down to sleep. In the morning I came up soon after dawn. It was a lovely summer Mediterranean morning, with the sun rising up in a gorgeous golden rage, and the sea so blue, so fairy blue, as the Mediterranean is in summer. We were approaching quite near to a rocky, pale yellow island with some vineyards, rising magical out of the swift blue sea into the morning radiance. The rocks were almost as pale as butter, the islands were like golden shadows loitering in the midst of the Mediterranean, lonely among all the blue.

M—— came up to my side.

"Isn't it lovely! Isn't it beautiful!" he said. "I love approaching these islands in the early morning." He had almost recovered his assurance, and the slight pomposity and patronizing tone I had first known in him. "In two hours I shall be free! Imagine it! Oh what a beautiful feeling!" I looked at him in the morning light. His face was a good deal broken by his last month's experience, older looking, and dragged. Now that the excitement was nearing its end, the tiredness began to tell on him. He was yellowish round the eyes, and the whites of his round, rather impudent blue eyes were discoloured.

Malta was drawing near. We saw the white fringe of the sea upon the yellow rocks, and a white road looping on the yellow rocky hillside. I thought of St. Paul, who must have been blown this way, must have struck the island from this side. Then we saw the heaped glitter of the square facets of houses, Valletta, splendid above the Mediterranean, and a tangle of shipping and Dreadnoughts and watch-towers in the beautiful, locked-in harbour.

We had to go down to have passports examined. The officials sat in the long saloon. It was a horrible squash and squeeze of the first and second-class passengers. M—— was a little ahead of me. I saw the American eagle on his passport. Yes, he passed all right. Once more he was free. As he passed away he turned and gave a condescending affable nod to me and to the Commander, who was just behind me.

The ship was lying in Valletta harbour. I saw M——, quite superb and brisk now, ordering a porter with his luggage into a boat. The great rocks rose above us, yellow and carved, cut straight by man. On top were all the houses. We got at last into a boat and were rowed ashore. Strange to be on British soil and to hear English. We got a carriage and drove up the steep highroad through the cutting in the rock, up to the town. There, in the big square we had coffee, sitting out of doors. A military band went by, playing splendidly in the bright, hot morning. The Maltese lounged about, and watched. Splendid the band, and the soldiers! One felt the splendour of the British Empire, let the world say what it likes. But alas, as one stayed on even in Malta, one felt the old lion had gone foolish and amiable. Foolish and amiable, with the weak amiability of old age.

We stayed in the Great Britain Hotel. Of course one could not be in Valletta for twenty-four hours without meeting M——. There he was, in the Strada Reale, strutting in a smart white duck suit, with a white piqué cravat. But alas, he had no white shoes: they had got lost or stolen. He had to wear black boots with his summer finery.

He was staying in an hotel a little further down our street, and he begged me to call and see him, he begged me to come to lunch. I promised and went. We went into his bedroom, and he rang for more sodas.

"How wonderful it is to be here!" he said brightly. "Don't you like it immensely? And oh, how wonderful to have a whisky and soda! Well now, say when."

He finished one bottle of Black and White, and opened another. The waiter, a good-looking Maltese fellow, appeared with two syphons. M—— was very much the signore with him, and at the same time very familiar: as I should imagine a rich Roman of the merchant class might have been with a pet slave. We had quite a nice lunch, and whisky and soda and a bottle of French wine. And M—— was the charming and attentive host.

After lunch we talked again of manuscripts and publishers and how he might make money. I wrote one or two letters for him. He was anxious to get something under way. And yet the trouble of these arrangements was almost too much for his nerves. His face looked broken and old, but not like an old man, like an old boy, and he was really very irritable.

For my own part I was soon tired of Malta, and would gladly have left after three days. But there was the strike of steamers still, we had to wait on. M—— professed to be enjoying himself hugely, making excursions every day, to St. Paul's Bay and to the other islands. He had also made various friends or acquaintances. Particularly two young men, Maltese, who were friends of Don Bernardo. He introduced me to these two young men: one Gabriel Mazzaiba and the other Salonia. They had small businesses down on the wharf. Salonia asked M—— to go for a drive in a motor-car round the island, and M—— pressed me to go too. Which I did. And swiftly, on a Saturday afternoon, we dodged about in the car upon that dreadful island, first to some fearful and stony bay, arid, treeless, desert, a bit of stony desert by the sea, with unhappy villas and a sordid, scrap-iron front: then away inland up long and dusty roads, across a bone-dry, bone-bare, hideous landscape. True, there was ripening corn, but this was all of a colour with the dust-yellow, bone-bare island. Malta is all a pale, softish, yellowish rock, just like bathbrick: this goes into fathomless dust. And the island is stark as a corpse, no trees, no bushes even: a fearful landscape, cultivated, and weary with ages of weariness, and old weary houses here and there.

We went to the old capital in the centre of the island, and this is interesting. The town stands on a bluff of hill in the middle of the dreariness, looking at Valletta in the distance, and the sea. The houses are all pale yellow, and tall, and silent, as if forsaken. There is a cathedral, too, and a fortress outlook over the sun-blazed, sun-dried, disheartening island. Then we dashed off to another village and climbed a church-dome that rises like a tall blister on the plain, with houses round and corn beyond and dust that has no glamour, stale, weary, like bone-dust, and thorn hedges sometimes, and some tin-like prickly pears. In the dusk we came round by St. Paul's Bay, back to Valletta.

The young men were very pleasant, very patriotic for Malta, very Catholic. We talked politics and a thousand things. M—— was gently patronizing, and seemed, no doubt, to the two Maltese a very elegant and travelled and wonderful gentleman. They, who had never seen even a wood, thought how wonderful a forest must be, and M—— talked to them of Russia and of Germany.

But I was glad to leave that bone-dry, hideous island. M—— begged me to stay longer: but not for worlds! He was establishing himself securely: was learning the Maltese language, and cultivating a thorough acquaintance with the island. And he was going to establish himself. Mazzaiba was exceedingly kind to him, helping him in every way. In Rabato, the suburb of the old town – a quiet, forlorn little yellow street – he found a tiny house of two rooms and a tiny garden. This would cost five pounds a year. Mazzaiba lent the furniture – and when I left, M—— was busily skipping back and forth from Rabato to Valletta, arranging his little home, and very pleased with it. He was also being very Maltese, and rather anti-British, as is essential, apparently, when one is not a Britisher and finds oneself in any part of the British Empire. M—— was very much the American gentleman.

Well, I was thankful to be home again and to know that he was safely shut up in that beastly island. He wrote me letters, saying how he loved it all, how he would go down to the sea – five or six miles' walk – at dawn, and stay there all day, studying Maltese and writing for the newspapers. The life was fascinating, the summer was blisteringly hot, and the Maltese were most attractive, especially when they knew you were not British. Such good-looking fellows, too, and do anything you want. Wouldn't I come and spend a month? – I did not answer – felt I had had enough. Came a postcard from M—— : "I haven't had a letter from you, nor any news at all. I am afraid you are ill, and feel so anxious. Do write ——" But no, I didn't want to write.

During August and September and half October we were away in the north. I forgot my little friend: hoped he was gone out of my life. But I had that fatal sinking feeling that he *hadn't* really gone out of it yet.

In the beginning of November a little letter from Don Bernardo – did I know that M—— had committed suicide in Malta? Following that, a scrubby Maltese newspaper, posted by Salonia, with a marked notice: "The suicide of an American gentleman at Rabato. Yesterday the American

M—— M——, a well-built man in the prime of life, was found dead in his bed in his house at Rabato. By the bedside was a bottle containing poison. The deceased had evidently taken his life by swallowing prussic acid. Mr. M—— had been staying for some months on the island, studying the language and the conditions, with a view to writing a book. It is understood that financial difficulties were the cause of this lamentable event."

Then Mazzaiba wrote asking me what I knew of M——, and saying the latter had borrowed money which he, Mazzaiba, would like to recover. I replied at once, and then received the following letter from Salonia. "Valletta, 20 November, 1920. My dear Mr. Lawrence, some time back I mailed you our *Daily Malta Chronicle* which gave an account of the death of M——. I hope you have received same. As the statements therein given were very vague and not quite correct, please accept the latter part of this letter as a more correct version.

"The day before yesterday Mazzaiba received your letter which he gave me to read. As you may suppose we were very much astonished by its general purport. Mazzaiba will be writing to you in a few days, in the meantime I volunteered to give you the details you asked for.

"Mazzaiba and I have done all in our power to render M——'s stay here as easy and pleasant as possible from the time we first met him in your company at the Great Britain Hotel. [This is not correct. They were already quite friendly with M—— before that motor-drive, when I saw these two Maltese for the first time.] He lived in an embarrassed mood since then, and though we helped him as best we could both morally and financially he never confided to us his troubles. To this very day we cannot but look on his coming here and his stay amongst us, to say the least of the way he left us, as a huge farce wrapped up in mystery, a painful experience unsolicited by either of us and a cause of grief unrequited except by our own personal sense of duty towards a stranger.

"Mazzaiba out of mere respect did not tell me of his commitments towards M—— until about a month ago, and this he did in a most confidential and private manner merely to put me on my guard, thinking, and rightly, too, that M—— would be falling on me next time for funds; Mazzaiba having already given him about £55 and would not possibly commit himself any further. Of course, we found him all along a perfect gentleman. Naturally, he hated the very idea that we or anybody else in Malta should look upon him in any other light. He never asked directly, though Mazzaiba (later myself) was always quick enough to interpret rightly what he meant and obliged him forthwith.

"At this stage, to save the situation, he made up a scheme that the three of us should exploit the commercial possibilities in Morocco. It very nearly materialized, everything was ready, I was to go with him to Morocco, Mazzaiba was to take charge of affairs here and to dispose of transactions we initiated there. Fortunately, for lack of the necessary funds the idea had to be dropped, and there it ended, thank God, after a great deal of trouble I had in trying to set it well on foot.

"Last July, the Police, according to our law, advised him that he was either to find a surety or to deposit a sum of money with them as otherwise at the expiration of his three months' stay he would be compelled to leave the place. Money he had none, so he asked Mazzaiba to stand as surety. Mazzaiba could not as he was already guarantor for his alien cousins who were here at the time. Mazzaiba (not M——) asked me and I complied, thinking that the responsibility was just moral and only exacted as a matter of form.

"When, as stated before, Mazzaiba told me that M—— owed him £55 and that he owed his grocer and others at Notabile (the old town, of which Rabato is the suburb) over £10, I thought I might as well look up my guarantee and see if I was directly responsible for any debts he incurred here. The words of his declaration which I endorsed stated that 'I hereby solemnly promise that I will not be a burden to the inhabitants of these islands, etc.,' and deeming that unpaid debts to be more or less a burden, I decided to withdraw my guarantee, which I did on the 23rd ult. The reason I gave to the police was that he was outliving his income and that I did not intend to shoulder any financial responsibility in the matter. On the same day I wrote to him up at Notabile saying that for family reasons I was compelled to withdraw his surety. He took my letter in the sense implied and no way offended at my procedure.

"M——, in his resourceful way, knowing that he would with great difficulty find another guarantor, wrote at once to the police saying that he understood from Mr. Salonia that he (S) had withdrawn his guarantee, but as he (M) would be leaving the island in about three weeks' time (still intending to exploit Morocco) he begged the Commissioner to allow him this period of grace, without demanding a new surety. In fact he asked me to find him a cheap passage to Gib. in an ingoing tramp steamer. The police did not reply to his letter at all, no doubt they had everything ready and well thought out. He was alarmed in not receiving an acknowledgment, and, knowing full well what he imminently expected at the hands of the Italian police, he decided to prepare for the last act of his drama.

"We had not seen him for three or four days when he came to Mazzaiba's office on Wednesday, 3rd inst., in the forenoon. He stayed there for some time talking on general subjects and looking somewhat more excited than usual. He went up to town alone at noon as Mazzaiba went to Singlea. I was not with them in the morning, but in the afternoon about 4.30, whilst I was talking to Mazzaiba in his office, M—— again came in looking very excited, and, being closing time, we went up, the three of us, to town, and there left him in the company of a friend.

"On Thursday morning, 4th inst., at about 10 a.m., two detectives in plain clothes met him in a street at Notabile. One of them quite casually went up to him and said very civilly that the inspector of police wished to see him *re* a guarantee or something, and that he was to go with him to the police station. This was an excuse as the detective had about him a warrant for his arrest for frauding an hotel in Rome, and that he was to be extradited at the request of the authorities in Italy. M—— replied that as he was in his sandals he would dress up and go with them immediately, and, accompanying him to his house at No. I Strada S. Pietro, they allowed him to enter. He locked the door behind him, leaving them outside.

"A few minutes later he opened his bedroom window and dropped a letter addressed to Don Bernardo which he asked a boy in the street to post for him, and immediately closed the window again. One of the detectives picked up the letter and we do not know to this day if same was posted at all. Some time elapsed and he did not come out. The detectives were by this time very uneasy and as another police official came up they decided to burst open the door. As the door did not give way they got a ladder and climbed over the roof, and there they found M—— in his bedroom dying from poisoning, outstretched on his bed and a glass of water close by. A priest was immediately called in who had just time to administer Extreme Unction before he died at 11.45 a.m.

"At 8.0 a.m. the next day his body was admitted for examination at the Floriana Civil Hospital and death was certified to be from poisoning with hydrocyanic acid. His age was given as 44, being buried on his birthday (7th Novr.), with R. Catholic Rites at the expense of *His Friends in Malta*.

"Addenda: Contents of Don Bernardo's letter: —

"'I leave it to you and to Gabriel Mazzaiba to arrange my affairs. I cannot live any longer. Pray for me.'

Document found on his writing-table:

"'In case of my unexpected death inform American consul.

"'I want to be buried first class, my wife will pay.

"'My little personal belongings to be delivered to my wife. (Address.)

"'My best friend here, Gabriel Mazzaiba, inform him. (Address.)

"'My literary executor N—— D——. (Address.)

"'All manuscripts and books for N—— D——. I leave my literary property to N—— D—— to whom half of the results are to accrue. The other half my debts are to be paid with:

"'Furniture etc. belong to Coleiro, Floriana.

"'Silver spoons etc. belong to Gabriel Mazzaiba. (Address.).'

"The American Consul is in charge of all his personal belongings. I am sure he will be pleased to give you any further details you may require. By the way, his wife refused to pay his burial expenses, but five of his friends in Malta undertook to give him a decent funeral. His mourners were: The consul, the vice-consul, Mr. A., an American citizen, Gabriel Mazzaiba and myself.

"Please convey to Mrs. Lawrence an expression of our sincere esteem and high regard and you will kindly accept equally our warmest respects, whilst soliciting any information you would care to pass on to us regarding the late M——. Believe me, My dear Mr. Lawrence, etc."

[Mrs. M—— refunded the burial expenses through the American consul about two months after her husband's death.] '

When I had read this letter the world seemed to stand still for me. I knew that in my own soul I had said, "Yes, he must die if he cannot find his own way." But for all that, now I *realized* what it must have meant to be the hunted, desperate man: everything seemed to stand still. I could, by giving half my money, have saved his life. I had chosen not to save his life.

Now, after a year has gone by, I keep to my choice. I still would not save his life. I respect him for dying when he was cornered. And for this reason I feel still connected with him: still have this to discharge, to get his book published, and to give him his place, to present him just as he was as far as I knew him myself.

The worst thing I have against him, is that he abused the confidence, the kindness, and the generosity of unsuspecting people like Mazzaiba. He did not want to, perhaps. But he did it. And he leaves Mazzaiba swindled, distressed, confused, and feeling sold in the best part of himself. What next? What is one to feel towards one's strangers, after having known M—— ? It is this Judas treachery to ask for sympathy and for generosity, to take it when given – and then: "Sorry, but anybody may make a mistake!" It is this betraying with a kiss which makes me still say: "He should have died sooner." No, I would not help to keep him alive, not if I had to choose again. I would let him go over into death. He shall and should die, and so should all his sort: and so they will. There are so many kiss-giving Judases. He was not a criminal: he was obviously well intentioned: but a Judas every time, selling the good feeling he had tried to arouse, and had aroused, for any handful of silver he could get. A little loving vampire!

Yesterday arrived the manuscript of the Legion, from Malta. It is exactly two years since I read it first in the monastery. Then I was moved and rather horrified. Now I am chiefly amused; because in my mind's eye is the figure of M—— in the red trousers and the blue coat with lappets turned up, swinging like a little indignant pigeon across the drill yards and into the canteen of Bel-Abbès. He *is* so indignant, so righteously and morally indignant, and so funny. All the horrors of the actuality fade before the indignation, his little, tuppenny indignation.

Oh, M—— is a prime hypocrite. *How* loudly he rails against the *Boches! How* great his enthusiasm for the pure, the spiritual Allied cause. Just so long as he is in Africa, and it suits his purpose! His scorn for the German tendencies of the German legionaries: even Count de R. secretly leans towards Germany. "Blood is thicker than water," says our hero glibly. Some blood, thank God. Apparently not his own. For according to all showing he was, by blood, pure German: father and mother: even Hohenzollern blood!!! Pure German! Even his speech, his *mother-tongue*, was German and not English! And then the little mongrel —— !

But perhaps something happens to blood when once it has been taken to America.

And then, once he is in Valbonne, lo, a change! Where now is sacred France and the holy Allied Cause! Where is our hero's fervour? It is *worse than* Bel-Abbès! Yes, indeed, far less human, more hideously cold. One is driven by very rage to wonder if he was really a spy, a German spy whom Germany cast off because he was no – , good.

The little *gentleman!* God damn his white-blooded gentility. The legionaries must have been gentlemen, that they didn't kick him every day to the lavatory and back.

"You are a journalist?" said the colonel.

"No, a *littérateur*" said M—— perkily.

"That is something more?" said the Colonel.

Oh, I would have given a lot to have seen it and heard it. The *littérateur!* Well, I hope this book will establish his fame as such. I hope the editor, if it gets one, won't alter any more of the marvellously staggering sentences and the joyful French mistakes. The *littérateur!* – the impossible little pigeon!

But the Bel-Abbès part is alive and interesting. It should be read only by those who have the stomach. Ugly, foul – alas, it is no uglier and no fouler than the reality. M—— himself was near enough to being a scoundrel, thief, forger, etc., etc. – what lovely strings of names he hurls at them! – to be able to appreciate his company. He himself was such a liar, that he was not taken in. But his conceit as a gentleman *keeping up appearances* gave him a real standpoint from which to see the rest. The book is in its way a real creation. But I would hate it to be published and taken at its face value, with M—— as a spiritual dove among vultures of lust. Let us first put a pinch of salt on the tail of this dove. What he did do in the way of vice, even in Bel-Abbès, I never chose to ask him.

Yes, yes, he sings another note when he is planted right among the sacred Allies, with never a German near. Then the gorgeousness goes out of his indignation. He takes it off with the red trousers. Now he is just a sordid little figure in filthy corduroys. There is no vice to purple his indignation, the little holy liar. There is only sordidness and automatic, passionless, colourless awful mud. When all is said and done, mud, cold, hideous, foul, engulfing mud, up to the waist, this is the final symbol of the Great War. Hear some of the horrified young soldiers. They dare hardly speak of it yet.

The Valbonne part is worse, really, than the Bel-Abbès part. Passionless, barren, utterly, coldly foul and hopeless. The ghastly emptiness, and the slow mud-vortex, the brink of it.

Well, now M—— has gone himself. Yes, and he would be gone in the common mud and dust himself, if it were not that the blood still beats warm and hurt and kind in some few hearts. M—— "hinted" at Mazzaiba for money, in Malta, and Mazzaiba gave it to him, thinking him a man in distress. He thought him a gentleman, and lovable, and in trouble! And Mazzaiba – it isn't his real name, but there he is, real enough – still has this feeling of grief for M——. So much so that now he has had the remains taken from the public grave in Malta, and buried in his own, the Mazzaiba grave, so that they shall not be lost. For my part, I would have said that the sooner they mingled with the universal dust, the better. But one is glad to see a little genuine kindness and gentleness, even if it is wasted on the bones of that selfish little scamp of a M——. He despised his "physical friendships ——" though he didn't forego them. So why should anyone rescue his physique from the public grave? But there you are – there was his power: to arouse affection and a certain tenderness in the hearts of others, for himself. And on this he traded. One sees the trick working all the way through the Legion book. God knows how much warm kindness, generosity, was showered on him during the course of his forty-odd years. And selfish little scamp, he took it as a greedy boy takes cakes off a dish, quickly, to make the most of his opportunity while it lasted. And the cake once eaten: *buona sera!* He patted his own little paunch and felt virtuous. Merely physical feeling, you see! He had a way of saying "physical" – a sort of American way, as if it were spelt "fisacal" – that made me want to kick him.

Not that he was mean, while he was about it. No, he would give very freely: even a little ostentatiously, always feeling that he was being a *liberal gentleman*. Ach, the liberality and the gentility he prided himself on! *Ecco!* And he gave a large tip, with a little winsome smile. But in his heart of hearts it was always himself he was thinking of, while he did it. Playing his rôle of the gentleman who was awfully *nice* to everybody: so long as they were nice to him, or so long as it served his advantage. Just private charity!

Well, poor devil, he is dead: which is all the better.

He had his points, the courage of his own terrors, quick-wittedness, sensitiveness to certain things in his sur-soundings. I prefer him, scamp as he is, to the ordinary respectable person. He ran his risks: he had to be running risks with the police, apparently. And he poisoned himself rather than fall into their clutches. I like him for that. And I like him for the sharp and quick way he made use of every one of his opportunities to get out of that beastly army. There I admire him: a courageous, isolated little devil, facing his risks, and like a good rat, *determined* not to be trapped. I won't forgive him for trading on the generosity of others, and so dropping poison into the heart of all warm-blooded faith. But I am glad after all that Mazzaiba has rescued his bones from the public grave. I wouldn't have done it myself, because I don't forgive him his "fisacal" impudence and parasitism. But I am glad Mazzaiba has done it. And, for my part, I will put his Legion book before the world if I can. Let him have his place in the world's consciousness.

Let him have his place, let his word be heard. He went through vile experiences: he looked them in the face, braved them through, and kept his manhood in spite of them. For manhood is a strange quality, to be found in human rats as well as in hot-blooded men. M—— carried the human consciousness through circumstances which would have been too much for me. I would have died rather than be so humiliated, I could never have borne it. Other men, I know, went through worse things in the war. But then, horrors, like pain, are their own anaesthetic. Men lose their normal consciousness, and go through in a sort of delirium. The bit of Stendhal which Dos Passos quotes in front of *Three Soldiers* is frighteningly true. There are certain things which are *so* bitter, *so* horrible, that the contemporaries just cannot know them, cannot contemplate them. So it is with a great deal of the late war. It was so foul, and humanity in Europe fell suddenly into such ignominy and inhuman ghastliness, that we shall *never* fully realize what it was. We just cannot bear it. We haven't the soul-strength to contemplate it.

And yet, humanity can only finally conquer by realizing. It is human destiny, since Man fell into consciousness and self-consciousness, that we can only go forward step by step through realization, full, bitter, conscious realization. This is true of all the great terrors and agonies and anguishes of life: sex, and war, and even crime. When Flaubert in his story – it is so long since I read it – makes his saint have to kiss the leper, and naked clasp the leprous awful body against his own, that is what we must at last do. It is the great command *Know Thyself*. We've got to *know* what sex is, let the sentimentalists wiggle as they like. We've got to know the greatest and most shattering human passions, let the puritans squeal as they like for screens. And we've got to know humanity's criminal tendency, look straight at humanity's great deeds of crime against the soul. We have to fold this horrible leper against our naked warmth: because life and the throbbing blood and the believing soul are greater even than leprosy. Knowledge, true knowledge is like vaccination. It prevents the continuing of ghastly moral disease.

And so it is with the war. Humanity in Europe fell horribly into a hatred of the living soul, in the war. There is no gainsaying it. We all fell. Let us not try to wriggle out of it. We fell into hideous depravity of hating the human soul; a purulent small-pox of the spirit we had. It was shameful, shameful, shameful, in every country and in all of us. Some tried to resist, and some didn't. But we were all drowned in shame. A purulent small-pox of the vicious spirit, vicious against the deep soul that pulses in the blood.

We haven't got over it. The small-pox sores are running yet in the spirit of mankind. And we have got to take this putrid spirit to our bosom. There's nothing else for it. Take the foul rotten spirit of mankind, full of the running sores of the war, to our bosom, and cleanse it there. Cleanse it not with blind love: ah no, that won't help. But with bitter and wincing realization. We have to take the disease into our consciousness and let it go through our soul, like some virus. We have got to realize. And then we can surpass.

M—— went where I could never go. He carried the human consciousness unbroken through circumstances I could not have borne. It is not heroism to rush on death. It is cowardice to accept a martyrdom to-day. That is the feeling one has at the end of Dos Passos' book. To let oneself be absolutely trapped? Never! I prefer M——. He drew himself out of the thing he loathed, despised, and feared. He fought it, for his own spirit and liberty. He fought it open-eyed. He went through. They were more publicly heroic, they won war medals. But the lonely terrified courage of the isolated spirit which grits its teeth and stares the horrors in the face and *will* not succumb to them, but fights its way through them, *knowing* that it must surpass them: this is the rarest courage. And this courage M—— had: and the man in the Dos Passos book didn't *quite* have it. And so, though M—— poisoned himself, and I would not wish him *not* to have poisoned himself: though as far as warm life goes, I don't forgive him; yet, as far as the eternal and unconquerable spirit of man goes, I am with him through eternity. I am grateful to him, he beat out for me boundaries of human experience which I could not have beaten out for myself. The *human* traitor he was. But he was not traitor to the spirit. In the great spirit of human consciousness he was a hero, little, quaking and heroic: a strange, quaking little star.

Even the dead ask only for *justice*: not for praise or exoneration. Who dares humiliate the dead with excuses for their living? I hope I may do M—— justice; and I hope his restless spirit may be appeased. I do not try to forgive. The living blood knows no forgiving. Only the overweening spirit takes on itself to dole out forgiveness. But Justice is a sacred human right. The overweening spirit pretends to perch above justice. But I am a man, not a spirit, and men with blood that throbs and throbs and throbs can only live at length by being just, can only die in peace if they have justice. Forgiveness gives the whimpering dead no rest. Only deep, true justice.

There is M——'s manuscript then, like a map of the lower places of mankind's activities. There is the war: foul, foul, unutterably foul. As foul as M—— says. Let us make up our minds about it.

It is the only help: to realize, *fully*, and then make up our minds. The war was *foul*. As long as I am a man, I say it and assert it, and further

I say, as long as I am a man such a war shall never occur again. It shall not, and it shall not. All modern militarism is foul. It shall go. A man I am, and above machines, and it shall go, forever, because I have found it vile, vile, too vile ever to experience again. Cannons shall go. Never again shall trenches be dug. They *shall* not, for I am a man, and such things are within the power of man, to break and make. I have said it, and as long as blood beats in my veins, I mean it. Blood beats in the veins of many men who mean it as well as I.

Man perhaps *must* fight. Mars, the great god of war, will be a god forever. Very well. Then if fight you must, fight you shall, and without engines, without machines. Fight if you like, as the Roman fought, with swords and spears, or like the Red Indian, with bows and arrows and knives and war paint. But never again shall you fight with the foul, base, fearful, monstrous machines of war which man invented for the last war. You shall not. The diabolic mechanisms are man's, and I am a man. Therefore they are mine. And I smash them into oblivion. With every means in my power, except the means of these machines, I smash them into oblivion. I am at war! I, a man, am at war! – with these foul machines and contrivances that men have conjured up. Men have conjured them up. I, a man, will conjure them down again. Won't I? – but I will! I am not one man, I am many, I am most.

So much for the war! So much for M——'s manuscript. Let it be read. It is not this that will do harm, but sloppy sentiment, and cant. Take the bitterness and cleanse the blood.

Now would you believe it, that little scamp M—— spent over a hundred pounds of borrowed money during his four months in Malta, when his expenses, he boasted to me, need not have been more than a pound a week, once he got into the little house in Notabile. That is, he spent at least seventy pounds too much. Heaven knows what he did with it, apart from "guzzling." And this hundred pounds must be paid back in Malta. Which it never will be, unless this manuscript pays it back. Pay the gentleman's last debts, if no others.

He had to be a gentleman. I didn't realize till after his death. I never suspected him of royal blood. But there you are, you never know where it will crop out. He was the grandson of an emperor. His mother was the illegitimate daughter of the German Kaiser: D—— says, of the old Kaiser Wilhelm I, Don Bernardo says, of Kaiser Frederick Wilhelm, father of the present ex-Kaiser. She was born in Berlin on the 31 October, 1845: and her portrait, by Paul, now hangs in a gallery in Rome. Apparently there had been some injustice against her in Berlin – for she seems once to have been in the highest society there, and to have attended at court. Perhaps she was discreetly banished by Wilhelm II, hence M—'s hatred of that monarch. She lies buried in the Protestant Cemetery in Rome, where she died in 1912, with the words *Filia Régis* on her tomb. M— adored her, and she him. Part of his failings one can *certainly* ascribe to the fact that he was an only son, an adored son, in whose veins the mother imagined only royal blood. And she must have thought him so beautiful, poor thing! Ah well, they are both dead. Let us be just and wish them Lethe.

M— himself was born in New York, 7th November, 1876; so at least it says on his passport. He entered the Catholic Church in England in 1902. His father was a Mr. L— M—, married to the mother in 1867.

So poor M— had Hohenzollern blood in his veins: close kin to the ex-Kaiser William. Well, that itself excuses him a great deal: because of the cruel illusion of importance *manqué*, which it must have given him. He never breathed a word of this to me. Yet apparently it is accepted at the monastery, the great monastery which knows most European secrets of any political significance. And for myself, I believe it is true. And if he was a scamp and a treacherous little devil, he had also qualities of nerve and breeding undeniable. He faced his way through that Legion experience: royal nerves dragging themselves through the sewers, without giving way. But alas, for royal blood! Like most other blood, it has gradually gone white, during our spiritual era. Bunches of nerves! And whitish, slightly acid blood. And no bowels of deep compassion and kindliness. Only charity – a little more than kin, and less than kind.

Also, M— ! Ich grüsse dich, in der Ewigkeit. Aber hier, im Herzblut, hast du Gift und Leid nachgelassen – to use your own romantic language.

D. H. Lawrence
Taormina, Sicily

About the Authors

Charles Maurice Liebetrau Magnus (1876–1920) was born in New York City. His father, Charles Ferdinand Magnus, had immigrated from German Poland in the 1860s and died in 1904; his mother, Hedwig Rosamunde Liebetrau (1845–1912), was raised by Lutheran parents and was said to be the illegitimate daughter of Kaiser Wilhelm I. He published an early comic sketch *Zu den Waffen!* (1893) and a romantic drama *Eldyle* (1898). He contributed to two reference works and was on the staff of the magazine *The Smart Set*. Around 1903 he left New York for Europe. There he served as foreign correspondent for several newspapers and magazines and supplemented his income by giving language lessons. He met and became a business manager for theatrical producer Gordon Craig, the sponsor and lover of Isadora Duncan. For a while, Magnus ran a literary agency, but struggled financially. In 1907 he accompanied Duncan on her tour of Russia. Returning to the West, he collaborated with Craig on an unsuccessful literary magazine, *The Mask,* and tutored Duncan's children. In 1912 Magnus's mother died in Rome and was buried in the Protestant cemetary there. In 1913 Magnus married Lucy Seraphine Ardoine Bramley-Moore of London, seven years his senior; they were officially separated in 1917.

In March 1916, Magnus, then 39 years old and living in Italy, travelled to Tunis to join the French Foreign Legion and serve in the First World War. The United States had not yet entered the war, and the Italian, French, Russian, and Serbian armies had all rejected him. The Foreign Legion allowed him to retain his American citizenship while serving in the Allied forces. In May he was transferred from North Africa to Valbonne, France, near the Italian border. In June 1916, he deserted, crossed the border, and made his way back to Rome by way of Spain. He renewed acquaintance with Norman Douglas in 1917 and the men shared lodgings for a period and continued literary pursuits. In October 1917, Magnus took up residence in the monastery of Monte Cassino and returned there at various times through 1920. In 1918 he sailed to the United States as agent for an Italian filmmaker and came under suspicion for his wartime associations and relationship with Isadora Duncan. He returned to Europe in 1919, accompanied Duncan on a tour of Switzerland, and was introduced to D. H. Lawrence by

Norman Douglas. Continually beset by financial problems, he passed a series of bad checks. In April 1920, learning of warrants for his arrest, Magnus fled Monte Cassino for Sicily and then Malta, running up more debts along the way. He remained in Malta from May until November, when facing extradition to Italy on charges of fraud, he ended his life November 4, 1920, by drinking hydrogen cyanide. He named Norman Douglas his literary executor, and Douglas and Lawrence managed to have his *Memoirs* manuscript published in hopes of raising enough money to clear his debts.

Memoirs of the Foreign Legion by M. M., With an Introduction by D. H. Lawrence (London: Martin Secker, 1924)

D.H. Lawrence, *Memoir of Maurice Magnus,* ed. Keith Cushman (Santa Rosa, CA: Black Sparrow Press, 1987)

Louise E. Wright, *Maurice Magnus: A Biography* (Newcastle, UK: Cambridge Scholars, 2007).

David Herbert Lawrence (1885–1930) English novelist, poet, short story writer, and essayist. Born the fourth child of a Nottinghamshire coal miner, he earned a teaching certificate from University College Nottingham. After moving to London in 1908 he published the novels *The White Peacock* (1910), The Trespasser (1911), *Sons and Lovers* (1913), *The Rainbow* (1915), *Women in Love* (1920), *The Plumed Serpent* (1926), *Lady Chatterley's Lover* (1928), as well as poetry, short story, and essay collections, including the influential *Studies in Classic American Literature* (1923). In 1912 he met Frieda von Richthofen Weekley, who left her husband and three children to elope with him. During the First World War Lawrence was harassed by British authorities for his opposition to militarism. Financial success eluded him, and his works were suppressed or condemned for obscenity. After the war the couple spent most of their remaining years in voluntary exile from England, living in Italy, Australia, France, Mexico, and the United States. He died of tuberculosis at Vence, France, in 1930.

www.ingramcontent.com/pod-product-compliance
Lightning Source LLC
LaVergne TN
LVHW091052080826
845145LV00002B/718

* 9 7 8 1 6 0 9 6 2 2 7 6 3 *